Kingdom Learning

DAVID HEYWOOD

Kingdom Learning

scm press

© David Heywood 2017

Published in 2017 by SCM Press
Editorial office
3rd Floor, Invicta House,
108–114 Golden Lane,
London EC1Y 0TG, UK
www.scmpress.co.uk

SCM Press is an imprint of Hymns Ancient & Modern Ltd
(a registered charity)

Hymns Ancient & Modern® is a registered trademark of
Hymns Ancient & Modern Ltd
13A Hellesdon Park Road, Norwich,
Norfolk NR6 5DR, UK

All rights reserved. No part of this publication may be reproduced,
stored in a retrieval system, or transmitted,
in any form or by any means, electronic, mechanical,
photocopying or otherwise, without the prior permission of
the publisher, SCM Press.

The Author has asserted his right under the Copyright,
Designs and Patents Act 1988
to be identified as the Author of this Work

Scripture quotations are from the New Revised Standard Version of the
Bible, Anglicized Edition, copyright © 1989, 1995 by the Division of
Christian Education of the National Council of the Churches of Christ in
the USA. Used by permission. All rights reserved.

British Library Cataloguing in Publication data

A catalogue record for this book is available
from the British Library

978 0 334 05480 1

Typeset by Manila Typesetting
Printed and bound by
CPI Group (UK) Ltd

Contents

Acknowledgements   vii
'Setting God's People Free': Author's note   xi
Introduction: Learning for Discipleship and Ministry   1
1   Adult Learning in God's Kingdom   25
2   Learning to Connect Life and Faith   75
3   Leading the Learning Community   119
4   Learning for Ministry Together   179
Index of Names and Subjects   223

Acknowledgements

The third chapter of my book *Reimagining Ministry* includes a section entitled 'The learning church' and another entitled 'Reflective discipleship'. These placed reflective learning at the heart of the church's life. This book takes up and expands on the themes I briefly dealt with there. It has been written in the midst of my role as a teacher in ministerial education and expands on the themes I try to develop with students when teaching them mission and ministry, leadership, education and theological reflection. I have also tried to be mindful of my experience of 20 years in parish ministry and to write for my fellow clergy, facing the challenges of rapid change in the life of our society and the place of the church within it.

I have not attempted to write a practical 'how-to-do-it' manual, nor yet a theoretical study. What I have attempted is to explain how learning actually takes place and offer some principles for teaching and learning in the context of a local church based on this. This means that alongside the more practical sections and interspersed with them there are sections of deeper exploration. I hope readers will find these interesting in themselves as well as offering guidance for the practice of teaching and learning. Towards the end of the book I have made some comments on the way my own Church, the Church of England, approaches the training of its clergy. This topic requires another book to do it full justice. I hope what I have included here is enough to indicate the main lines of what my argument would be.

No book like this could be written without a good deal of help. I am grateful to successive cohorts of students at Ripon College Cuddesdon and on the Monmouth Ministry Area Leaders' Course, who have challenged and helped to develop my thinking in these areas. In particular, I would like to thank Karen Charman, Andrew Down, Mark Lawson-Jones, Gill Nobes, Alex Williams and Clive Watts for permission to quote their experiences and in some cases their college assignments in this book. I am also profoundly grateful to Rob Gallagher for permission to use the story from his ministry as the basis for my study of theological reflection in Chapter 2.

Tina Hodgett, Rowena King, Debbie McIsaac, Tim Treanor and Janet Williams read an early draft of this book and gave me valuable feedback, which has helped to shape the final draft. Needless to say, they are not responsible for the many shortcomings that remain.

There are also three written sources that have been particularly influential. In my opinion, Anton Baumohl's *Making Adult Disciples* is the best book written on adult learning in the church in a British context, although it has been out of print for many years.[1] Sylvia Wilkey Collinson's *Making Disciples* is a detailed study of the New Testament evidence, which offers some profound insights into the teaching methods of Jesus and the early church.[2] Thomas Hawkins' *The Learning Congregation* applies system theory to the Christian congregation to show how adaptive change is possible.[3] In all three cases there is, as far as I am aware, nothing quite like any of these books. I hope I have been able to build successfully on the work of these authors.

My usual practice is to alternate between male and female for the representative person, thus avoiding the ugly 'him or her'. This is what I have done in this book. Accordingly, the representative disciple, teacher, church leader and theologian is sometimes 'he' and sometimes 'she'. I hope readers will bear with me if this should be confusing.

I have used 'church' with a lower-case 'c' to refer to both the local church and the wider church. 'Church' with a capital 'C' refers to specific denominations and most often to the Church of England, the Church of which I am a member and from which most of my examples are drawn. I hope what I write will have some relevance to Churches of other denominations and to Scotland and Wales, but I leave the reader to judge.

ACKNOWLEDGEMENTS

Without the support of my wife Meg, neither the writing nor the experience of ministry on which it is based would have been possible.

David Heywood
December 2016

Notes

1 Anton Baumohl, *Making Adult Disciples*, London: Scripture Union, 1984.

2 Sylvia Wilkey Collinson, *Making Disciples: The Significance of Jesus' Teaching Methods for Today's Church*, Eugene, OR: Wipf & Stock, 2006 (originally Milton Keynes: Paternoster Press, 2004).

3 Thomas Hawkins, *The Learning Congregation*, Louisville, KY: Westminster John Knox Press, 1997.

AUTHOR'S NOTE

'Setting God's People Free'

In the past few years, my hope was that whole-life-discipleship would be the next aspect of mission to crystallize in the Church's understanding and practice. But this hope, expressed in my earlier book *Reimagining Ministry*, has not been realized. The Church's next step forward was to be chaplaincy ministry, which is rapidly taking off in a variety of informal settings, helping to bridge the ever-widening gap between the Christian faith community and wider society. But just as *Kingdom Learning* was being published, the Archbishops' Council of the Church of England issued the report 'Setting God's People Free',[1] drawing attention to the need to 'empower, liberate and disciple the 98 per cent of the Church of England who are not ordained' and 'set them free for fruitful, faithful mission and ministry' (p. 1).

As the report makes clear, and I argue in the Introduction to this book, accomplishing this goal will require a 'seismic revolution in the culture of the Church' (p. 3). In particular, it requires the Church of England to name and confront the culture of clericalism, which is deeply embedded in its modes of operating, especially in the training of its clergy (p. 22). I would go further and urge that the Church, perhaps represented by its bishops, publicly acknowledges this damaging aspect of its inherited culture and determines to adopt a new mindset and new practice.

The report laments that, although 'Lay engagement and influence in the workplace, community and society is vast', there is nevertheless 'very little curiosity, affirmation, prayer, theological or practical resourcing for these roles at local church level' (p. 12). It notes that 'most clergy want to release lay leaders, but genuinely struggle to do so' (p. 17), and raises the question of 'the most appropriate models of theological education and formation for an empowered and confident laity' (p. 15). 'Few churches', the report declares, 'are equipped with the kind of "action learning" approaches that we see in Jesus' disciple-making and in best practice in adult learning models in wider society' (p. 18).

The report includes an implementation plan, which may mean that I have to revise my assessment of the Church's performance in this area so far: namely that despite well thought-out policy aspirations, nothing of substance has been achieved. The weakness of the report, however, is that the quotation given above about the need for best practice in adult learning is almost the only mention of the importance of skills in this area.

It has long been my conviction that the Church as a whole needs to take on board the theory and practice of adult education if it is to be adequately equipped for ministry and mission. As I argue in Chapter 4, training for ordination that ignores educational best practice disempowers the Church, in particular making it more difficult for clergy to exercise collaborative models of ministry. But equally important, clergy require skills of adult education to achieve their aspiration to release the laity for mission. The aim of this book is to put those skills into the hands of all who wish to practise them.

'Setting God's People Free' begins with a quotation from Paul's letter to the Colossians: 'He is the one we proclaim, admonishing and teaching everyone with all wisdom, so that we may present everyone fully mature in Christ' (Colossians 1.28, NIV). It is my prayer that this book might provide a resource for achieving this goal in the present day, setting free the 98 per cent of the Church, who currently receive very little in the way of effective learning for discipleship and ministry, to play their part in the outpouring of God's love to the world.

Note

[1] Archbishop's Council, 'Setting God's People Free', General Synod Paper 2056 February 2017, www.churchofengland.org/media/3858033/gs-2056-setting-gods-people-free-pdf.

Introduction:

Learning for Discipleship and Ministry

An Adaptive Zone

The past two generations have seen a quiet revolution in the life of the church in Britain that is still gathering pace. Not only are we rediscovering the priority of mission in God's purposes, we are also discovering the breadth of all that is involved, from fresh expressions to Street Pastors, chaplaincy to Messy Church, retreats and quiet days to community engagement. To take fresh expressions of church as just one aspect of the church's renewed confidence in mission, it is estimated that four times as many churches were started in the year 2013–14 as were started in 2004, the year of the *Mission-shaped Church* report.[1] A model of mission that revolved around the invitation to 'come' to church is being replaced by a model that emphasizes the responsibility of the church to 'go': to witness to its faith through engagement with the wider community.

This re-emphasis on mission and renewed understanding of the *missio Dei*, the mission of God, is one aspect of the church's response to a wider change. The church is currently in what Ann Morisy has called an 'adaptive zone'.[2] It faces a series of interrelated and unfamiliar challenges, whose novelty and interrelatedness mean that the solutions are far from obvious. The past two or three generations have witnessed an ever-widening gap between the culture of contemporary society and the tradition of Christian faith. At a basic level, this period has seen the loss of a previously widespread acquaintance with the basic tenets of Christianity. More profoundly, the differences between society and the church on moral issues, not simply areas of personal morality, such as divorce, euthanasia and sexual orientation, but on social issues, such as materialism, individualism, competition and inequality, have become a substantial gulf. With the rise of pluralism, churches now have to compete in the marketplace of ideas as one voice among many, adapting to society's view of them as one interest group among many, advocating one truth among a kaleidoscopic variety of religious and quasi-religious positions. Moreover, the commitment of society to tolerance of diversity as the basis of social cohesion tends to fuel a growth in suspicion towards religious faith, typified by the hostile reception in some sections of the media of Tim Farron as leader of the Liberal Democrats in 2015, since religious believers are seen to appeal to sources of authority outside social control as arbiters of truth and conduct.

Not only are the changes taking place in society profound but the pace of change is becoming faster. As long ago as 1997, Thomas Hawkins could write: 'We no longer experience the river of time as a slow, peaceful stream with quiet eddies and calm pools . . . we are instead white-water rafting through the rapids of social, technological and demographic change.'[3] Until the 1970s it was reasonable to assume that most people would have learned most of what they needed for adult life by their early twenties. From the 1980s onwards, and especially since the development of the internet, bringing the possibility of instant worldwide communication, the pace of change has rapidly increased. The pace of economic and social change now not only requires individuals to become lifelong learners but organizations to learn continuously in order to adapt nimbly to the challenges of continual change. The pressure is on the church to become a 'learning church' in order to find adaptive solutions, ways of being and doing suited to the challenges of a new and unfamiliar situation.[4]

All this means that traditional and inherited ways of understanding church and mission, discipleship and ministry need to be 'reimagined' or 'relearned'. In 2010 the Archbishops' Council of the Church of England noted the paradox of an increasingly secular society in which attempts to marginalize religion are on the increase, with a growing interest in the spiritual dimension of life as well as some specifically religious issues.[5] In order to equip the Church to grow both spiritually and numerically and to contribute to the common good of society, the Council saw the need to both reimagine the Church's ministry and deepen the discipleship of every Christian.[6] In 2015 the report 'Released for Mission' identified five priorities for the rural church, including 'building a culture of discipleship appropriate to the rural context' and 'envisioning, enabling and equipping the ministry of lay people'. 'This', the report went on, 'requires the church nationally to reconceive its ministry, rethink how it trains its ministers and how it releases them for mission.'[7] In a similar way, writing about the role of local ministry in a church equipped for mission, Adrian Dorber declares, 'This new form of ministry is a quiet revolution that makes for systemic change at every level.'[8]

These calls for 'reconceiving' ministry and 'systemic change' point to the need for a process of adaptive change: the kind of change where solutions are not obvious and there is a need for far-reaching adjustments in the way we understand the problems before the way forward becomes clear. Adaptive change is far from easy: it involves facing inertia and risking conflict. Nevertheless, the key elements in the process have been well charted by writers in management studies and are not difficult to apply in the life of the church. While adaptive solutions may represent a break with the immediate past, they will nevertheless remain faithful to the Churches' core purpose and identity. In fact that core purpose and identity will be a key resource in steering the process of change. It will involve the recovery of some important elements of Christian tradition, such as the centrality of God's mission in the life of the church; the call to discipleship of all God's people, lay and ordained alike; and the nature of the church as a community of learning, rooted in Scripture and tradition.

The rediscovery and renewed emphasis on these in the life of the contemporary church is evidence of a process of adaptive change already in progress. But they also point the way to the need for the church to face the cost of further change. Adaptive change requires the ability to discern the hidden assumptions rooted in current ways of doing things and to weigh these in the light of the tradition. It requires the willingness to arrive at *metanoia*, a deep-rooted change of heart and mind leading to new ways of acting.

Finally, in distinction from mere technical change, adaptive change is essentially non-hierarchical: it requires the participation of the grass roots in recognizing and responding to outdated and inauthentic ways of working and the willingness to experiment with new ways.[9]

In this book I want to suggest four ways in which God is calling the church to become a 'learning church', drawing in each case on the practice of adult education. I want to suggest that understanding the way people learn provides a key resource and potentially the confidence we need to face the challenges of the present day. I also want to point to some of the deep-rooted assumptions at the heart of our church life that currently hold us back and have the potential, if not addressed, seriously to impede the progress of God's mission.

This book builds on my previous book, *Reimagining Ministry*.[10] There I charted the progress of the church's participation in God's mission over the previous 20 to 30 years. I suggested that one of the key elements of Christian tradition we need to recover is a vision of God's kingdom and of the church as the 'sign, agent and foretaste' of the kingdom.[11] I suggested that this vision also provides a very different perspective on ministry: not simply the ministry of the ordained, but the ministry of the whole church in the service of God's mission. I was writing specifically for the Church to which I belong, the Church of England, in the hope that what I had to say would also be of help to other denominations. Our challenge, I suggested, is not simply to 'restructure' the Church's ministry but to 'reimagine' it: to understand the purpose and nature of ministry in a whole new way. The years since *Reimagining Ministry* have seen the church gradually moving in the kind of direction I suggested, and I take this to be a sign that the book was broadly in tune with what the Spirit is saying to the Churches. In some ways I have been proved wrong: most particularly, I did not foresee the mushrooming of opportunities for informal chaplaincy in a wide variety of settings. I see this as a significant development in the Churches' mission, a key way God is providing a bridge across the ever-widening gulf between the Christian faith community and the wider society in which we are set.[12]

INTRODUCTION

The first of the four ways I believe God is calling us to adapt to the challenges of today is in the area of discipleship. In the words of 'Released for Mission', it is about 'building a culture of discipleship'. The challenge here is enormous. For generations, most regular worshippers have been disempowered: they have been encouraged to see the responsibility for the life and mission of the church in the hands of the trained clergy. A church in mission requires these same worshippers to see themselves as 'missionary disciples',[13] called to play their part in the church's ministry. Already the need for programmes to enable and encourage ordinary Christian believers to grow in discipleship is an item that is firmly on the agenda for the Churches. Progress, however, is slow and stumbling, characterized by thoughtful statements of intent and patchy to non-existent follow-up. Although this book is not a 'how-to-do-it' manual, I set out some basic principles of adult learning and a set of broad guidelines to help those who want to encourage discipleship learning in their churches. I also point to some reasons why I believe the progress in this area has been so disappointing.

An indispensable element in discipleship is Jesus' call to join him in his mission. Ministry and discipleship, as I will explain shortly, belong together. As part of discipleship learning, God's people also need to be resourced to live as followers of Christ in the course of their daily lives and work, and many will need training for their involvement in specific aspects of ministry. Here I am referring to the ministry of all God's people in and through the local church. Each denomination has courses of training in place to prepare people for licensed ministry, lay and ordained. In this book I focus on the wider and less formal ministry churches are called to undertake both to build up the life of the church as a worshipping, loving community and also to serve the wider community and networks in which they are set. I also suggest why the model of training for ministry offered at national level, the kind of training most existing clergy have received, reflects a poor model of learning, and some of the ways this needs to change.

The context in which discipleship learning and much training for ministry takes place is the life of the local church. But the church's corporate life is not only the context for learning, it plays a vital part in the learning itself. Disciples learn what it means to follow Christ through participating in the life of the church. A vital task for those entrusted with the leadership of the churches is, therefore, to maintain the faithfulness of the church's life. Church leaders need continually to be asking whether 'the way we do things here' faithfully reflects our understanding of the gospel. It is not only individuals who learn: whole churches learn together what it means to embody the love of God and the good news we have received in Christ in the shared life of the community. Therefore a third element in the book is the exploration of how this takes place: how church leaders can facilitate this corporate learning that allows churches to adapt and change. The key tool in this, I suggest, is the skill of theological reflection. In Chapter 2 I set out at length how I understand this process and in Chapters 3 and 4 apply it to the task of enabling and guiding learning in the local church.

From here it is a short step to my fourth concern. The pace of change is relentless and, as a result, the need for churches to evaluate their own life and mission is continual. Local churches and whole denominations need to become 'learning organizations', capable of adapting and changing without losing sight of their core purpose and identity. Leaders at all levels need to be equipped to lead adaptive change. In Chapter 4, I will argue that we are prevented from attaining this by our assumptions about the nature of leadership, the nature of learning and the nature of theology. Here again, theological reflection plays a central role for what it tells us about the nature of knowledge. Over the course of the book I hope to guide the reader into a way of seeing knowledge not as a grand theoretical construct but as a continuous feedback loop by means of which we orientate ourselves to the world in which we live, make sense of and manage its tasks and relationships. The one, being essentially static, impedes our ability to respond to adaptive challenges; the other, being fluid and dynamic, aids it. A book on the nature of adaptive leadership would be a separate project and help is available from a variety of sources.[14] My concern here is simply to point to the very considerable obstacles that stand in our way.

INTRODUCTION

The Story so Far

The story of the Churches' attempts to encourage discipleship learning is one of thoughtful, well-grounded recommendations and frustrating lack of progress. I am writing specifically about the Church of England, with which I am most familiar, but the picture does not appear to be too different in most of the other denominations.

The year 2003 saw a major study of the future of training for ordination in the Church of England with the title *Formation for Ministry within a Learning Church*, a report that came to be known, after its principal author, as the 'Hind Report'.[15] The title of the report was important in two ways. First, it consciously adopted the word 'formation' for the process by which candidates were to be trained for ordained ministry; and formation was understood to include growth in the virtues of character required for ministry as well as in knowledge and skills. Second, it placed this process of formation in the context of a 'learning church', a whole church committed to learning its faith and growing in discipleship. The amount of attention given to discipleship learning, however, is disappointingly small, amounting to some five or six pages and linking it, for the most part, with training for ministry, whether lay or ordained. But it did begin a process by which discipleship learning once again became a focus of attention for the Church.

As a direct outcome of this renewed recognition of the importance of learning for discipleship, an ecumenical working party was set up with representatives from the Methodist and United Reformed Churches, and its report was included in the next major document from the Church of England, *Shaping the Future*.[16] The report was headed 'Education for Discipleship', and aspired to lay the foundations for a nationwide provision of opportunities for discipleship learning. Its definition of discipleship was 'the whole-life response of Christians to Jesus Christ', a definition intended to cover 'everything a Christian believes and does', including her participation in ministry in the world as part of the mission of God. The report's authors carefully differentiated this from a 'preliminary foundation stage' for training for licensed ministry. Lay discipleship and ministry should be seen to have a value in themselves independent of formal training and recognition. They also deliberately distanced themselves, as I also wish to do, from the style of church life that sees discipleship in terms of discipline, in which leaders have sought to oversee the lives of their followers in intrusive and authoritarian ways.[17]

The aim of 'Education for Discipleship' was to be 'to help students, individually and in community, to develop a habit of informed, critical and creative engagement with issues of faith, morality, discipleship, mission and ministry'. Students were to learn about the Bible and Christian tradition, and be equipped to relate these to the 'varied contexts of contemporary culture', the life of the church and their own daily lives. The underlying principles to which the report draws attention are worth quoting at length because they echo the principles I have taken for granted in the writing of this book:

- Every human being has a capacity for learning, which is part of what it means to be human.
- Those who respond to God's call to follow him share explicitly in his mission in the world.
- Christian discipleship has both an individual and a corporate dimension, and is a collaborative as well as an individual response to Christ's call.
- All God's people are called to discipleship; all are valuable; all are gifted.
- Communities and networks of learning are an invaluable resource to the Church.
- The Church is resourced by the mutuality of learning between public ministers (lay and ordained) and the rest of the people of God.
- Learning designed to enhance discipleship needs to be rooted in understandings of the Christian tradition and the Bible.
- Learning is life-long.[18]

The report then went on to outline an ambitious programme of regional provision for discipleship learning, with the possibility of assessment for those who wished it, which would also dovetail

INTRODUCTION

with formal training for licensed ministry. Unfortunately, virtually no progress was made in implementing it, so that five years later a strategy document for the Diocese of Carlisle entitled 'Growing Disciples' made no mention of any regional provision, and a survey of 2013 concluded that 'lay development and discipleship are not clearly articulated as strategic priorities in most dioceses.'[19]

In 2015 the Church made another attempt, this time in a General Synod Paper entitled 'Developing Discipleship'. As well as quoting the 2013 survey, this also concluded that 'there is no well-developed authoritative source for the theology of discipleship to which the contemporary Church of England can readily look to inform its teaching.' As a result, the report continued, the Church's vision of discipleship is unclear; its understanding of service neglects the calling of Christians to live out their Christian faith in the world; the Church's understanding of ministry becomes 'lopsided', with far too much attention devoted to ordained ministry; and, most serious of all, the witness and mission of the Church is impoverished.[20]

The main cause of this situation and 'the biggest obstacle in lay development' was widely perceived to be 'the clericalised culture of church and ministry'.[21] This is the situation to which I drew attention in *Reimagining Ministry*. At the heart of clericalism lies the assumption that ministry is the prerogative of the clergy, so that ministry comes to be defined as 'what the clergy do'. The consequences of clericalism are many:

- Many clergy are reluctant to devolve responsibility and involve others in ministry.
- Many congregations are reluctant to engage in ministry.
- Lay ministry, when it does take place, is seen as 'helping the clergy'.
- Training courses for lay ministry are designed to reproduce the training of the clergy.
- Schemes of pastoral reorganization concentrate on the deployment of the clergy rather than the mission of the whole church.
- Ordained ministry consumes the overwhelming proportion of the Church's financial resources, time and energy.

And in summary: the vital ministry of the whole church is seen as relatively insignificant; so much so that ordained ministry is routinely referred to as 'the' ministry.

'Developing Discipleship' led to a working group under the title of 'Serving Together', which produced an interim report the following year. Once again it was clear that far more of the Church's energy needed to be devoted to lay discipleship and ministry. Most significantly, the obstacles to progress were recognized to lie in the Church's corporate mindset. The 'three essential changes' required all had to do with the need to 'reimagine' or 'reconceive' what we mean by 'ministry'. They are outlined as follows:

- 'Corporate and institutional *reflection on the current theology and practice* of lay ministry needs to continue and gain momentum, strength and a sense of purpose.'
- 'Encouraging through practical action and embedding at all levels the belief that all ministry is best understood and practised as a *collegiate and corporate endeavour*.'
- 'Shifting discourse about lay ministry from concerns about role and identity to the *undertaking of tasks and acts of service* in response to particular missional needs.' In other words, ceasing to think of lay ministry in terms of offices, like Readers or Eucharistic assistants, but starting to think in terms of the ministry required in each local context to fulfil the mission of God in that place.[22]

While the Church continues in its failure to get to grips with the problem of clericalism, mature Christians become frustrated. An online survey of lay church members in the Diocese of St Alban's in 2014 may be taken as representative.[23] The survey demonstrated that the 1,385 lay Christians who completed it had a sound grasp of the theological basis for ministry. By and large they understood that baptism is the basis of the Christian's authorization for ministry, agreed that every Christian has a distinctive call from God and recognized that 'ministry' involved both contributing to the growth of the church and serving God in the wider world. Almost 90 per cent saw lay ministry as important in the life of the church. And significantly there was also a considerable measure of disagreement with the idea that ministry is about 'helping the vicar'.

INTRODUCTION

The survey also revealed considerable frustration, in some cases amounting to impatience, with the failure of the clergy in many places to recognize the place of lay ministry, especially of ministry in the wider world, or to enable and equip lay people for ministry.

In some cases, the frustration is so great that lay people leave the church. In his book *The Invisible Church*, Steve Aisthorpe reports on his survey of over 800 Scottish Christians who continued to practise their faith but had left their churches, in many cases after years of active service, often in positions of leadership. In the cases of more than half of the people he interviewed, the decisive factor in the decision to leave had been a desire to respond to missional opportunities in the area, opportunities their local church was ignoring. One-third agreed with the statement: 'Not being involved in a traditional church congregation frees me to pursue what I believe is my Christian calling.'[24]

The idea that Christians of many years' standing are contemplating or actually leaving their churches in order to free up time to respond to God's call to mission emphasizes the urgency of the challenges posed by 'Serving Together'. It is to those challenges that this book is addressed. My hope is that Christians will not find it necessary to leave their churches, because those churches will be providing the stimulating discipleship learning they look for and recognizing the priority of enabling and equipping them for ministry in the world. But this can only happen effectively when we also reflect on the patterns of our church life with an eye to evaluating their faithfulness to the gospel, ready to face the cost of change should that become necessary.

Discipleship and Ministry

Before embarking on the exploration of how all this can take place, it is important to be clear about the understanding of ministry and discipleship I am taking for granted. What do we mean by ministry and discipleship? And what is the relationship between them?

1 Ministry is the church's participation in the mission of God

Over the last 50 years or so the church has rediscovered the basic truth that mission is primarily the action of God. Mission begins in the heart of God the Trinity; it is an expression of the Trinitarian movement of God towards the world in both creation and redemption. It is not just something God does: it is an aspect of God's character, an overflow of the love of Father, Son and Holy Spirit towards the world God has created. The church does not initiate mission: it is called into being by mission. It has no essence in itself: its nature is derived from its relation to God's mission. 'The Church derives its being from the missionary God and is created and shaped to share in the *missio Dei*, the goal of which is the coming of the kingdom.'[25]

The mission of God goes before the church. The 'chief actor', the 'director of the whole enterprise', is the Holy Spirit.[26] But the church is called to participate: it is a 'privileged instrument' in God's mission.[27] In the words of Rowan Williams, 'mission is finding out what the Holy Spirit is doing and joining in.'[28] We thus encounter that familiar mystery, the relation between divine and human action. Mission is the work of God, and yet also the work of the church: something God initiates in which we are called to participate, and in which our response becomes part of his action. Our response, the work of the whole church, is what we call 'ministry'.

The word most commonly translated 'ministry' in the New Testament is the Greek word *diakonia*. Traditionally, *diakonia* has been understood as 'humble service', and the ministry of 'deacons' as humble service to others in both church and community. More recently, based on an extensive survey of the way the word *diakonia* was ordinarily used in the first century, the New Testament scholar John Collins has proposed that the root meaning of *diakonia* is not so much 'humble' as 'commissioned' service, the carrying out of a 'mandated task'.[29] The person engaged in *diakonia* may simply be an 'assistant', but is often an 'agent' or 'emissary'. This understanding of the word provides an obvious link with the mission of God. It implies that the 'ministry' of the church derives from the fact of its being 'sent'. The church's role as a 'foretaste, sign and agent' of the kingdom of God is expressed through its ministry. Wherever the church participates in the mission of God, there is 'ministry'.

INTRODUCTION

This is the definition of ministry I will be using when we consider learning for ministry. It is a broad one and brings a wide range of activity within its scope: not only participation in church-based programmes of evangelism and service but learning to express Christian love and live out Christian community in the course of everyday life; to discern the presence of God and the signs of God's kingdom in places of daily work; and service on Christ's behalf alongside people of all faiths and none in a variety of community contexts. However, it is not indiscriminately broad: it is related to and defined by the *missio Dei*, another concept with a broad reach, not always easy to define but nevertheless fundamental for the life of the church. It has the merit of relating to and being defined by the call and action of God rather than of the church. It also helps to guard against some of the church's historical errors and shortcomings, especially its tendency to collapse the ministry of the whole church into the ministry of the ordained. Its starting point is the ministry of the *whole church*, shaped by the *missio Dei*.

2 Discipleship is the call to follow Christ by developing Christlike character and a godly pattern of life

In the words of *Shaping the Future*, it is a 'whole-life response to Jesus Christ'.[30] At the heart of the New Testament is the call to Christians to be 'transformed' into the image of Jesus Christ. One of the most remarkable features of Paul's letters is that, convinced as he was of his own calling to preach the gospel and found churches throughout the Roman world, in his letters he never urges the members of those churches to engage in personal evangelism. Rather, his continuous theme is the call to live a transformed life. To the Colossians he writes that he is toiling and struggling 'with all the energy that [Christ] powerfully inspires within me' to present everyone 'mature in Christ' (Colossians 1.28–29). To the Galatians he writes that he is 'in the pain of childbirth until Christ is formed in you' (Galatians 4.19).

This call and process of transformation is a corporate one. The verbs of Paul's exhortations are plural verbs: he is calling them to respond not simply as individuals but as whole communities. To the Philippians he writes of his confidence that he who began a good work 'among you' will bring it to completion in the day of Christ (Philippians 1.6). Later in the letter he urges the fledgling church to aim at unity of heart and mind. And in Ephesians the writer looks forward to the day when, 'all of us come to the unity of the faith . . . to maturity, to the measure of the full stature of Christ . . . we must grow up in every way into . . . Christ, from whom the whole body . . . promotes the body's growth in building itself up in love' (Ephesians 4.13–16).

Partly, the reason for this has to do with mission. Paul clearly wanted his churches to be distinctive in their manner of life so that others would be drawn to Christ, to 'shine like stars in the world' (Philippians 2.15). This mission emphasis is an important element in contemporary calls for distinctive Christian lifestyle. Lesslie Newbigin asks:

> How is it possible that the gospel should be credible, that people should come to believe that the power which has the last word in human affairs is represented by a man hanging on a cross? I am suggesting that the only answer, the only hermeneutic of the gospel, is a congregation of men and women who believe it and live by it.[31]

And Graham Tomlin writes:

> God has chosen to work out his will for the world not through a bunch of individuals being sent out to persuade others to believe in him, but by creating a community made up of very different people, giving them his Spirit who enables them to live together in unity, to develop a new way of life and to live this life publicly.[32]

But the call to transformation is not simply functional, for the sake of effectiveness in mission. The deeper reason has to do with the nature of the Christian life. Baptism symbolizes and effects not just salvation from sin but incorporation into Christ. It calls and requires us to live a new life: the life of Jesus himself, given to us by his Holy Spirit. There is simply no other way of being a Christian.

INTRODUCTION

The compass and content of our vision for the Church is Jesus Christ. In times of uncertainty and confusion, if we navigate by this compass we are likely to stay on course . . . It is Jesus who gives the church its DNA, its genetic code. While the Church may need to take a variety of shapes as our culture changes, it will be on course providing we discern that the risen Christ is at the centre.[33]

We have seen that church, ministry and discipleship are all defined by the mission of God. In the words of Emil Brunner, 'The church exists by mission as a fire exists by burning.'[34] Mission, as the 'overflowing of God's being and nature into God's purposeful activity in the world',[35] calls the church into existence and individuals to discipleship and ministry. But within this overarching framework of understanding, the relationship between ministry and discipleship requires a closer look. The relationship is integral: the disciple's gradual change of inward character and its outward expression in a godly life that reflects the character of Jesus and her participation in the mission of God are part of a single process of gradual formation and reorientation of life.

3 Ministry arises from discipleship

Discipleship is not only an inward and outward transformation into the likeness of Christ, it is at the same time the discovery of our true selves, the people God created us each to be. We are never free until we submit our hearts and minds in obedience to Christ, and we are never so much our true selves as when becoming more like him. One aspect of this discovery of all God made us to be is the discovery of God-given vocation. To some extent this arises through the recognition of the gifts God gives us for his service, some of which are listed in passages in the New Testament such as Romans 12.3–8; 1 Corinthians 12.4–11; Ephesians 4.11. But at a deeper level is the God-given passion or desire that causes us to 'hunger and thirst for righteousness' in a particular corner or aspect of his world.

Francis Dewar lists a number of features of personal calling, among them:

- You will be doing what in your heart of hearts you love to do.
- It will be a generous giving of what you truly are and could be.

- It will be prompted by God.
- It will be something that in *some* way enriches the impoverished, or gives sight to the blind, or release to the prisoners, or freedom for the oppressed.
- It is more likely, statistically speaking, to be in the secular sphere than in the Church, simply because there is more of it.[36]

When speaking about a sense of personal calling, there is a danger that this might become individualistic and even proprietorial: a case of 'my ministry' as the expression of my own particular passions. Dewar's description makes clear that the discovery of genuine God-given passion is neither of these. It is, rather, a generous giving, directed towards the service of God and others. Moreover, his reference to the ministry of God's servant described in Isaiah 61 and quoted by Jesus in the synagogue at Nazareth makes clear that genuine God-given passion is kingdom-shaped, a desire to serve his loving rule. Crucially, for most people the calling is to serve God in the 'secular' sphere: if not in their places of work or lives, then in the wider community.

4 Ministry contributes to discipleship

Rarely can there have been a group of people less prepared for the ministry to which Jesus called them than the apostles. Right up to the time of the Ascension, they still expected the coming of the kingdom to involve the restoration of rule to the people of Israel (Acts 1.6). Only through a painful process of change and conflict did they gradually discover God's purpose that the Gentiles should be included among his people. Earlier, while Jesus was recommissioning Peter for the part he was to play as leader of the apostles, Peter was still looking sideways at the beloved disciple and asking what his future was to be (John 21.20–21)!

But part of the purpose of their ministry was to contribute to their transformation into the people Christ intended them to be. This is expressed perhaps most clearly in Paul's second letter to the Corinthians. The ministry to which God had called him and his companions had brought them to a place of despair. Paul writes: 'we were so utterly, unbearably crushed that we despaired of life itself. Indeed, we felt that we had received the sentence of death so that we would rely not on ourselves but on God who raises the dead' (2 Corinthians 1.8–9). For Paul and his companions, experience of ministry had the effect of refining and deepening their personal discipleship. Later he writes to the Romans: 'we also boast in our sufferings, knowing that suffering produces endurance, and endurance produces character, and character produces hope' (Romans 5.3–4). Later still, to the Philippians he writes: 'I have learned the secret of being well-fed and of going hungry, of having plenty and of being in need' (Philippians 4.12). The experience of ministry had contributed to his growth in discipleship, tried and tested him and developed his character.

Ann Morisy provides a contemporary illustration of the capacity of ministry to facilitate our growth in discipleship in her description of a group of people who had committed themselves to a project providing debt advice.

> One by one, as the volunteers were confronted by the insidiousness with which debt claims its victims and the destruction which results, they found that the pattern of their weekend changed. No longer could they find the motivation to spend Saturday afternoon going round the shops, indulging the extraordinary pleasure which comes from spending money. Each time they looked in the shop window, the slogans which spelt out the availability of instant credit and the discounts for those taking on a charge card churned their stomachs . . . shopping became a functional task, no longer a psychological fix, and its power over them evaporated.[37]

In this case, ministry had the effect of alerting those involved to the influence of secular culture in a particular area of their lives. Involvement in ministry can be expected to have a number of more general effects. It challenges us through the calling to serve, to put the needs of others before our own. It teaches us more of the nature of sin, both the structural sin of society and also the sinful tendencies of our own hearts. It teaches us more of the goodness and mercy of God, his compassion for the poor and marginalized and his strength in our weakness.

Ministry in the Whole of Life

I have suggested that it is impossible to make a clear distinction between ministry and discipleship. Ministry both arises from and contributes to personal discipleship. The distinction between them is fluid: often they will be seen to be complementary aspects of the same situation. In this respect I differ from the accepted position of the Church of England, in which the term 'ministry' is reserved for 'licensed ministry', lay or ordained; that is, for ministry officially recognized by the Church.[38]

It is arguable that using the word 'ministry' for publicly licensed ministry, 'with its key focus on the nurture, development and leadership of the Church and equipping others for service',[39] and 'discipleship' for Christian service in the world preserves a helpful distinction. But there are dangers in this usage of which it is important to be aware. One is the danger of forgetting the integral relationship between discipleship and ministry. Another is thinking of 'ministry' purely in terms of activities that build up the life of the gathered church and forgetting the vital role of the church dispersed in the world. A third is seeking to control the work of the Holy Spirit by insisting, in effect, that he works within our structures. Finally, perhaps the worst danger is that of falling into theological error, the error that sees the life of the church as prior to and independent of God's call to mission.

The church is not an end but a means. It is a foretaste of the kingdom, the first fruits of a salvation that will ultimately extend to the reconciliation of the whole creation under the lordship of Jesus Christ. The goal of mission is the kingdom of God, and ministry is the way the church participates with God the Holy Spirit in working for the coming of the kingdom.

This insight is evocatively and cogently expressed in the work of Miroslav Volf on the significance of 'work in the Spirit'.[40] According to Volf the purpose of human work in the new creation is 'co-operation with the Spirit in the renewal of creation'. The Spirit is the giver of diverse gifts, whose purpose is to enable each person to pursue a God-given vocation to work for the coming of God's kingdom in co-operation with the Holy Spirit. For Volf, as for Dewar, vocation is not a general calling to a particular type of work – the vocation to teach, to be a lawyer, to the church's ministry. It is a specific calling, empowered by the Spirit, to work in an area of passion. Equally, for Volf, the potential for daily work to become a contribution to the coming of the kingdom is for *all* people, not only Christians. Since the kingdom is an expression of our deepest human longings, it is open to all to make their daily occupations a means of working for it.

As Bishop of Durham, Tom Wright rejoiced that so many of the Christians he used to meet:

> went straight from worshipping Jesus in church to making a radical difference in the material lives of people down the street, by running playgroups for children with single-parent working mums, by organizing credit unions to help people at the bottom of the financial ladder find their way to responsible solvency, by campaigning for better housing, against dangerous roads, for drug rehab centres, for wise laws relating to alcohol, for decent library and sporting facilities, for a thousand other things in which God's sovereign rule extends to hard, concrete reality.[41]

All these are examples of 'ministry', not because a local church has organized or even recognized these activities but because they are part and parcel of the mission of God, whose goal is the coming of the kingdom.

But in an ideal world local churches *will* recognize, support and perhaps organize such activities. This will mean encouraging and training Christians to pray for the coming of the kingdom in the places they live and work, to discern the signs of God's kingdom and to work for the kingdom in co-operation with the Holy Spirit, one another and all those who desire the well-being of others. In such instances the line between 'discipleship' and 'ministry' is well and truly blurred: both are taking place, as different aspects of the same situation and activity.

Kingdom Learning

In this book I shall suggest how the ministry of all God's people within a 'collegiate and corporate' pattern of mission and ministry, which the Church of England and its partner denominations aspire to, can become a reality. In part this will be through offering some general principles to guide programmes of discipleship learning and ministerial training. At a deeper level I will be examining the discipline of theological reflection (TR) to show how TR reflects the way people learn most effectively and how, because it is specifically *theological* reflection, TR enables us to grow not only in our understanding of God but also in the realm of feelings and values. I hope to show the way TR enables and challenges us to develop Christian character and so forms us in the likeness of Christ. I will also show the centrality of TR in whole-church learning: the kind of learning through which a local church or whole denomination is enabled to reflect on its own life.

Chapter 1 begins by asking what discipleship meant for the first disciples, the followers of Jesus and members of the New Testament churches. I will be examining the Gospels to tease out Jesus' characteristic teaching methods, Paul's aspirations for his churches, and the ways discipleship learning was expected to take place. I then explore the vision that lies behind discipleship learning: the vision of God's kingdom as the Christian understanding of what it means to live a fully human life in community. Part of any vision for learning is an understanding of the learner. Accordingly, I look at the way adult learning has been understood in the past hundred years and ask how this compares with what we know about the nature of God's kingdom. Finally in Chapter 1, I will raise the subject of character, showing how character development is once again becoming part of the agenda for education in this country, and the part it plays in learning for discipleship and ministry. Recognizing the vital importance of character and virtue as an element in learning raises the question of what knowledge actually is, what approach to learning best facilitates the development of virtue, and how growth in virtue is to be understood in relation to growth in knowledge.

I then devote the whole of Chapter 2 to an exploration of theological reflection. TR is the way we connect life and faith: the way we learn to see our everyday lives through the lens of Christian faith, and the way we recognize and respond to the challenges to faith daily life is continually throwing at us. Although I use an example of TR from ordained ministry, it is a tool equally

INTRODUCTION

adapted for lay and ordained, discipleship and ministry. The example I have chosen allows me to investigate what is going on in TR from several different points of view. I will be exploring the place of Scripture, the role of the church and the involvement of the Holy Spirit. At the heart of the exploration, however, lies the investigation of what knowledge actually is, the way we hold and deploy our knowledge and what is actually going on when we learn.

In Chapter 3, I begin to bring together the exploration so far in order to put it into practice. I begin by showing how TR echoes the widely recognized cycle of experiential learning: how TR can be understood as bringing an intentionally Christian dimension to both formal planned learning and to the informal learning that people engage in all the time. I then look specifically at planned programmes of Christian learning and offer some general guidelines to help those whose responsibility it is to promote discipleship learning in the local church.

However, it is important to be aware that while such programmes have their undoubted value, they are not the most important source of learning in the life of the church. The most important learning comes about as a result of participation in the life of the church, in the course of which people learn to recognize, consciously or unconsciously, the shared perspectives at the heart of the church's life, the meaning of Christian faith for the members of this particular community, their shared expectations for Christian conduct, their vision of mission and ministry. I suggest that the most powerful experiences of learning are likely to be those that come about when these shared assumptions are examined with a view to testing their faithfulness to the gospel. They take the form of 'interventions' with the potential for transformative change in the life of individuals and in the church as a whole. Using theological reflection as a learning tool to enable the church to reflect together on its own life is the key to adaptive change. When used wisely it has the power to overturn the culture of clericalism in which church members are expected to rely on the expertise of the clergy, and to empower and equip ordinary lay Christians for mission and service.

The next section of this chapter takes us deeper still. Here I introduce the concept of a 'practice', first put forward by Alasdair

MacIntyre, an idea that is becoming increasingly influential in discussion of Christian ministry. I show how practices bring together knowledge, skills and virtues in a unified whole. I go on to look at the local church as a 'community of practice' and show how this can make sense of the corporate element of learning, the way we learn together and from one another. Moreover, by exploring the boundaries between the church and the other communities of faith in which people take part, it can also help us to think about the way Christians can be equipped to live out their faith in the varied contexts of their daily life and work.

In Chapter 4, I turn to look specifically at learning for ministry. First I show that ministry itself can be understood as a practice, or rather as a related cluster of practices, and that this has important implications for the way people are trained most effectively for ministry. I then look at the challenges that face the church as we seek to come to terms with the assumptions we have inherited from the past that prevent us from enabling the ministry of the whole church. I show how our existing understanding of leadership, of the nature of knowledge itself and of the nature of theology, conspire together to inhibit the changes we need to make, and suggest how we need to 'reimagine' all three if we are to rise to the challenges that face us. Finally, I suggest some of the ways church leaders can help to equip their congregations for ministry.

Kingdom Learning is not, as I have said, a straight 'how-to-do-it' book, but nor is it a work of pure theory. What I am hoping for is that, by understanding what is going on when people learn, and thus by understanding better what is required to help them to learn, church leaders will be equipped to respond flexibly to the challenge of change, the challenge to reimagine ministry in order to participate more effectively in the mission to which God calls us.

Notes

1 George Lings, 'The Day of Small Things, Church Army, 2016, p. 4, www.churcharmy.org/Groups/244966/Church_Army/Church_Army/Our_work/Research/Fresh_expressions_of/Fresh_expressions_of.aspx.
2 Ann Morisy, *Journeying Out*, London: Continuum, 2004, pp. 1–4.

INTRODUCTION

3 Thomas Hawkins, *The Learning Congregation*, Louisville, KY: Westminster John Knox Press, 1997, p. 3.

4 For the distinction between 'technical' and 'adaptive' situations, see the work of Ronald Heifetz in *Leadership Without Easy Answers*, Cambridge, MA: Harvard University Press, 1994; and Ronald Heifetz, Alexander Grashow and Marty Linsky, *The Practice of Adaptive Leadership*, Boston: MA: Harvard Business Press, 2009.

5 Archbishops' Council, 'Challenges for the New Quinquennium', General Synod Miscellaneous Paper 1815, 2010, § 1.

6 'Challenges for the New Quinquennium', § 11.

7 Archbishops' Council, 'Released for Mission', General Synod Miscellaneous Paper 1092, 2015, p. 3.

8 Adrian Dorber: 'Why is Local Ministry Important for a Mission-Shaped Church?', in *Local Ministry: Story, Process and Meaning*, ed. Robin Greenwood and Caroline Pascoe, London: SPCK, 2006.

9 Peter Senge, *The Fifth Discipline: The Art and Practice of the Learning Organisation*, 2nd edn, New York: Random House, 2006, pp. 13–14 on *metanoia*; pp. 171–4 and 228–9 on hierarchy.

10 David Heywood, *Reimagining Ministry*, London: SCM Press, 2011.

11 This way of describing the relationship of church and kingdom is that of Lesslie Newbigin and first appears in 'On Being the Church for the World', in *The Parish Church*, ed. Giles Ecclestone, London: Mowbray, 1988, pp. 37–8; reprinted in *Lesslie Newbigin: Missionary Theologian*, ed. Paul Weston, London: SPCK, 2006, pp. 137–8. In the documents of Vatican II, *Lumen Gentium* refers to the church as 'sacrament – a sign and agent of communion with God and of unity with all men' and the 'seed and beginning' of the kingdom: *Documents of Vatican II*, ed. Austin Flannery, pp. 350, 353. According to the Lima document, *Baptism, Eucharist and Ministry*, 'The Church is called to proclaim and prefigure the kingdom of God'; Geneva: World Council of Churches, 1982, p. 16.

12 For a survey and reflection on the rapidly growing phenomenon of informal chaplaincy, see Victoria Slater, *Chaplaincy Ministry and the Mission of the Church*, London: SCM Press, 2015.

13 Pope Francis, *Evangelii Gaudium*, London: Catholic Truth Society, 1913, § 24, 119–21; taken up by Steven Croft in 'Developing Disciples', General Synod Paper 1977, § 20, 40.

14 See the work of Ronald Heifetz and Peter Senge, mentioned in notes 4 and 9. For a briefer and more accessible introduction written from a Christian standpoint, see Hawkins, *Learning Congregation*.

15 Archbishops' Council, *Formation for Ministry within a Learning Church*, London: Church House Publishing, 2003.

16 Archbishops' Council, *Shaping the Future: New Patterns of Training for Lay and Ordained*, London: Church House Publishing, 2006.

17 *Shaping the Future*, p. 4.

18 *Shaping the Future*, p. 6.

19 Diocese of Carlisle, *Growing Disciples*, 2011; General Synod Paper 1977, 'Developing Discipleship' § 33.

20 'Developing Discipleship' §§ 33, 37, 38.

21 'Developing Discipleship' § 33.

22 Update on 'Serving Together' for the joint meeting of the House of Bishops and Archbishops' Council, November 2016; emphasis in original.

23 Presented to St Alban's Diocesan Synod on 14 March 2014 by Revd Canon Dr Tim Bull, Director of Ministry for the diocese.
24 Steve Aisthorpe, *The Invisible Church*, London: SCM Press, 2016, pp. 167–83.
25 Martyn Atkins, 'What is the Essence of the Church?', in *Mission-Shaped Questions*, ed. Steven Croft, London: Church House Publishing, 2008, p. 19.
26 John V. Taylor, *The Go-between God*, London: SPCK, 1972, p. 3.
27 The Faith and Order Advisory Group of the Church of England, *The Mission and Ministry of the Whole Church*, London: Church House Publishing, 2007, p. 56.
28 Rowan Williams, Presidential address to the Church of England General Synod, July 2003.
29 John Collins, *Diakonia: Re-interpreting the Ancient Sources*, Oxford: Oxford University Press, 1990.
30 *Shaping the Future*, p. 4.
31 Lesslie Newbigin, *The Gospel in a Pluralist Society*, London: SPCK, 1989, p. 227.
32 Graham Tomlin, *The Provocative Church*, London: SPCK, 2002, p. 69
33 Steven Croft, *Jesus' People: What the Church Should Do Next*, London: Church House Publishing, 2009, p. 8; and see also Peter Allen's opening chapter in George Guiver et al., *The Fire and the Clay*, London: SPCK, 1993, in which he explores the Christian's new identity in Christ.
34 Emil Brunner, *The Word in the World*, London: SCM Press, 1931, p. 138.
35 *Mission and Ministry of the Whole Church*, p. 58.
36 Francis Dewar, *Called or Collared?*, London: SPCK, 1991, pp. 5–6.
37 Ann Morisy, *Beyond the Good Samaritan*, London: Mowbray, 1997, pp. 17–18.
38 See, for example, Archbishops' Council, *Shaping the Future*, pp. 4–5; *Mission and Ministry of the Whole Church*, pp. 62, 64; Martin Davie, *A Guide to the Church of England*, London: Continuum, 2008, p. 108.
39 *Shaping the Future*, p. 4.
40 Miroslav Volf, *Work in the Spirit*, Eugene, OR: Wipf & Stock, 1991; see especially chapter 4, 'Work, Spirit, and New Creation'.
41 Tom Wright, *Surprised by Hope*, London: SPCK, 2007, p. 205.

1

Adult Learning in God's Kingdom

Following Jesus

From the very beginning of his ministry, Jesus called people to 'follow' him. He rarely if ever referred to himself as a 'leader', perhaps because he was extremely critical of the models of leadership on offer in his culture, whether that of the Jewish religious leaders or the Roman occupiers; but he did call 'followers', and the presence of these followers or 'disciples' is a prominent feature of his life and ministry as recorded in all four Gospels.

It is important to remember that the Gospel narratives are not intended simply as records of the things Jesus did and said but as theologically structured accounts in which the principles of arrangement and in many cases the very words chosen are intended to convey profound reflections on Jesus' life and ministry. So it is significant that in both Matthew and Mark the story of the call of the first disciples immediately follows the commencement of Jesus' ministry and his announcement that the 'kingdom of God has come near' (Matthew 4.17; Mark 1.14). The call of a group of disciples who would eventually 'fish for people' is clearly a key part of what we are probably justified in calling Jesus' long-term strategy.[1] John, who structures his Gospel entirely differently, nevertheless conveys the same point: immediately after the prologue of chapter 1, the Fourth Gospel focuses on Jesus' relationship with John the Baptist and then on the call of the first disciples. The account of his call of Peter and Andrew, Philip and Nathaniel leads into that of the first sign at the wedding at Cana, where Jesus 'revealed his glory; and his disciples believed in him' (John 2.11).

KINGDOM LEARNING

Learning from Jesus

From the very beginning Jesus is accompanied in his ministry by a group of followers he has called to be with him. And there are indications that although the twelve named as apostles were all men, the wider discipleship group also included women (Matthew 27.55-56; Mark 15.40-41; Luke 8.1-3). The context in which their call to follow took place was Jesus' mission. Jesus was proclaiming the arrival of the kingdom of God and inviting people to respond in repentance and faith. The miracles he performed were signs of the kingdom's approach, in which sickness and disability were healed, sins were declared forgiven, evil cast out and outcasts restored to their community. The ministry of Jesus marked the inauguration of a new age in which the kingdom of God was present in the person of the King himself. But the presence of the kingdom was discerned only by faith, which typically meant that those who trusted in their own wisdom or righteousness missed the signs while the poor, needy and simple-hearted responded with gratitude.

The disciples' role was to accompany and assist Jesus in this mission: to 'be with him, and to be sent out to proclaim the message' (Mark 3.14). In the course of their life together as an informal band of helpers they were to learn from Jesus about the nature of the kingdom he had come to announce and the mission they were to undertake. Their 'sending out' was an integral part of their discipleship, their serving and learning from him a preparation for mission. Discipleship and ministry overlapped and reinforced one another in the context of a shared mission.

As Sylvia Wilkey Collinson has shown, we can learn a great deal by observing the methods Jesus used to help the disciples to learn what he expected of them.[2] The context in which they learned was a common life centred on Jesus as leader and teacher with the shared purpose of assisting him in his God-given mission. Within this context it is clear that Jesus' teaching methods consisted of a balance of formal instruction and informal learning. The Gospels record a number of memorable and pithy sayings that sum up aspects of Jesus' teaching (Matthew 6.19-24; 7.7-8; 16.24-26). We are shown Jesus giving them instruction about specific areas of life, such as prayer (Luke 11.1-13), money

ADULT LEARNING IN GOD'S KINGDOM

(Matthew 6.24–34) and sexual ethics (Matthew 5.27–32; 19.1–12). We are told that after speaking to the crowd in parables he took his disciples aside and explained everything to them (Mark 4.33–34). And we are particularly told that after his resurrection he spent a considerable period with them teaching them about the kingdom of God (Acts 1.3).

But alongside the formal teaching, occasions for learning occurred spontaneously through questions, disputes, misunderstandings and demonstration. Even the practical task of organizing the crowds who flocked to Jesus had a learning dimension, as we see at the feeding of the 5,000 (Mark 6.35–36; 8.14–21) and when Jesus rebukes the disciples for turning away children and their carers (Mark 10.13–16). In Luke's account the formal teaching that includes the Lord's Prayer arises from a question provoked by Jesus' own example. An important lesson on attitudes to wealth arises from observing the contrast between people giving to the Temple treasury (Mark 12.41–44). New insights on exorcism arise from an instance of failure after previous successes (Mark 9.28–29). Opportunities for teaching might arise when one or more disciples asked advice about tricky situations (Mark 9.38–41; Matthew 17.24–27). The countercultural nature of the life Jesus invited them to share exposed them to frequent questioning, in particular from the guardians of the religious status quo, which required Jesus to explain the nature of their calling (Matthew 8.18–22; 9.10–17). And their common life threw up tensions whose resolution involved important lessons in the attitudes required by the kingdom (Mark 10.35–45).

Moreover, as Collinson suggests, it is likely that Jesus deliberately set out to prepare the disciples for their role in announcing the kingdom by arranging some important learning opportunities. The parable of the sower and those that follow prepare them for a mixed reception (Mark 4.1–32); the action of taking them to sea with a storm imminent and then calming the storm assures them of his power to protect them in danger (4.35–41); three major miracles demonstrate his power to heal and cast out evil spirits (5.1–43); and finally his reception at Nazareth is an example of the rejection they are to expect in some places (6.1–6). 'Each of these lessons was imperative for the Twelve to learn if they were to fulfil his mission and realistically be prepared to face the variety of responses to their message.'[3] At a later stage, in the context of the journey to Jerusalem, Jesus is teaching them about the nature of life together in the kingdom of God, challenging their desire to direct the course of their own lives (Mark 8.31–38); their competitiveness (9.33–41); their social attitudes (10.2–16); their attitudes to wealth (10.17–31); their desire for power and position (10.35–45). All this learning took place in the course of discussion, question and answer, challenges from outsiders, comments and correction.

In summary, the Gospels reveal Jesus to have been a master of the action-reflection approach to learning. It is often remarked that his choice of his disciples defies the kind of rationale that makes sense in our contemporary culture. The men and women he gathered around him do not seem to have been particularly intelligent or gifted. Rather, the Gospels draw attention to the variety of their social backgrounds, their hesitancy and frequent failure to understand. They appear to be united only by their 'ordinariness', their response to Jesus' call and their willingness to share the conditions of his mission. Together they formed a learning community, learning from Jesus in the context of a shared life in which formal instruction took place in the midst of shared experience, action and reflection. Collinson draws attention to this as the heart of Jesus' approach, the key method by which he was able to facilitate the development of a genuine learning community among this mixed group of people: 'The action-reflection method . . . provides a solution to every caring teacher's problem, that of encouraging those not gifted academically to learn and operate successfully at their own level of giftedness.'[4]

Learning in the early church
At the end of Matthew's Gospel the evangelist records that Jesus instructed his followers to 'make disciples' of all nations, 'baptizing them in the name of the Father, the Son and the Holy Spirit, and teaching them to obey everything that I have commanded you', remembering that he promises to be with them at all times 'to the end of the age' (Matthew 28.19–20). Clearly Matthew

implies that the disciples' pattern of life as a learning community gathered around Jesus is to continue as the Christian community grows by the addition of men and women who will themselves become disciples. This is precisely what we observe in Luke's account of the earliest church in the book of Acts. The major difference is that Jesus is no longer present in person, so the task of discipling others and of discerning the direction for his discipleship community falls on those who are now usually called the 'apostles'. Even so, the word 'disciples', which occurs 28 times in the book, continues to be the standard term for Christian believers. Significantly, the word is nearly always plural: 'disciples' are members of a community who learn together. Most significant of all, believers continue to be disciples of Jesus, not of the apostles: the risen Lord continues to be present as the focus of their devotion, even though the work of teaching devolves to others.[5]

In the context of their community life it is clear that formal teaching occupied an important place. The earliest believers 'devoted themselves to the apostles' teaching' (Acts 2.42). Paul frequently uses his letters to remind the members of his churches of the instructions he has given them (1 Corinthians 11.23–26; 15.1–7; 1 Thessalonians 4.1–2). The presence of the 'household tables', those instructions as to how Christian faith applies to believers in their roles as masters and slaves, husbands and wives, parents and children, as well as to their attitude to civil authorities (Colossians 3.18–4.1; Ephesians 5.21–6.9; 1 Peter 2.11–3.12), suggests that a commonly accepted pattern of Christian teaching soon developed. So too do fragments of what appear to be baptismal instruction (Romans 6.1–11; Colossians 3.5–11; 1 Peter 3.18–22). To strengthen the faithful through teaching, especially the instruction of recent converts, was an important element in the life of the churches, and one to which some were specifically called (Romans 12.7; Ephesians 4.11; Hebrews 5.12; 13.7; James 3.1).

This formal teaching took place in the context of a shared life in which mutual exhortation and correction were important elements (2 Corinthians 2.5–8; 1 Thessalonians 5.12–13; Hebrews 3.12–13). The book of Acts shows the early church learning through action and reflection the demands of shared community: how to respond to persecution (Acts 4.23–31), divergences of wealth among themselves (4.32–37), deceit within the community (5.1–11) and division along ethnic lines (6.1–7). Just as Paul's letters provide evidence of the formal teaching he gave his churches, so they show him responding to particular problems and providing guidance for the churches in specific situations. As Collinson summarizes, 'The life of the community itself and its members became agents for discipling to take place.'[6]

There was, moreover, 'no attempt to set up a school to carry on the task of teaching those who came into the faith or to train future leaders'. Partly this was due to circumstances: the early church quickly began to experience persecution and consequent dislocation; it was also growing at a rate that would have outstripped any possibility of forming an institution. In such a situation, the methods pioneered by Jesus were sufficient: the formation of small, family-like groups of believers committed to Jesus, capable of growing in love for one another and supporting one another in the face of opposition and persecution. In these groups, each learned to contribute their various gifts for the benefit of all, and teaching and learning took place in both formal and informal ways. As Collinson comments:

> A schooling model would have severely limited the potential for growth within the faith communities. The discipling model had a capacity for encompassing a wide variety of people from different ethnic, cultural and educational backgrounds. It was not confined to buildings, curriculum or specific methods of teaching. It was ideally suited to the rapidly changing experience of those early communities.[7]

Transformation

But what was the goal of discipleship now that the immediate purpose of participation in Jesus' Galilean ministry no longer applied? What was to be the aspiration of those whose conversion did not mean leaving their homes or abandoning their jobs and families? On this point the New Testament epistles, especially those of Paul,

ADULT LEARNING IN GOD'S KINGDOM

are clear: the goal is personal and corporate transformation into the image of Jesus. In the words of Jesus himself, disciples are to become 'like the teacher' (Matthew 10.24–25; Luke 6.40).

As I noted in the Introduction, it is remarkable that Paul, who was consumed by a zeal for the gospel and convinced of his own call to travel the Mediterranean world establishing churches in places not yet evangelized, should nowhere in his correspondence exhort the members of those churches to engage in personal evangelism. Instead his message is clear in every one of his letters: 'be transformed' (Romans 12.2). The pattern for that transformation was to be the character of Christ himself. To the Romans he writes that all who are called are 'predestined to be conformed to the image of his Son' (Romans 8.29). To the Galatians he writes of his deep concern, like the pain of childbirth, 'until Christ is formed in you' (Galatians 4.19). The power by which such a transformation is to be accomplished is that of the Holy Spirit at work within them. To the Galatians he writes that the qualities to which they should aspire are the 'fruit of the Spirit' (Galatians 5.22–23); and in Romans 8 he demonstrates that the Spirit is the means through which we are enabled to overcome the power of sin and so fulfil the righteous demands of the Law.

Finally, and perhaps most important, this transformation is corporate: it is not as individuals but as disciples together that we grow in our likeness to Christ. In 1 Corinthians 12, Paul contrasts the working of God's Holy Spirit with the spirits they had encountered in their pagan past. The characteristic of the Holy Spirit is first that he acknowledges Jesus as Lord, and then that he leads us to unity in diversity, a common life in which all are valued, all contribute their gifts in service to one another and, 'If one member suffers, all suffer together . . .; if one member is honoured, all rejoice together' (1 Corinthians 12.26). And in Ephesians, which if not written by Paul was written by someone close to him who knew his mind, the goal of discipleship is accomplished when 'all of us come to the unity of the faith and of the knowledge of the Son of God, to maturity, to the measure of the full stature of Christ . . . from whom the whole body . . . as each part is working properly, promotes the body's growth in building itself up in love' (Ephesians 4.13,16).

Delving more deeply into Paul's writing, it is possible to discern something of the learning process through which he expected this transformation to take place. The letter to the Colossians is especially instructive. It opens with Paul's prayer for the Colossians' growth in the Christian life:

> For this reason, since the day we heard of it [the response of the Christians at Colossae to the preaching of the gospel], we have not ceased praying for you and asking that you may be filled with the knowledge of God's will in all spiritual wisdom and understanding, so that you may lead lives worthy of the Lord, fully pleasing to him, as you bear fruit in every good work and as you grow in the knowledge of God. (Colossians 1.9–10)

Reading Colossians is rather like listening to one side of a telephone call: it is generally agreed that Paul is responding to a group of false teachers, who had introduced at Colossae something they called a 'philosophy' (Colossians 2.8). It is far from clear what this 'philosophy' consisted of, since the only evidence we have is the arguments Paul uses to refute it in the letter itself.[8] But it appears that it offered an esoteric 'wisdom' capable of raising believers to a new level of Christian maturity. It was therefore important for Paul to remind the church of the true nature of such terms as 'knowledge' (in Greek *epignosis*), 'wisdom' (*sophia*) and 'understanding' (*synesis*).

As a student of the Hebrew Scriptures, Paul would have been well aware that the Hebrew word for 'to know', *yada*, is a relational concept. According to Rabbi Abraham Heschel:

> In Hebrew *yada* means more than the possession of abstract concepts . . . It involves both an intellectual and an emotional act. An analysis of the usage of the verb in biblical Hebrew leads to the conclusion that it often, though not always, denotes an act involving concern, inner engagement, dedication or attachment to a person.[9]

In the next section I will explore the importance of our relationships with God and one another as a vital element in all human life. The point to be made here is that in the Bible, 'knowing' takes place in the context of relationships. It is not abstract and objective but related to valuing and loving.

Accordingly, in the passage above, Paul rebukes the Colossians for their erroneous understanding of what it means to 'know' God. First, he reminds them that 'knowledge', 'wisdom' and 'understanding' are centred on and derived from God himself. Knowledge is knowledge of God's will, and understanding is 'spiritual' (*pneumatikos*), derived from the Holy Spirit.[10] Second, these qualities are practical: knowledge, wisdom and understanding issue in lives worthy of the Lord, fully pleasing to him, bearing fruit in every good work. The words 'so that' express an outcome: genuine knowledge of God's will is bound to result in lives of a certain quality. But they also express a purpose: the point of knowing God's will is obedience and changed lives.

Third, it is possible to discern a cycle at work in these verses. Paul assumes that by responding to what they know of God's will in lives worthy of him, his readers will thereby gain further knowledge. Not only does right knowledge lead to right action, right action leads to deeper knowledge.[11] It would be anachronistic to claim that Paul is pointing to what has become known as the 'learning cycle' or making a claim for the importance of praxis, or reflected action, but it would appear that, like Jesus, he expected his converts to learn through a process of action and reflection; at the very least he expects knowledge of God to be acted upon if we wish to grow in wisdom and understanding.

At the centre of Christian learning lies 'Christ himself, in whom are hidden all the treasures of wisdom and knowledge' (Colossians 2.2–3). This is because of Jesus' place in God's plan for his creation. As 'the image of the invisible God, the firstborn of all creation' (1.15), Jesus is the one through whom the true nature not only of God but also of humanity is revealed.

> He is the very centre and crown of the creation, because he is man as God from the beginning designed man to be . . . He is the embodiment of that purpose of God which underlies the

whole creation, and so he supplies the principle of coherence and meaning in the universe.[12]

Today we are so used to living in a pluralist society, in which claims to ultimate truth are treated with suspicion and even ridicule, that it is perhaps necessary to remind ourselves of this important element of both Jewish and Christian tradition. At least 500 years before the birth of Christ, and in the view of many scholars considerably earlier, the Jewish people were claiming that the tribal god of their relatively insignificant state was the creator and ruler of the entire universe, the one to whom every people and their gods would have to give account. The early Christians aroused the hostility of the Roman Empire by claiming that Jesus and not the Emperor was 'Lord'. And towards the end of the first century the writer of John's Gospel made perhaps the most astonishing claim of all. In the Stoic philosophy dominant in his time, the *logos* or 'Word' was the rational principle through which the world had been made and by which human beings were enabled to understand it. John's prologue insists that the pre-existent and incarnate Jesus *is* that rational principle, the ultimate source of all truth (John 1.1–18).

So Paul warns the Colossians against 'human tradition', which he characterizes as 'empty deceit', whose source is the 'elemental spirits of the universe' (Colossians 2.8). Christ is the measure of all truth and wisdom; the riches we have in him are not to be measured by any earthly system of philosophy. Our goal is to understand the truth as we have it in Jesus himself, something that can only come about as we obediently live it out. He likens this process to a stripping off of the 'old self' and a putting on of the 'new self', 'which is being renewed in knowledge according to the image of its creator' (3.9–10). Christian discipleship, in other words, involves a transformation of identity, which comes about as we live from a centre in Christ rather than in our old self.

Practical wisdom

Paul's vision of discipleship is further filled out in the letter to the Philippians. Here again Paul is looking for transformed lives with love at the centre:

And this is my prayer, that your love may overflow more and more with knowledge and full insight to help you to determine what is best, so that on the day of Christ you may be pure and blameless, having produced the harvest of righteousness that comes through Jesus Christ for the glory and praise of God. (Philippians 1.9–11)

Once again, love and knowledge, intellectual understanding and quality of life are held together. Neither will grow without the other: understanding is an outcome of love and love requires insight in order to determine what is best. The measure of both love and knowledge is Jesus himself. In chapter 2, Paul draws on what was perhaps an early hymn describing the way Jesus 'emptied himself' out of obedience to God the Father in order to become a slave to all (2.6–8). His purpose is to exhort the Philippians to serve each other in the same way, looking not to their own interests but to the interests of others. The 'mind' they should have is the same as that of Christ himself (2.4–5).

One of the distinctive characteristics of Philippians is the frequent use of the Greek verb *phronein*, the verb form linked with the noun *phronesis* or 'practical wisdom'. As Marianne Meye Thompson points out, the ancient Greek philosopher Aristotle had spoken of *sophia*, *synesis* and *phronesis* as the three highest virtues.[13] For Aristotle, *phronesis* was a wisdom that goes beyond the purely intellectual. According to Gordon Fee, 'it has to do with having or developing a certain "mind-set", including attitudes and dispositions.'[14] Stephen Fowl explains it as a form of practical moral judgement in which thinking, feeling and acting are united.[15] In 4.10, Paul rejoices that the Philippians' 'disposition' of concern for him and partnership in the gospel had taken the form of the financial gift he had received through their messenger Epaphroditus. By way of reply he assures them of his own 'disposition' of love and affection towards them (1.7) and then goes on to place this relationship in the context of the disposition all should hold in common (2.2), exemplified in Jesus Christ's sacrificial suffering for us (2.5–11). 'Let this be your pattern of thinking, acting and feeling, which was also displayed in Christ Jesus' is Fowl's translation of 2.5, leading into the hymn of Jesus' humiliation and exaltation.[16]

And yet there is more to *phronesis* than this uniting of intellect, feeling and action. Moral judgement requires right valuing. To be 'of one mind' involves agreement on what is good and what is best. So in 1.7, Paul writes to the Philippians about the value he places on them; in 1 Corinthians 4.6 he urges his readers not to value himself or Apollos more highly than each other; in Romans 12.3 he urges them not to value themselves more highly than they should; in 1 Corinthians 13 the idea that as a child he 'thought' like a child carries the overtones of childish values; and in Mark 8.33 and its parallel in Matthew 16.23 the Gospel writers have Jesus rebuking Peter because his values, and with them his thoughts and desires, are not in tune with God's. Outlining his response to Jesus' sacrificial death and resurrection, Paul expresses his desire 'to know Christ and the power of his resurrection and the sharing of his sufferings by becoming like him in his death' (Philippians 3.10). He may not yet have attained this, and others may disagree, but, he affirms, to set one's affections on this state of mind and heart is true Christian maturity (3.15).

By means of 'practical wisdom' Christians are enabled to emulate those qualities of Christ not through slavish imitation but as a guide to discerning the way Jesus calls them to live in any given situation. In Philippians, Paul gives four examples of the 'mind' or 'disposition' of Christ, two from his own life and one each from the life of Timothy and Epaphroditus. The Philippians should not be alarmed or upset by Paul's imprisonment or the possibility of his condemnation and death. In fact, he writes, his imprisonment is serving the gospel and, like Jesus, he is content to die if need be in God's service (1.12–14, 21–26). Timothy is 'genuinely concerned for your welfare' (2.20), while Epaphroditus was willing to risk his life in order to serve Paul (2.29). Finally, Paul sees all his earthly advantages and qualifications as mere rubbish beside the surpassing worth of knowing Christ in his suffering and resurrection (3.7–11).

And yet at the end of the day we do not achieve this conformity to Christ in our own power and strength or even our own wisdom: 'it is God who is at work in you, enabling you both to will and to work for his good pleasure' (Philippians 2.13). The power and discernment is that of God's Holy Spirit. This is why Dietrich Bonhoeffer can write:

> To be conformed to Christ is not an image to be striven after. It is not as though we had to imitate him as well as we could. We cannot transform ourselves into his image; it is rather the form of Christ which seeks to be formed in us, and to be manifested in us. We must be assimilated to the form of Christ in its entirety, the form of Christ incarnate, crucified and glorified.[17]

Discipleship in the New Testament
What may we conclude from this brief exploration of the example of Jesus and the early church? First, that the goal of Christian discipleship was transformation. Far more than a change of religious allegiance, commitment to Christ involved a change of personal orientation: a step on the journey of *metanoia*, a change of mind and heart resulting in outwardly changed behaviour. Second, the knowledge that resources Christian growth was more than intellectual: it was rooted in right desiring or right valuing, which united thought, feeling and action. And it was intended to produce a practical outcome in the shape of lives dedicated to the worship of God, bearing good fruit and bringing glory to God. Moreover, such kingdom learning was self-reinforcing: knowledge acted upon led to further growth in knowledge. Conversely, to approach Christian learning as merely speculative, treating the knowledge gained from it as neutral and divorcing it from action, was to introduce a block to further learning.

The journey of discipleship was a shared journey, which took place in small groups, united by commitment to Christ, meeting together in homes and sharing a common life. Although formal instruction played an important role, the context was of informal learning. The ideal presented in the New Testament is of a community in which all contribute their gifts and experience; all seek to encourage one another and share the care of one another; all submit to the discipline of a shared life and the need for occasional admonition, rebuke and repentance. Moreover, all share in discernment about the challenges of maintaining the community's well-being and corporate life together in the face of persecution or hostility, the attraction of other ways of life and the subtle influence of worldly ways of thinking inherited from the surrounding culture. This transformation, which is the goal of discipleship, is corporate rather than individual, visible in relationships within the community and between the community and those outside. The choice of such informal communities and the method of action and reflection appear to be the most advantageous context for the kind of growth in character and commitment that is the aim of Christian learning.

Finally, despite the lack of emphasis on personal evangelism, the context for discipleship in the early church, just as for the original disciples, was mission. As Graham Tomlin remarks, 'The true location of Christian behaviour is not in the doctrine of salvation but in the doctrine of mission.'[18] A few Christians were members of teams like Paul's, enduring for short or longer periods the hardships of mission, developing qualities of Christlikeness, as did Timothy and Epaphroditus, through responding to the challenges of missionary service.[19] The majority were members of local churches for whom inward growth in the fruits of the Holy Spirit were reflected in transformed relationships, creating communities of wholeness and healing through which rich and poor, women and men, slave and free were called and enabled to relate as brothers and sisters. In theological terms the purpose of these transformed communities was to make known the wisdom of God to the 'rulers and authorities in the heavenly places' (Ephesians 3.10). In practical terms it was to have an impact on the society of which they were a part through the transformation of family, working and civic life, in the process drawing others to the acknowledgement of Christ as Lord and the journey of discipleship.

The Adult Learner

Like all the great teachers of antiquity, Jesus was a teacher of adults. In contrast to the United States, where adult Christian education has been an integral part of church programmes for many years, it is only relatively recently that the church in Britain has begun to recognize the importance of adult learning. When I began to work in the field of 'Christian education' in the 1980s, almost everyone I spoke to about it assumed I was referring to work with children. In the case of the Church of England, while there have been 'adult education advisers' or their equivalent at diocesan and national level for many years, it is only recently that lay discipleship has begun to be seen as a vital element in the Church's life. Like the neglect of mission, this is another area where a national Church with a guaranteed place as part of the 'establishment' has allowed itself to lose touch with its inheritance of faith and now finds itself facing the need for radical change. Jesus' message, and that of the apostles who followed him, was directed towards adults and called them to transformation. For adults, as much if not more than for children, discipleship is a process of learning leading to changed understanding, attitudes and way of life.

Any programme of education presupposes a vision for human life. Schools and universities are guided by a vision of the kind of society for which their task is to prepare children and young people, something currently a subject of considerable uncertainty and controversy in Britain. In the same way, a programme of learning for discipleship and ministry requires a vision to sustain it. This vision will have at least two aspects:

- It will include an account of the goal of learning: a vision of the fully flourishing human life for both individuals and the community of which they are a part.
- It will include an account of the nature of the learner: what motivates people to learn, and how best does learning take place?

Accordingly, an approach to adult discipleship requires an account of both the purpose of discipleship and the nature of the adult Christian learner. In this section I will lay some basic foundations for an approach to Christian adult learning by suggesting what that overall vision might be.

The nature of God's kingdom

The Christian understanding of fully flourishing human life for both individual and society is summed up in the vision of God's kingdom: a vision for what life would be like were God fully in charge and, we believe, will be like when his rule is finally established. The roots of this vision are to be found in the Old Testament. In Micah 4.1–4, the nations beat their swords into ploughshares and their spears into pruning hooks, and in this world of universal peace, 'they shall all sit under their own vines and their own fig trees, and no one shall make them afraid.' In Isaiah 11.1–9, God's appointed king judges righteously on behalf of the poor and the meek. The harmony thus established extends to nature, with the wolf and the lamb, the leopard and the kid, the cow and the bear, and the lion and the ox dwelling peacefully together. In Psalm 72 the righteous ruler again judges with justice and righteousness, delivering the poor, the weak and the needy. Here too the vision includes prosperity, with grain growing even to the tops of the mountains. Isaiah 65.20–23 presents a vision of economic justice in which people receive fair rewards for their labour, children are born healthy and old people live out their days in peace.[20]

All these glimpses of God's promised future are summed up by the concept of *shalom:* just and harmonious relationships. *Shalom* is 'The substance of the biblical vision of one community embracing all creation . . . all those resources and factors which make communal harmony joyous and effective.'[21] To this we can add the institution of the Sabbath, the command to rest that lies at the heart of Israel's corporate life, a command that not only instituted a rhythm of work and worship but also served as a continual reminder of their dependence on his blessing for their well-being, and an invitation to find the space and time to enjoy his bounty.[22]

At the heart of Jesus' preaching was his announcement that God's kingdom was 'approaching' or 'drawing near' (Matthew 4.17; Mark 1.15). The challenge or invitation to welcome the coming rule of God was a constant theme. His parables of the kingdom describe the way under God's rule 'the last will be first, and the first will be last' (Matthew 20.16), enemies become neighbours, repentant sinners are forgiven, the poor receive a heavenly reward while the rich and prosperous are condemned for their selfishness, those formerly entrusted with the knowledge of God are judged faithless and the benefits of the kingdom are extended to all nations. In his formal teaching to the disciples he instructs them on the way God would have them live under his rule: trusting him for material provision, giving generously, forgiving freely and accepting hardship and persecution for his sake. Through his works he demonstrates the nature of God's rule: compassion to those in need, relief and restoration to the sick and those on the margins, authority over the forces of nature, rebellious spiritual powers, sickness and even death.

In fact not only does Jesus proclaim and demonstrate the coming of God's kingdom, he *is* the presence of the kingdom. He claims to have come to fulfil the Law and the prophets (Matthew 5.17); his presence is what many prophets and righteous men have longed to see (13.17); the way to eternal life includes following him (19.21); and one day he will return in glory to judge all nations (25.31–32). From Jesus' own words it is a short step to those of the apostles, who proclaim him as king, seated at God's right hand in the heavenly realms (Colossians 1.13–14; Ephesians 1.20; Hebrews 2.9; Revelation 1.5). His death and resurrection are the means by which the kingdom of God is established and men and women enjoy the benefits of that rule (Romans 6.5; Colossians 2.13–15; Ephesians 2.6–8; Hebrews 4.14–16; 1 Peter 3.18).

As we have already seen, Jesus himself is the ultimate source and measure of truth. This means that Christian faith rejects some of the most fundamental assumptions of our pluralist society, just as it did many of the assumptions of the first-century Roman world. But in fact, as I hope to show in the course of this book, the idea that truth ultimately resides in a Person is a surer guide to the nature of knowledge and the way people learn and grow than is the prevailing approach to knowledge in contemporary Western society. The foundation for any truth claim is an account of human identity, a vision of what it means to be human, and Jesus is the one through whom the true nature of humanity is revealed. He is 'Man as God from the beginning designed man to be'.[23] In the next chapter we shall note the important role of 'exemplars' in the way we interpret and interact with the world, standard examples that enable us to make sense of the situations we encounter. Jesus is the ultimate exemplar of what it means to be a human being in relationship with God. As we have seen in the previous section, Paul uses him in just this way in his letter to the Philippians, pointing to himself, Timothy and Epaphroditus as examples of Christians exhibiting the qualities of Jesus, each in their different way.

In the words of Dietrich Bonhoeffer, the church is 'Christ existing as community'.[24] 'The church is God's new will and purpose for humanity.'[25] It is the place where the revelation of God in human history becomes visible and comprehensible. God the creator of the universe is a relationship of love. And God has provided indications of his relational nature throughout the created world, from the relativity of space and time, the way electrons occur in matched pairs and plants and animals inhabit ecological niches. Most significant of all, God has created persons like himself. Genesis 1 tells us, in what is clearly intended as a programmatic statement, that human beings are created 'in the image of God'. Like God, we share the mystery of personhood. We have individuality, symbolized by our personal names. We know ourselves and are able to reflect on ourselves as the subjects of our own unique experience, which we hold in our memories. We are aware of having a destiny and the future of our individuality is supremely important to each one of us.

However, none of these things originates in persons understood simply as individuals. Just as God exists in relationship, so the origin of our personal identity lies in relationships. Of supreme importance is the relationship we all have, whether we acknowledge it or not, with God as creator. In addition, we are each born into a network of earthly relationships and it is in and through these relationships that our identity or sense of self comes to be. We literally cannot exist without being sustained by a network of relationships. Our relationships are not incidental to our lives but actually constitute them. We become who we are only in and through relationships with others.[26]

Some relationships are extremely beneficial and help us to thrive and flourish as people; others can be toxic, stifling and destructive, leaving us less well able to face the world. The relationships that enable us to thrive are those where love is present. We are created in relationships and fulfilled in loving relationships: made both to love and be loved. And our experience of loving relationships gives us a further clue to what God is like, because they are a reflection of his character and being.

The New Testament suggests that when we become Christians, something radical happens to us in the realm of relationships. We are placed in right relationship with God the Father through being incorporated 'into' Christ; and as an integral part of this incorporation we receive the gift of the Holy Spirit, who makes this relationship an actuality and empowers us to live from a centre in that new, right relationship. The Spirit's presence has the potential to transform all our relationships as 'the love of God is poured into our hearts' (Romans 5.5). In relation to other Christians we are placed in *koinonia* or fellowship, in which the love of God operating in us is reciprocally given and received, leading to relationships of a different quality, capable of witnessing to the presence of God. In relation to others, the quality of God's love for the loveless, broken, marginalized and enemies becomes a possibility for us, and we are both commanded and empowered to act as agents of that love and of the gospel, the message that explains it.

As God's redeemed community, the church is to be a sign to the world of God's being and purpose. In the words of Lesslie Newbigin, the church is to be a 'foretaste' of God's coming kingdom, witnessing in the quality of its common life to the purpose of God for the whole of creation.[27] As Newbigin writes:

> This community has at its heart the remembering of [Jesus'] words and deeds . . . It exists in him and for him. He is the centre of its life. Its character is given to it, when it is true to its nature, not by the characters of its members but by his character. In so far as it is true to its calling, it becomes the place where men, women and children find that the gospel gives them the framework of understanding, the 'lenses' through which they are able to understand and cope with the world.[28]

Just as the mission of God is an overflow of the love of the Father, Son and Holy Spirit and an expression of his character, so the church's participation in that mission is to be an overflow of the love the church experiences in its common life. Our first call is to receive God's love and be changed by it: the desire to share that love with the wider community is to be a natural overflow of the Trinitarian life in which we participate. Mission undertaken simply for the sake of mission misses the point. The church's vocation is to love God, to seek the coming of his kingdom and to love the wider community. When we respond to this calling under the guidance of the Holy Spirit, mission is the result.[29]

The church is a network of people called into friendship with God and with one another, informed and motivated by a transformed understanding of the world. Admitted to the privilege of friendship with Jesus, we receive insight into God's purposes (John 15.15) and the vision of his kingdom becomes our primary reference point, the lens through which we view every other part of our lives. We learn to see others as those whom God loves: to see Jesus 'in the face of the other' and to seek to love them with the love he gives. We learn to see our daily work as a calling from God to co-operate with the Holy Spirit for the renewal of creation and the coming of the kingdom.[30] As Newbigin again writes:

> The major role of the Church in relation to the great issues of justice and peace . . . will be in its continual nourishing and sustaining men and women who will act responsibly as believers in the course of their secular duties as citizens.[31]

Our vision of the purpose of Christian learning is, therefore, a vision of God's kingdom and for the way his loving rule is to be embodied in the life of the church. Discipleship learning is learning that acknowledges the biblical vision of God's kingdom as a description of what it means to live a fully flourishing human life. But it is more than that: it is the process of transformation through which we learn to live under God's rule. This transformation is intellectual, emotional and behavioural, consisting in the development of habitual patterns of thought, feeling and action that reflect those of Jesus himself. In the words of Paul, it means clothing ourselves, 'with the new self, which is being renewed in knowledge according to the image of its creator' (Colossians 3.10). Or to put it another way, it involves the gradual development of Christian character, marked by the qualities of Jesus himself.

Visions of adult learning
This is not the way adult learning is normally viewed in contemporary British society. In the context of the wider society of which the church is a part, Christian discipleship as an approach to adult learning is countercultural. The past 30 years have seen two broad approaches to adult learning. The first is based on a vision of the self-directed adult learner, in which learning contributes both to a richer and more rounded individual life and to the culture of democracy. The second, which is currently threatening to supplant the other, is a view of adult learning as primarily directed to economic goals: equipping the skilled workforce required in today's global economy.

The second of these approaches may be illustrated by the way the goals set by government for the universities have changed over the past 50 years. In 1961 the Robbins Report listed as the aims and objectives for the universities: instruction in the skills required for the economy taught in such a way as to 'promote the general powers of the mind'; the 'advancement of learning' or the 'search for truth'; and finally:

> There is a function which is more difficult to describe concisely, but that is none the less fundamental; the transmission of a common culture and common standards of citizenship . . . that background of culture and social habit upon which a healthy society depends.[32]

In 1997 the Dearing Report described the aims of higher education in similar terms. Alongside the preparation of individuals to achieve personal fulfilment and serve the needs of the economy, the authors assigned the universities a major role in shaping a democratic, civilized, inclusive society.[33] Just over ten years later, this balance between the economic and the social and cultural purposes of higher education had radically changed. The Labour government had moved control of the university sector to the Department of Business, Innovation and Skills (BIS), and in the 2009 report from BIS, 'Higher Ambitions: The Future of the Universities in a Knowledge Economy', the social and cultural role of higher education institutions had shrunk to the provision of sporting facilities and the prevention of extremism. In many ways the title says it all: the universities are seen as part of the 'knowledge economy', equipping people with the high-level skills required for global competition.[34] The Browne review of university funding the following year saw the purposes of higher education as: 'Sustaining future economic growth and social mobility in an increasingly competitive global economy.'[35]

The trend in thinking with regard to the universities is paralleled in government thinking about the 'adult education' sector. One of the most significant factors in adult education is the need for workers in virtually every sector of the economy continually to upgrade their skills. In economically straitened circumstances, resources previously allocated to the voluntary sector are being redirected towards work-based learning, whose aim is either continuing professional development or 'human resource development'. The idea of human capital is one that has developed steadily since the 1960s, reflected in the increasing number and variety of courses and qualifications designed to equip the learner with work-related skills.[36]

This emphasis on the need to equip adult learners to contribute to the needs of the national economy threatens to displace an older vision of adult learning, whose origins lie in the early twentieth century with the work of John Dewey and then Eduard Lindeman.[37] This approach is based on a vision of adults as self-directed learners. Unlike children, who are expected to learn what they are told they will need for adult life, adults have reached a stage of autonomy at which they choose their own learning goals. Adults' orientation to learning is therefore life-centred: they learn the things they want and need for a more fulfilling and successful life. And learning not only fulfils the need to be self-directing but

ADULT LEARNING IN GOD'S KINGDOM

enhances their ability to achieve it. At the same time, these thinkers believed, because a democratic society is based on as many of its citizens as possible exercising mature judgement, adult learning aimed at building self-direction and critical faculties and thus facilitating rational choice plays a key role in building democratic societies.[38]

The great disadvantage of this model is that it is based explicitly on a rationalist and individualist theory of human nature. It assumes that adults are motivated to learn principally by their own needs rather than the needs of others. It is the product of Western society, in which adulthood is understood as a progression from childhood conformity to individual autonomy, in contrast, for example, to traditional societies, in which adulthood is seen as the stage at which the individual takes responsibility for upholding social norms.[39]

On the other hand, its great advantage is that it pays explicit attention to the factors that contribute to effective learning, and in particular the link between learning and identity. Adults are learning all the time. Research by Allen Tough in the 1970s revealed that almost every adult engages in at least two learning projects every year, and sometimes as many as 15 or 20, and that about 70 per cent of these were planned by the learners themselves. These might be as various as learning the culture of a country and its language in preparation for a foreign holiday, developing parenting skills on the birth of a child, learning a musical instrument or acquiring a technical skill like boat-building. With the rapid development of new technologies and the availability of information on the internet since the time of Tough's research, it can safely be assumed that these learning episodes have in no way been reduced.[40]

If we ask why adults continue to learn in adulthood, often at considerable cost of time and effort, the answer seems to lie more in the direction of identity than of economics. As Tough concluded, 'In each episode more than half of the person's total motivation is to gain and retain certain fairly clear knowledge and skill, or to produce some other lasting change in himself.'[41] In the 1990s two studies of adult learners identified the person's dissatisfaction with themselves, desire for change or to better themselves as a primary source of motivation. Linden West summarizes:

> The learners used a variety of language and metaphor to describe how they felt and why they wished to change direction. They talked of emptiness at home, of personal inadequacy and dissatisfaction in relationships, of lost status through unemployment; or of being unable to cope with insecurities in their working lives and wanting to escape into a different career... Many students talked of distressing gaps between who they felt they were and what they wanted to be.[42]

The role of identity in learning provides an explicit link with Christian discipleship. The journey of discipleship involves discovering and learning to live out our true identity in Christ. There is therefore a lot in common between the vision of adult education as self-discovery and the vision of discipleship. Both reflect the conditions of creation, in which God places the world under the dominion of humanity and grants human beings the freedom to shape the world to their own purposes. In both, the underlying themes are those of journey and self-discovery. In both, the goal is individual flourishing.

The differences lie in the vision of what constitutes human flourishing and in particular the role of relationships. God's kingdom is the realm of restored relationships, with God and others. It is in these relationships that the Christian finds identity and fulfilment. Moreover, these are relationships of service: it is in humility regarding others as better than ourselves and looking to the interests of others rather than our own (Philippians 2.3–4) that we express the mindset of Christ. Without denying the autonomy that is God's gift in creation to every human being, the Christian vision is of persons-in-relation, finding our true identity not through striving for self-fulfilment but in service and self-giving.

Characteristics of adult learners

With this in mind it is possible to draw on the work done in the field of adult education over the past 100 years to set out some key characteristics of adults as learners and to place these in the context of learning for discipleship and ministry in the kingdom of God.

Learning in adulthood is natural and all-pervasive
People are learning all the time: at least two and sometimes many more consciously planned learning projects each year. Allen Tough's findings about deliberately planned learning are only the tip of the iceberg. Most learning is unplanned and completely informal: it is the way we adapt to our environment and make sense of situations in order to cope with them. As we shall see in later chapters, people are learning all the time in ways of which they may not be consciously aware.

This observation has a powerful bearing on people's *motivations* to learn. 'Extrinsic' motivations, the desire for things other than the learning itself, play a certain role. People frequently engage in learning – and are encouraged to by their employers and national government – in order to gain entry to a particular career, promotion, a qualification entitling them to a higher salary, or because they are required to upgrade their skills. They also sometimes join a learning programme for social reasons: the satisfaction of being part of the group and of building relationships, perhaps even overcoming loneliness.

But the most powerful motivations are 'intrinsic' and have to do with identity. Sometimes this is about remedying a deficiency, real or imagined: perhaps to make up for what they missed out on at school. Often there is a desire to become a 'better person' in some way, whether through the mastery of some skill such as learning a foreign language or developing creative writing, or simply to become a more educated person. In almost all adult learning, motivation to learn is integrally connected to a sense of 'Who I am' and 'Who I want to become'.[43]

From this point of view, Christian discipleship is a paradigm example of adult learning. To be a child of God and follower of Jesus is our ultimate identity, the one we receive now and will take with us into eternal life with God. In relational terms it is a new allegiance, a conscious commitment to the church and its purposes, including its role in the mission of God. We are therefore justified in seeing learning and transformation as the natural state of Christian believers and programmes of learning as an essential aspect of Christian life. The observation that in many places this is not our experience therefore requires some explanation. Why has the church become so dysfunctional that many of its members fail to see the need for transformation and service, and what can we do to change this?

Adults need to see the relevance of what they are learning
Learning is an effort and a challenge. It involves the possibility of discovering our own ignorance and, even worse, having it exposed before others. It means facing the possibility of change in ways we may not be able to predict. Thus the positive reasons for learning need to outweigh the potential risks. Adults need to see the relevance of the potential learning to their needs, interests and desires.

In addition, most adults are aware of the complexity of the world and the demands it makes on them. They need a strong belief that the effort devoted to learning is going to be worthwhile: that it will help them to achieve their aims and to become the people they want to be. This means that any programme of learning has to sell itself. There have to be good reasons for people to believe that it will fulfil their own learning goals.

Although most programmes of learning are built around 'subjects', the goals learners bring are likely to be related to life situations: learning French, for example, in preparation for holidaying abroad, computing skills in order to cope with new technology, or woodwork in order to make one's own furniture. Developing an interest, such as in history or politics, may be part of an exploration of identity; learning creative writing the outcome of a desire for self-expression. Some of the most significant situations adults face are those life stages, such as marriage, parenthood or bereavement, that require both new skills and significant personal readjustment.

This is an aspect of adult self-directedness. Whereas children learn what society tells them they will need for adult life, in Western society adults are used to exercising personal choice, and adult education has been seen not only as a sphere in which the power of choice is rightly exercised but as contributing to the capacity to be self-directed and to pursue personal goals.

This is why the idea of call and vocation is so important in learning for Christian discipleship and ministry. Christians are called to become the people God wants them to be and to use their gifts to serve God and others. But for most people this is a gradual process. Only gradually, and as the outcome of the very process of repentance and transformation that is Christian discipleship, are our personal goals redirected. This means that the Christian educator has to work with the goals and sources of motivation actually present in the lives of the potential learners, and trust to God to reshape these in his own good time and in the course of the learning process.

It also means that subject-centred learning must be clearly related to Jesus' call. A group may come together to study the New Testament, but the reason for doing so is not to understand the New Testament for its own sake but to learn from it more about what it means to be a Christian disciple. I once led a Bishop's Certificate course in which the fourth term of the course was a study of church history. My initial expectation was that the group would struggle to find any relevance in it to their own life situations. I could not have been more wrong! They found it fascinating: not only did it help them to understand why and how the church had arrived at its present position but, in the words of one member, 'These are our brothers and sisters in Christ!' Their excitement arose from the way the course was affirming and building their identity as members of Christ's worldwide Body.

Adults bring considerable experience to their learning
Any new learning has to enable us to make sense of our past experience. Even children bring experience to learning, and what they learn has to build on what they already know. In the case of adults, the amount of past experience is usually much greater. This is encapsulated by an example given by Jenny Rogers in her introductory textbook on adult learning, quoting the words of a teacher of adults from some years ago:

> My most enjoyable groups have always been with women students who want to take up teaching after rearing their families. They simply will not accept the pat theories of child development because all the time they are asking, 'Did my children do that?' or, 'Was that true when my children were four?' Whereas a 20-year-old will write it straight down in her notebook, the mature woman always pauses to weigh and consider against her own and other people's experience . . . They bring a depth and humour to rather dry theories which younger people could never attain.[44]

In Christian adult learning, whatever may be the subject under discussion, a parable from the Gospels, the possible reordering of part of the church building, the Christian response to migration or human trafficking or the possibility of embarking on a youth project or fresh expression, those involved will always bring with them considerable prior experience and existing attitudes and opinions, sometimes strongly held. Neither individual learning nor shared corporate decisions will take place unless that prior experience is acknowledged and brought into the learning experience.

In practical terms this often means that it can take adults much longer to learn than we expect. This is because adult learners need time to work with their prior experience, time to see the implications of the new experience or information for all they have previously believed. Often it involves 'unlearning': if not the recognition that their previous ideas have been wrong, then at least the reconstruction of their beliefs to take account of new insights, or the making and exploring of new connections with things they already know and believe.

This means that all adult learning is transformational in some way. Sometimes the outcome is a small adjustment of what we already knew and believed, at other times it can involve a profound reorientation: the kind of 'transformative learning' associated with the American writer Jack Mezirow. For Mezirow, transformative learning begins with a disorientating event or dilemma, which means that existing perspectives and ways of dealing with life are revealed as inadequate. This results in a profound reassessment of these perspectives, leading to a reframing or restructuring of one's conception of reality and one's place within it. Such transforming life events might include divorce or redundancy; alternatively, they might outwardly appear relatively unimportant but nevertheless carry great significance for the person concerned.[45]

Clearly Christian discipleship shares in this transformative aspect of learning. Learning for discipleship involves a considerable amount of 'unlearning' and the transformation of both identity and perspectives on life. But it is important to realize that the changes that take place in discipleship are not exceptional in this respect. Not only is transformative learning a common experience outside the Christian context, but this is so because all learning involves some degree of reconstruction and reordering of what we know and the way we see the world.

Perhaps the best metaphor to characterize adult learning in the conditions of contemporary society, with the continual need to adapt to challenge and change, is the journey: a journey of development and self-discovery, not excluding the possibility of wrong turnings, personal crises, disruption and disconnection. The assumption of our society is that on this journey it is the learner himself who is in charge, the one making all the key decisions about when and how he wishes to engage with learning opportunities. This means that the teacher of adults is a companion and facilitator. She carries the authority that belongs to her knowledge of the subject and her expertise in facilitating learning, but places this at the service of the learner, guiding but not directing.

This does not rule out the possibility of challenge. Stephen Brookfield, who is one of the principal advocates of 'self-directed learning', nevertheless resists the idea that all teachers have to do is supply resources to enable adults to take ownership of their own learning. There is also an important role for challenge:

> The particular function of the facilitator is to challenge learners with alternative ways of interpreting their experience and to present to them ideas and behaviors that cause them to examine critically their values, ways of acting, and the assumptions by which they live.[46]

What teachers must strive to do, and what is perhaps the most difficult of all pedagogic balances to strike, is to prompt adults to consider alternatives and to encourage them to scrutinize their own values and behaviors, without making this scrutiny such a disturbing and personally threatening experience as to become a block to learning.[47]

Clearly this requires a relationship of trust. The learner must have confidence in the teacher's integrity and in her concern for his well-being. That integrity requires the teacher to share the journey in such a way that the learning event becomes a place where teacher and learner engage in a shared process of discovery, animated by a mutual love of the subject. The teacher's willingness to go on learning and her concern for the learners will spring from the virtue of humility: the ability to value her own expertise while placing it at the disposal of the learners; her willingness to be challenged in the process of learning; and, in a Christian context, her desire to continue growing in the likeness of Christ.

People learn in relationships
Our discussion of the role of experience in learning has highlighted another key element: the importance of relationships. We are relational beings, whose identity is formed in relationship with others. For the adult learner, not only is the relationship with the teacher significant but also relationships with fellow learners on the same journey of exploration and discovery. Although it is possible to learn on one's own, and most internet-based learning assumes this, relationships are still involved. The learner must trust the sources of information made available to him, and his learning will affect his relationships with others, such as colleagues and family members.

Most learning, however, takes place in groups. A group is far more than a random collection of individuals. A group rapidly becomes an entity in itself, with its own norms and expectations. As a context for learning, the shared life of the group can have significant advantages, but there are also some potential disadvantages, which are capable of obstructing learning. On the plus side:

- The group can provide a supportive environment, creating a climate of acceptance, a sense of solidarity, reinforcing the motivation to learn, supporting exploration and experiment and affirming success.
- Each member brings their own experience, which together provide a rich resource for learning.
- The group may provide an appropriate challenge, in which the learner encounters a range of different views and perspectives.
- Loyalty to the group may provide a significant motivation for an individual to continue the learning in the face of adverse circumstances.

On the other hand, groups may also impede learning:

- Groups tend to develop shared norms, which may discourage exploration, experiment and challenge in favour of comfortable conformity. Some group members' fear of conflict may inhibit disagreement. Prejudices and expectations may go unchallenged for fear of 'rocking the boat'.
- The potential strength of the group in providing a place of affirmation for its individual members may turn into a weakness if members become typecast, expected to play a particular role from which it is difficult to break out.
- The prevailing learning style, or pace of learning, may not suit all the members.[48]

Many churches encourage their members to join small groups and see these as places of significant learning. However, small groups do not work for everyone. Even those churches that most actively encourage small groups rarely see membership rise above 40 per cent of their congregation. The reasons for this are related to the disadvantages of group learning listed above. While small groups can affirm they can also exclude; while they can encourage learning they can also stifle it.

Research on small groups strongly suggests that they are very good at some things and not good at others. Small groups tend to act as friendship networks providing personal support, but at the same time enforcing conformity, usually conformity to the church's expectations about Christian life and behaviour. For these very reasons they are not good at encouraging learning or involvement in mission. In a survey of small-group members by Roger Walton, whereas 104 of the 645 respondents mentioned 'fellowship' or 'friendship' as the best part of belonging to a small group, fewer than 40 included the word 'Bible' in their response, and only 18 per cent thought the group had helped get them more involved in local issues such as poverty or loneliness.[49]

Joseph Myers suggests that although everyone has a fundamental need to belong, people 'belong' in four different 'spaces':[50]

- The first is public space, in which people meet occasionally for shared purposes. In public space people are usually strangers to each other, but this does not mean that they do not belong or have a sense of connection. Members of political parties and supporters of the same football team may not know each other personally but share a passionate sense of belonging and commitment. Churches encounter people in public space on a regular basis: at Christmas services, for example, or for baptisms, weddings and funerals. It is easy to assume that these people do not 'belong' in any meaningful way to the church – until we encounter the passions stirred up by a threat to close a church building. Public space provides significant opportunities for learning: Christmas and Remembrance events; Open the Book assemblies in schools; and at a marriage preparation event, even though conversation between the couples themselves may be at an intimate level, the relationship between them and those leading the event may well be located in 'public space'.
- In 'social space' most conversation takes the form of small talk. It is the sphere of 'neighbour relationships', in which people know each other sufficiently well to provide help when needed but rarely share personal information. And yet social space is essential: it is the space in which we belong to entities like our neighbourhood, our workplace or school parents' association. One of the functions of social space is to provide opportunities for people to explore the possibility of forming friendships. A church congregation is a social space, consisting of people we recognize as fellow believers, with several of whom we are being

drawn into friendship. Most of the Christian learning I will be considering in this book takes place in social space. It does not require participants to be friends but it will often encourage a sense of belonging and may include occasional personal sharing.
- Personal space is the space of friendships, the space in which we share likes and dislikes, hopes and fears. It is the space in which we look for emotional support and offer it to others. Ideally this is the space in which a ministry team operates, building close-knit and supportive relationships at the same time as working together in ministry. It is also the space in which small church groups are situated, with the expectation that people will get to know one another and provide pastoral support. Clearly, small groups are a place of some significant learning, especially where people receive the support they need to engage with personal challenges. However, as we have seen, the group dynamic may actually inhibit learning by rewarding conformity.
- Intimate space is reserved for a very few. Myers sees this as the space where we are 'naked and not ashamed', emotionally if not bodily. Some of the most profound Christian transformation may take place in intimate space, but this requires deeply trusted companions: a mentor, spiritual director or trusted friend.

Healthy Christian community, Myers suggests, exists in all four spaces. It is possible to 'belong' in all four. Even though small groups in personal space are held up in some church circles as an ideal, in fact the journey of discipleship involves all four, and most learning takes place in social space. The ideal would be a group capable of functioning in both social and personal space, with the additional possibility of public and intimate belonging. This would be a group that serves together, learns together and plays together, is capable of joining with people who are not part of the group in shared enterprises, and where it is possible to find intimate support and companionship from some few of the members when needed.[51]

Adult learners bring considerable 'baggage' to learning
Adults have been alive for much longer than children. They have had time to accumulate a great deal of varied experience. They

have developed well-established likes and dislikes, tried-and-tested ways of approaching situations.

Most have clear expectations of learning. For some, their memories of school are memories of success. They excelled at learning and enjoyed it, and they come to adult learning with confidence and perhaps the expectation that they will 'shine' as they did at school. For others, their memories of school are not so happy. They are memories of failure and embarrassment, making them extremely reluctant to commit to any further learning. They bring with them the fear of being made to look ignorant and stupid. Some will expect adult learning to be like school: perhaps they expect the teacher to be an authority figure, capable of supplying the 'right answers'. Yet others, with different experiences of previous learning, expect more active learning styles with the opportunity to explore. And others may not expect adult learning to be like school at all. But in every case it is likely that anxiety will be a factor: fear of the unknown and the unexpected. This is one reason why it is important wherever possible to let people know what to expect: to clarify what will actually happen in the learning event and, where possible, to explain why; and equally important, to plan space at the beginning of any learning event to explore participants' hopes and fears.

Some of the 'baggage' people bring are the wounds of the past, from disappointed expectations to actual abuse. When people are vulnerable, as they usually are in a learning situation, these may come to the surface in unexpected ways. Even as a teacher in ministerial education, with highly motivated students who have arrived in training only after a rigorous process of discernment, I have to manage the learning environment carefully, clarifying expectations, regulating the scope of class activity and occasionally responding on a one-to-one basis to individual problems. But partly that is because I am continually challenging my students, introducing new ways of thinking about ministry and giving them activities that stretch their capacity.

Effective learning requires the right balance of support and challenge. It requires a 'holding environment' in which challenges can be faced and change take place. In part this holding environment is provided by adequate facilities: well-lit comfortable meeting rooms and sufficient refreshments. The skill of the teacher, her ability to make people feel 'safe' by defusing the anxieties they bring, her ability to establish an expectation of love and justice in which group members respect and listen to each other, will be a vital factor. In the context of adult discipleship, the Christian congregation ideally provides a loving community in which each person is accepted as they are, valued in all their uniqueness and forgiven for their faults and failings. In loving community people are far more likely to become vulnerable enough to learn, to confront their ignorance and insecurity and embrace the possibility of change.

Loving community is not only the context for Christian learning, it is also the goal. The perfect community does not exist this side of heaven. All that is required for effective learning is 'good enough' community offering 'good enough' support and challenge. This will be a community of character, in which people are not simply growing in knowledge but experiencing personal transformation, growing into the likeness of Jesus himself, demonstrating the fruit of the Spirit: compassion, kindness, gentleness, humility and, above all, the love that puts the other first, bears and forgives.

Any programme of education requires a vision of human flourishing, for both individual and community. The vision that provides the foundation for Christian learning is the hope of God's coming kingdom. Adult Christian discipleship equips Christians both to understand and to live under God's just and loving rule. It involves learning to live out our identity as children of God and followers of Jesus, and in the process experiencing transformation by the power of God's Holy Spirit so as to be conformed to the likeness of Christ himself. Thus at the heart of discipleship learning is the idea of virtue or character. In contemporary society, however, these ideas are the subject of a good deal of misunderstanding. In the final section of this chapter, therefore, we turn to the subject of character and ask what we mean by it and how virtue is learned.

The Recovery of Virtue

Alasdair MacIntyre begins his seminal book *After Virtue* with what he calls a 'disquieting suggestion':

Imagine that the natural sciences were to suffer the effects of a catastrophe. A series of environmental disasters are blamed by the general public on the scientists. Widespread riots occur, laboratories are burnt down, physicists are lynched, books and instruments are destroyed. Finally a Know-Nothing political movement takes power and successfully abolishes science teaching in schools and universities, imprisoning and executing the remaining scientists. Later still there is a reaction against this destructive movement and enlightened people seek to revive science, although they have largely forgotten what it was. But all they possess are fragments . . .[52]

They know about a few experiments but no longer understand the purpose of these. They have the names of a few scientific terms, such as neutrino, mass, specific gravity or atomic weight, but don't understand what these actually mean. By piecing the fragments together they begin the process of recovery of what they call 'science'. At least at first, it is very little like the science with which we are familiar today, but they have no way of knowing that.

MacIntyre's disquieting suggestion is that this is precisely what happened to the moral understanding of Western civilization as a result of the intellectual movement we know as the 'Enlightenment'. His argument is that the Enlightenment was, in effect, a 'know-nothing' movement, which has abolished and corrupted our understanding of the true basis of human morality by robbing the language of virtue and character of its meaning. All we now possess is fragments. We still use the words, 'character' and 'virtue', and still talk about some specific virtues like 'courage' or 'patience', but we no longer understand what these words actually mean and have no framework within which language like this makes sense.

MacIntyre's thesis may be said to have been empirically verified by some research carried out in 2008–9 by the organization Learning for Life. This was 'an empirical enquiry into the values, virtues, dispositions and attitudes of a sample of students and employees who volunteered to be interviewed'. Asked about the concept of 'character', these young adults, all of whom had performed well in their final school examinations, became incoherent and confused. They recognized the language of character but were unable to make sense of it. They showed some ability to recognize and describe the qualities of good character but continually confused character with personality, leadership ability or the 'soft skills' of interpersonal relationships. They routinely confused friendship with friendliness. Several thought good business practice more important than good character. And there was no mention even of qualities like self-control, justice or courage. The students did recognize that personal values define both character and personal goals and translate into moral imperatives. Significantly, they also recognized the importance of role models such as parents and teachers in the learning of values. But taken as a whole their answers confirm MacIntyre's contention that many people in contemporary society lack a conceptual framework within which the language of character or virtue make sense.[53]

An ethic of character
As we have seen, the ethic of the New Testament is an ethic of character. The goal for which Paul strives, the subject of his prayers, is that all Christians grow to 'maturity in Christ', 'putting on' the character of Christ himself.[54] Nor is Paul out of step with the rest of the New Testament witness. In a variety of different ways, every book of the New Testament carries the same message. Christians live a distinctive way of life based on the character of Christ. In relation to the society in which they live they are 'aliens', 'strangers' or 'exiles', subject to marginalization and exclusion, treated as a threat to society because of their refusal to conform to its ways. Their witness to this society will take place largely through their transformed way of life. So they are firmly instructed not to withdraw into a religious ghetto but to use their roles in society, master or slave, husband, wife and citizen, to express Christian love through Christian character. This way of life does not involve following a set of rules, although it does include a set of guiding principles. It is empowered by the Holy Spirit, who indwells each believer and provides the power required for their behaviour to echo that of Jesus.

Although the Christian way of life contrasted sharply with the culture of the Roman world, the ethical theory that sustained it is typical of the ethics of the ancient world generally. Although that world was divided by a variety of ethical systems, such as Stoicism and Epicureanism, the philosophical basis for all these systems is most clearly articulated by Aristotle's *Nichomachean Ethics*. For Aristotle, virtues are the qualities or excellences required in order to live a good and satisfying life, which is the *telos* or purpose of human existence. Central to his account of moral decision-making is the faculty of *phronesis* or practical wisdom, which enables us to make judgements about the character of the good life and the behaviour that best exemplifies the virtues necessary to achieve it. The New Testament retains the idea that there is a highest form of life and that it is to be attained through developing specific qualities of character. But its vision of this highest form of life and of the qualities of character appropriate to the Christian life is radically transformed. The highest form of life, which will result in universal human well-being, is the kingdom of God, life under God's rule, as taught and demonstrated by Jesus himself. Some of the virtues by which the life of God's kingdom is to be lived out line up with those taught by Aristotle, in particular the cardinal virtues of courage, justice, prudence and temperance. But others differ radically from those most highly esteemed by Roman society, including humility and above all *agape*, now defined as sacrificial, self-giving love. Moreover, the Christian virtue tradition has a different account of how the virtues develop: they are not seen as latent human capacities to be developed simply by regular exercise. They are attainable only through *metanoia*, a radical change of direction echoing the pattern of Jesus' death and resurrection and empowered by the Holy Spirit.[55]

The reason for MacIntyre's contention that the Enlightenment has destroyed virtue ethics is straightforward: central to the Enlightenment is the dogma that reliable knowledge is available only through immediate experience and rational deduction. Anything not verifiable by a combination of these two methods forfeits any claim to knowledge and is consigned to the realm of subjective opinion. It is readily apparent that this dogma destroys the very possibility of *phronesis*. It rules out entirely the possibility of a faculty that *combines* knowing, feeling and acting.

According to the Enlightenment's account of human mental functioning, the roots and function of these faculties are entirely separate. It also rules out the possibility of anything whatever being objectively good, since what is deemed to be 'good' lies outside the sphere of immediate experience and rational deduction. In the course of this book, I hope to demonstrate the falsity of the Enlightenment's picture of what it means to 'know' something, and trace the influence of this on the church's approach to ministerial training. At this stage it is important to recognize that if we are to recover a concept of discipleship learning with growth in Christian character at its heart, this can only be done in the teeth of the Enlightenment's faulty description of human thinking, which has dominated Western culture for the past 200 years.

Character on the agenda
Thankfully, in the early years of the present century the tide is beginning to turn. Character is once again on the agenda. The Learning for Life study expressed disquiet about the lack of clarity surrounding the role of institutions of higher education: specifically, the extent to which universities should be concerning themselves with the formation of character or other life-related skills and helping students to 'create meaningful lives that integrate interests of the head with passions of the heart',[56] rather than concentrating on academic success and employability justified in strictly economic terms. This is just part of a significant re-emergence of interest in the place of character development in education at all levels from primary schools to universities. It is worth mentioning three studies in particular, on which the following discussion will draw: the 2015 report by Demos, the cross-party think tank, 'Character Nation'; the Jubilee Centre study 'Character Education in UK Schools', also of 2015, on which the Demos report draws heavily; and a stimulus paper from Kathleen Quinlan for the Oxford Learning Institute, 'Developing the Whole Student'.[57]

Each one draws on a considerable range of published work, much of which represents a profound cultural shift: a move beyond the postmodern suspicion of all-embracing meta-narratives towards a rediscovery of the value of community and character. In many ways this literature represents a tentative rebuilding of the language of virtue and character along the lines foreseen by MacIntyre, and much of it looks back explicitly to Aristotle's original formulation of virtue ethics. In the Foreword to the Jubilee Centre report, Professor Thomas Lickona acknowledges that 'One of the most important ethical developments of our time has been the recovery of ancient wisdom about the importance of character . . . We cannot live well or create a good society apart from acquiring and practicing virtue.'[58] And reviewing a variety of authors for her stimulus paper, Kathleen Quinlan concludes that 'Most authors espouse an integrative view, emphasising the connections and relationships between thinking, feeling and action.'[59]

The Demos report concludes:

> Evidence suggests that character matters hugely for a variety of later life outcomes. It can help boost educational attainment and motivation to learn among young people, as well as facilitating . . . good mental well-being, positive health behaviours and more success in the labour market.[60]

In other words, character is essential in order to achieve the good life. But just as in the ancient world, it remains unclear exactly what the good life consists of or the nature of the virtues required to attain it. What the research does is identify a set of demonstrably good outcomes, investigate the qualities of character associated with these, and then explore the specific ways through which these may be encouraged by schools and other educational institutions. The Jubilee Centre defines character as 'a set of personal traits or dispositions that produce specific moral emotions, inform motivation and guide conduct', and identifies four main categories of good behaviour: moral virtues, such as honesty, humility, empathy or gratitude; intellectual virtues, such as curiosity and critical thinking; performance virtues, such as resilience and self-regulation; and civic virtues, such as acts of service and volunteering.[61]

Quinlan also notes the variety of terminology in use in this area, including 'character education', 'values education', 'educating for citizenship' and 'holistic education'. The Demos report positively recommends that, despite the preference of many head teachers for terms like 'personal development' or 'developing skills for life', 'character' should be adopted as the description for this agenda: 'The term "character" has its strengths: a rich philosophical heritage, public familiarity, and inclusion of the moral and civic virtues that are often ignored in studies of "social and emotional learning".'[62] All the studies recognize that in proposing renewed emphasis on the development of character, they are swimming against the tide. The Jubilee Centre's report 'Building Character Through Youth Social Action' observes that 'Talking about moral virtues puts [some] providers outside their comfort zone.'[63] Some teachers thought that terms like 'character' could be seen as elitist or even militaristic, and carried overtones of private schools and social class.[64] And Kathleen Quinlan observes that 'higher education is a contested and conflicted sector' where the pressures of the market are towards commodification in the service of economic outcomes.[65]

How does the Church of England stand in relation to this move towards a recovery of character in education? Its research about its own life and learning is nothing like as extensive as that being generated by the Jubilee Centre. But in terms of an aspiration to place character at the centre of the curriculum, the Church has moved earlier and further than the secular educational world. The Church has significant, historically rooted involvement in two areas of education in particular: education in schools and 'theological education', or training for ministry. In both these areas it has made important statements of principle.

Like the Demos report, the Church's report, 'The Fruits of the Spirit', takes the Jubilee Centre report as its starting point.[66] It acknowledges the work of the Centre in defining the moral, intellectual, performance and civic virtues, but seeks to go beyond lists of specific traits to the vision of life within which these virtues make sense and from which they derive their value. It affirms God's kingdom as the heart of a distinctively Christian vision of life and quotes from the developers of the What If Learning programme:

Following Christ is not, in the final analysis, about keeping rules, nor even about following Christian principles and values . . . Rather it is being a particular type of person, one who is shaped by Jesus' teaching; someone whose life is an embodied anticipation of the Kingdom yet to come . . . Sometimes it is thought, wrongly, that character is only a moral dimension when, in fact, it manifests itself in the spiritual, social, intellectual and other dimensions of life. A person of Christian character is someone then who foreshadows God's wise rule in all these dimensions in the sort of person they are.[67]

The report also goes beyond the idea that the values listed in the Jubilee Centre report are universal and objective qualities valued by all, which it sees as a reflection of European and in particular British liberalism. Instead it recognizes that there will be disagreement between cultures about the relative value of various qualities of character, and proposes going beyond tolerance of difference to a real 'reconciliation', which will involve 'finding ways to disagree well'.[68] Finally, it draws attention to some successful examples of character education in Church of England schools as a first step towards establishing the methods by which character may most effectively be taught.

The second area in which character comes to the fore is in the Church's aspirations for ministerial education. In 1987 the authors of the report 'Education for the Church's Ministry' proposed that the goal of ministerial education be seen as the acquisition of 'the wisdom and godly habit of life which are engendered by God's self-presentation of himself in the world and by his grace in the Christian', along with the understanding of 'how they are to be exercised in and through the corporate ministry of the Church of England and for the world'.[69] The report is implicitly drawing on the work of Edward Farley who, in his book *Theologia*, sought to recover the ancient meaning of 'theology' as *habitus*, by which he meant 'a cognitive disposition and orientation of the soul'; 'a *practical*, not theoretical, habit having the primary character of wisdom'.[70] The report went on: 'Theological education should therefore seek to form the ordinand in this wisdom and godly habit of life as a virtue bestowed by the grace of God.'[71]

The idea of *habitus* is not an easy one to grasp, but is central to our understanding of what it means to live the Christian life. By *habitus* is meant a way of life informed by a vision of who God is and an ability to discern and respond to his presence, expressed in consistent patterns of behaviour and relating. When the Hind Report returned to the same question in 2003, it asked the Church's training institutions to seek to enable students to appropriate theology as 'inhabited wisdom' and called this a 'guiding principle' of ministerial education.[72] And in 2006, introducing the learning outcomes for ordained ministry, *Shaping the Future* explained, 'This approach is grounded in an understanding of theology as *habitus* which lays the stress not upon the acquisition of knowledge or skills, but upon the development of people of faith within communities that shape Christian living.'[73] These normative statements call for a certain *type* of knowing, practical rather than simply theoretical, arising from consistent ethical qualities. Rather than simply an academic discipline, they view 'theology' as something closer to the New Testament vision of discipleship learning: a habit of life, a virtue ethic for Christian discipleship and ministry.

Of similar significance is the Preface to the Common Awards, written in 2012 in preparation for the formation of a common curriculum for ministerial education. The Common Awards commit the Church to partnership with a higher education institution, Durham University, and the Preface, while acknowledging the potential of such a partnership to include the Church in 'a vibrant, interdisciplinary community of scholars', nevertheless cautions that while the Common Awards are 'in the world' of contemporary higher education, they are not thereby 'of that world'. The difference is specifically one of epistemology – that is, the way knowledge is understood – and the type of knowledge held to be appropriate to ministerial formation. The Preface observes that the epistemology of higher education can appear dualist, separating theory from practical skills. In contrast:

> A wider and deeper epistemology that also embraces affective knowledge underpins the Common Awards. Such knowledge shapes the emotions, hones virtue and fuels passion after the pattern of Christ . . . The Common Awards offer education

that (re-)asserts the necessary unity of faith and learning, of knowledge and divine revelation, of the pursuit of truth and the nurturing of virtue, and so must reach beyond the aims of prevailing models of higher education and, in some sense, return to its Christian roots . . .

The Common Awards adhere to an understanding of Christian education that is holistic, shaping intellect, spirit, affections, relationships and bodily life. It is more akin to the classical Greek conception of education – *paideia* – that was adopted and adapted by the early church, and within which attention is given to the formational dimensions of the pursuit of knowledge and the acquisition of skills. Formation relates to the transformation of learners into the likeness of Christ and into ways of being, knowing and doing that inhabit the kingdom of God and reflect the God-given callings for which learners are being prepared. It involves the cultivation of virtues, spiritual disciplines, self-mastery and self-awareness, but, above all, seeing the knowledge, love and worship of God as the only and ultimate goal of learning from which all other learning flows.[74]

Through its normative theological statements, then, the Church of England is decisively committed to a view of both public education and ministerial formation that gives central place to the formation of Christian character, and understands the Church as a learning community. Up to the present, however, the implementation of this commitment is only partial. By the nature of the task there is a long way to go in forming a consensus about how to put into practice the principles set out in 'The Fruits of the Spirit' in all Church of England schools. And in ministerial training, as we shall see in later chapters, the emphasis on 'wisdom and godly habit of life' is still somewhat overshadowed by an approach that owes much to the continuing influence of Enlightenment modes of thinking and learning.

Learning character
Character is at the heart of learning for discipleship and ministry, whether in the context of the local church or in more formal ministerial training. But *how* is character learned? What methods

and modes of teaching and learning best facilitate the development in Christian men and women of theology as *habitus*? The Preface to the Common Awards mentions *paideia*, the classical Greek concept of education taken over by the early church, as the key to the educational approach required. But what is entailed by *paideia*? And how easy or indeed appropriate is it to transfer the educational approach of the ancient world into contemporary society?

Some guidance is available from the research conducted into the way schools and other institutions successfully encourage the development of character in young people. The research of the Jubilee Centre demonstrates that teachers view an effective whole-school policy as of prime importance. In other words, character-building needs to be part of the warp and weft of the ethos of the institution. Teachers also see too high a priority given to measurable outcomes as a positive hindrance to the creation of such an ethos.[75] The Demos report supplies a list of 'what works', with whole-school ethos at the top. The list also includes student self-reporting and structured periods of reflection; the availability of personal mentors, whether staff or older pupils; voluntary involvement in programmes of social action; and explicit moral teaching through lessons in philosophy and ethics.[76] Kathleen Quinlan highlights 'active, engaged pedagogies, such as experiential education, service learning, problem-based learning and collaborative learning'. All these, she concludes, share basic principles of learning: they involve reflection on engagement in real-life situations, whether individually or collaboratively. Like the best adult-education approaches, they are life-centred rather than subject-centred.[77]

In the next chapter I want to begin by examining in particular the skill of theological reflection (TR). I believe that an exploration of TR will take us to the heart of discipleship learning and the Christian's call to grow in maturity after the pattern of Christ. There are a number of reasons for this choice:

- First, as Sylvia Wilkey Collinson points out, action-reflection was one of Jesus' most important teaching methods.
- Then too, reflection is specifically mentioned in the research on character-building as an effective element in the mix of methods involved.

- Third, the active pedagogies mentioned by Kathleen Quinlan are linked by a common approach to learning through reflection on action.
- TR honours a number of the characteristics of adult learners that we examined in the previous section. It is situation-related and integrates subject knowledge in a response to situations. It explicitly links the questions arising from present situations with previous experience. And it is inherently a corporate activity: not only does TR call on the wisdom of shared Christian tradition, it is best done with others.
- Fifth, and of crucial importance, the key issue at the heart of kingdom learning concerns our *way of knowing*, a way of knowing that 'shapes the emotions, hones virtue and fuels passion after the pattern of Christ',[78] and the exploration of TR as a way of knowing that unites knowing and feeling, valuing and acting serves as a way into a deeper study of what it really means to 'know' something.
- Following on from this, TR involves *reflexivity*: it requires the learner to be open to and reflect upon their own thoughts, feelings, actions and the deep assumptions that lie behind all these. It is a method that invites 'deep learning', real changes in the way the learner sees themselves in the world. In this way it is intimately related to 'transformative learning'.
- Finally, and following from the two previous considerations, TR plays a key role in the appropriation of Christian faith as *habitus:* a way of seeing the world, a disposition that is indwelt rather than a body of knowledge to which to refer.

In addition there is another series of more practical reasons for focusing on TR. In the first place TR is the skill of applying the learner's knowledge of Scripture and theology to the real and often messy problems of everyday life. In the words of Paul Ballard and John Pritchard, 'Theological reflection is . . . the art of making theology connect with life and ministry so that gospel truth comes alive.'[79] TR honours what Jeff Astley has called the 'ordinary' theology of congregations and believers untrained in formal theology.[80] It helps to bridge the gap between the learning of ordinary, untrained believers and those who have received specialist training for ministry. This is because the cycle of TR provides a structure within which the methods and insights of 'formal' academic theology can be appropriated and usefully applied to all manner of ordinary situations. Equally important, as we shall see, TR is based on sound pedagogical principles: it dovetails easily into those educational approaches most suitable to the learning of adults. And finally, reflection is also a key component of institutional learning. Skills of reflection enable organizations to examine the assumptions that drive their habitual practices, to recognize the potential gaps between their 'espoused theories' and their 'theories-in-use', leading to *metanoia*, a profound change of mind and new ways of seeing. If the Church is to become an effective 'learning organization', skills of reflection need to be widely taught and used.

Notes

1 In relation specifically to Mark's Gospel, R. T. France comments: 'The story Mark tells is to a large extent the story of Jesus as seen by his disciples. It is the story of their gradual "conversion", with its new insights and sacrificial commitments as well as its gaffes and failures . . . Mark sets those first disciples before his readers as a guide to their own following of Jesus' – *The Gospel of Mark*, Grand Rapids, MI: Eerdmans, 2002, p. 28.

2 Sylvia Wilkey Collinson, *Making Disciples: The Significance of Jesus' Educational Methods for Today's Church*, Eugene, OR: Wipf & Stock, 2006 (originally Milton Keynes: Paternoster Press, 2004).

3 Collinson, *Making Disciples*, pp. 37–8.

4 Collinson, *Making Disciples*, pp. 103–4.

5 Collinson, *Making Disciples*, pp. 109–10.

6 Collinson, *Making Disciples*, p. 111.

7 Collinson, *Making Disciples*, pp. 118–19.

8 See F. F. Bruce, *The Epistles to the Colossians, Philemon and to the Ephesians*, Grand Rapids, MI: Eerdmans, 1984, pp. 17–26 for a summary of speculations about the nature of the 'Colossians heresy'; also G. B. Caird, *Paul's Letters from Prison*, Oxford: Oxford University Press, 1976, pp. 160–4.

9 Abraham Heschel, *The Prophets*, New York: HarperCollins, 1962, vol. 1, p. 57.

10 For this point, see Bruce, *Epistles*, p. 45.

11 Bruce, *Epistles*, pp. 45–7

12 Caird, *Paul's Letters*, p. 172.

13 Marianne Meye Thompson, *Colossians and Philemon*, Grand Rapids, MI: Eerdmans, 2005, p. 23.

14 Gordon D. Fee, *Paul's Letter to the Philippians*, Grand Rapids, MI: Eerdmans, 1995, pp. 89f., 184f.

15 Stephen E. Fowl, *Philippians*, Grand Rapids, MI: Eerdmans, 2005, pp. 28f.

16 Fowl, *Philippians*, p. 88. On p. 28 Fowl quotes Wayne Meeks: 'Although Paul does not use the noun, we may say with some cogency that this letter's most comprehensive purpose is the shaping of Christian *phronesis*, a practical moral reasoning that is "conformed to (Christ's) death" in hope of his resurrection' – Meeks, 'The Man from Heaven in Paul's Letter to the Philippians', in *The Future of Early Christianity: Essays in Honor of Helmut Koester*, ed. Birger Pearson, Minneapolis, MN: Fortress Press, 1991, pp. 329–36; quotation from p. 333.

17 Dietrich Bonhoeffer, *The Cost of Discipleship*, London: SCM Press, 1959, p. 272.

18 Nick Spencer and Graham Tomlin, *The Responsive Church*, Leicester: InterVarsity Press, 2005, p. 99.

19 The context of the mission team is now becoming more generally known as 'sodal' as distinct from the 'modal' context of the local church, a distinction made by Ralph Winter in his 1974 article 'The Two Structures of God's Redemptive Mission', http://frontiermissionfellowship.org/uploads/documents/two-structures.pdf.

20 This passage from Isaiah 65 supplies the inspiration for the 'Isaiah Agenda', a programme for mission through community engagement. See Raymond Fung, *The Isaiah Agenda*, Geneva, WCC, 1992.

21 Walter Brueggemann, *Living Toward a Vision*, New York: United Church Press, 1976, p. 16.

22 For more on *shalom* and Sabbath as the twin characteristics of life under the rule of God, see my *Reimagining Ministry*, London: SCM Press, 2011, pp. 77–91.

23 G. B. Caird, *Paul's Letters for Prison*, Oxford: Oxford University Press, 1976, p. 172

24 Dietrich Bonhoeffer, *Sanctorum Communio*, Minneapolis, MN: Fortress Press, 2009, p. 199.

25 Bonhoeffer, *Sanctorum Communio*, p. 141.

26 As Stephen Pickard points out, this argument locates the basis for human community not in redemption but in creation. 'Indeed,' he writes, 'created sociality is exactly what we ought to expect from a Trinitarian account of creation and human life' – *Seeking the Church*, London: SCM Press, 2012, p. 89. He is drawing on the work of Daniel Hardy, who writes of a 'divine ordering' in creation, that 'ultimately implants in the human condition the "being with" which is natural to it' – 'Created and Redeemed Sociality', in Daniel Hardy and Colin Gunton (eds), *On Being the Church: Essays on the Christian Community*, Edinburgh: T. & T. Clark, 1989, p. 42.

27 Lesslie Newbigin, 'On Being the Church for the World', in Giles Ecclestone (ed.), *The Parish Church*, London: Mowbray, 1988, p. 37–8; reprinted in Paul Weston (ed.), *Lesslie Newbigin: Missionary Theologian*, London: SPCK, 2006, pp. 138–9.

28 Lesslie Newbigin, *The Gospel in a Pluralist Society*, London: SPCK, 1989, p. 227.

29 Ann Morisy refers to this as the 'principle of obliquity'. See her *Journeying Out*, London: Continuum, 2004, pp. 11–18.

30 See Miroslav Volf, *Work in the Spirit*, Eugene, OR: Wipf & Stock, 2001, especially pp. 74–5, 88–122.

31 Newbigin, *Gospel in a Pluralist Society*, p. 139.

32 Quoted in Stephen Heap, *What are Universities Good for?*, Cambridge: Grove, 2012, p. 12.

ADULT LEARNING IN GOD'S KINGDOM

33 Heap, *What are Universities Good for?*, p. 12.

34 Department for Business, Innovation and Skills, *Higher Ambitions: The Future of Universities in a Knowledge Economy*, 2009; see especially pp. 80–93.

35 Lord Browne of Madingly, *Securing a Sustainable Future for Higher Education: An Independent Review of Higher Education Funding and Student Finance*, 2010, p. 14.

36 See Peter Jarvis, *Adult Education and Lifelong Learning: Theory and Practice*, 4th edn, Abingdon: Routledge, 2010, pp. 46–52. It is significant that this particular chapter has changed radically in each edition of Jarvis' book.

37 The classic works of John Dewey include *Education and Democracy*, New York: The Free Press, 1916 and *Experience and Education*, London: Collier Macmillan, 1938. Lindeman's seminal work is *The Meaning of Education*, Montreal: Harvester House, 1961 (first published 1926).

38 See further Malcolm S. Knowles, Elwood F. Holton III and Richard A. Swanson, *The Adult Learner*, 8th edn, Abingdon: Routledge, 2015, pp. 18–50.

39 Alan Rogers and Naomi Horrocks, *Teaching Adults*, 4th edn, Maidenhead: Open University Press, 2010, p. 48.

40 See Knowles et al., *Adult Learner*, pp. 36–8.

41 Quoted in Knowles et al., *Adult Learner*, p. 36.

42 Linden West, *Beyond Fragments*, London: Taylor & Francis, 1996, pp. 34–5. See also Pam Coare and Alistair Thomson (eds), *Through the Joy of Learning*, Leicester: NIACE, 1996.

43 See further Jenny Rogers, *Adults Learning*, 5th edn, Maidenhead: Open University Press, 2007, pp. 18–24.

44 Rogers, *Adults Learning*, p. 36.

45 See Jack Mezirow, *Learning as Transformation*, San Francisco: Jossey-Bass, 2000; also James Loder, *The Transforming Moment: Understanding Convictional Experiences*, San Francisco: Harper & Row, 1981.

46 Stephen Brookfield, *Understanding and Facilitating Adult Learning*, Buckingham: Open University Press, 1986, p. 23.

47 Brookfield, *Understanding and Facilitating Adult Learning*, p. 136.

48 Rogers and Horrocks, *Teaching Adults*, pp. 196–9.

49 Roger Walton, *Disciples Together*, London: SCM Press, 2014, pp. 108–22.

50 Joseph Myers, *The Search to Belong*, Grand Rapids, MI: Zondervan, 2003, especially pp. 35–58.

51 This possibility closely echoes the vision for 'transforming communities' in Steven Croft's book of the same name, London: Darton, Longman & Todd, 2002.

52 Alasdair MacIntyre, *After Virtue*, 2nd edn, London: Duckworth, 1985, p. 1.

53 J. Arthur, K. Wilson and R. Godfrey, *Graduates of Character*, Birmingham University, 2009, pp. 22–48, http://learningforlife.org.uk/wplife/research/research-projects/graduates-of-character-values-and-character-higher-education-and-graduate-employment.

54 See, for example, Galatians 5.16–23; Ephesians 4.13–16; Colossians 1.28; 3.9–14.

55 For an introduction to Christian virtue ethics, see Tom Wright, *Virtue Reborn*, London: SPCK, 2010.

56 Kathleen M. Quinlan, 'Developing the Whole Student: Leading Higher Education Initiatives that integrate Heart and Mind', Oxford Learning Institute, University of Oxford, 2011, p. 5, www.lfhe.ac.uk/en/research-resources/publications/index.cfm.

57 Quinlan, 'Developing the Whole Student'; Jonathan Birdwell, Ralph Scott and Louis Reynolds, 'Character Nation: A Demos Report with the Jubilee Centre for Character and Virtues', London: Demos, 2015, www.demos.co.uk/publications/character-nation; James Arthur et al., 'Character Education in UK Schools', University of Birmingham, 2015, www.jubileecentre.ac.uk/1566/projects/previous-work.
58 Arthur et al., 'Character Education', p. 4.
59 Quinlan, 'Developing the Whole Student', p. 7.
60 Demos, 'Character Nation', p. 34.
61 Jubilee Centre for Character and Virtues, 'A Framework for Character Education in Schools', 2015, www.jubileecentre.ac.uk/432/character-education.
62 Demos, 'Character Nation', p. 10.
63 J. Arthur, T. Harrison and E. Taylor, 'Building Character Through Youth Social Action', Jubilee Centre for Character and Virtues, 2015, www.jubileecentre.ac.uk/464/character-education/research.
64 Demos, 'Character Nation', p. 20.
65 Quinlan, 'Developing the Whole Student', p. 4.
66 Church of England Education office, 'The Fruits of the Spirit: A Church of England Discussion Paper on Character Education,' October 2015, https://churchofengland.org/media/2386307/fruits_of_the_spirit.pdf.
67 What If Learning (no date), www.whatiflearning.co.uk/bigpicture/virtues, quoted in 'Fruits of the Spirit', p. 10.
68 'Fruits of the Spirit', pp. 12–15.
69 ACCM Occasional Paper 22, 'Education for the Church's Ministry', § 46.
70 Edward Farley, *Theologia*, Philadelphia, PA: Fortress Press, 1983, p. 35.
71 ACCM 22, § 47.
72 Archbishops' Council, *Formation for Ministry within a Learning Church*, London: Church House Publishing, 2003, § 4.14.
73 Archbishops' Council, *Shaping the Future: New Patterns of Training for Lay and Ordained*, London: Church House Publishing, 2006, p. 60.
74 'Preface to the Common Awards', www.churchofengland.org/clergy-office-holders/ministry/ministerial-education-and-development/common-awards-in-theology-ministry-and-mission/document-library.aspx, pp. 1–2.
75 Jubilee Centre, 'Framework for Character Education', p. 25.
76 Demos, 'Character Nation', p. 12.
77 Quinlan, 'Developing the Whole Student', pp. 10–12.
78 'Preface to the Common Awards', p. 1.
79 Paul Ballard and John Pritchard, *Practical Theology in Action*, 2nd edn, London: SPCK, 2006, p. 127.
80 Jeff Astley, *Ordinary Theology*, Aldershot: Ashgate, 2002.

2

Learning to Connect Life and Faith

Theological Reflection

The purpose of this chapter is to 'break open' the process of theological reflection, to explore the processes of learning involved and the kind of knowledge that results. I have been teaching TR now for over ten years and I know from experience how life-giving it can be. Using the techniques of TR helps students to make vital connections between their faith and the situations they encounter not only as part of their practical placements but also in their daily lives. In the words of one of our students:

> I found that the Pastoral Cycle can be a quick response in any situation, even simply taking a pause in proceedings to re-centre yourself theologically. I have found that using the Pastoral Cycle in a structured way means it is weaving itself into my everyday life. I feel it does not require setting aside a huge amount of time to specifically apply a process to a situation but enables me to more easily bring God into the heart of situations and moments. I recognize that some situations will need more time and a mixture of approaches, and being aware of a variety of reflective tools is crucial, but as a working model I can use even while driving from one place to the next, I am finding the Pastoral Cycle to be effective. I am aware of the limitation of reflecting on my own and think that like other approaches, theological reflection becomes most transformative when done with others.[1]

Over the course of two terms this student has learned to use a particular technique of TR in a flexible way to help her 're-centre':

to make sense of the situations she encounters in the light of faith, to be able to bring God more readily into situations. She also illustrates the way learning to work with a formal technique of TR can help to make our whole life more 'theologically centred', how the implicit question at the centre of TR, 'Where is God in this?', can become a habitual part of our thinking, fed by the confidence that we have well-tried ways of exploring and answering the question. As another student at a different institution testified:

> When I consider my use of this method over the last three years, I am struck as to how much it has, almost without thinking, shaped my reflections and in turn my actions and thus the narrative of the communities in which I have been placed.[2]

The crucial words here are 'almost without thinking'. The methods of TR she had learned had become her habitual way of relating life and theology. Theology had become an 'inhabited wisdom', enabling her to bring her understanding of God and his ways into any and every situation she encountered.

These students are discovering TR as a vital tool for ordained ministry. But it is equally important as an element in discipleship learning. In fact I regularly urge my students not to keep it to themselves, but rather to think of it as a gift to their congregations: to teach it and help others to use it as a regular part of their everyday Christian lives.

The 'pastoral cycle'

Before introducing a concrete example and looking in detail at its various facets, it may be helpful to begin with a brief description of TR, using the technique known as the 'pastoral cycle' as our standard example.[3] I have chosen the pastoral cycle because in my view all valid methods of TR are essentially cyclical, so that all the other various techniques are, in effect, variations on the pastoral cycle. And second, because the pastoral cycle is itself a variation on the well-known 'learning cycle' based on the work of David Kolb, which provides an account of the processes that apply to all learning.[4]

The pastoral cycle has four stages, which for the sake of simplicity we will call Experience, Exploration, Reflection and Response. It is usual to begin with the stage of Experience for the simple reason that so much theological reflection does in fact arise from concrete situations. But it is not necessary to begin there: it is equally possible to begin with any of the stages and follow the cycle round. And although, especially when working as a group, it can be helpful to take a careful step-by-step approach, following the cycle stage by stage, the cycle itself does not require this. In reality, every stage is in continual dialogue and interaction with all the others. It is also important to stress at this stage that using the pastoral cycle for TR is best seen as an aspect of prayer. Unless approached in a spirit of prayerfulness, it can become a dry and barren mechanical technique. But used prayerfully, it shares important characteristics with contemplative disciplines like *lectio divina*: above all the quest for God's presence in the midst of everyday life and experience.

In the Experience phase, the aim is to focus on the experience from which the reflection arises, be this a specific incident, an ongoing situation in the life of a church, family, workplace or organization, encountered in person or through the pages of a newspaper or a television bulletin. And here we need to allow the experience to speak for itself. This may begin with getting the facts straight: 'Where and when did this take place?', 'Who was involved?', 'What was actually said as far as we are able to remember?', 'What were the immediate feelings to arise from it?' At this stage it is important to avoid making judgements as far as possible, except to record any that may have been expressed in the situation itself, perhaps in the course of a conversation.

It can be difficult to separate out our perception of the incident or situation on which we want to reflect from our immediate judgements about it. To do so successfully takes discipline and openness. In this way it is like the discipline of attentive listening, in which we aim to give the person we are listening to our full attention. We put aside our own needs, perhaps to be able to solve their problem, our desire to point them to what seems to us the best path, in order simply to listen: to allow them to tell the story in their own words, to give value to the feelings they want to express, to offer a hospitable space for their bewilderment, anger or perhaps rejoicing. In another context the philosopher Iris Murdoch has written of 'a just and loving gaze', 'a patient and loving regard directed upon a person, a place or a situation'.[5] The words 'just', 'loving' and 'patient' alert us to the dispositions required truly to allow an experience to speak to us in its own terms without rushing on to use it as a springboard for our own reflections and judgements. Already we begin to see how our ability to reflect successfully is heavily dependent on qualities of character, and how the process of reflection calls forth those qualities.

The second phase of the pastoral cycle is Exploration. Here is the stage at which we do begin to bring to mind our previous experience. The purpose is to begin to connect the experience we have chosen to reflect on with previous experiences, both similar and dissimilar. Here we both examine our own feelings and the judgements we find ourselves making in response to the experience; and begin to call on what we already know. In relation to our own feelings and judgements, this is the stage at which reflection becomes reflexive: these judgements and feelings are as much part of the reflection as every other element, and part of the purpose of reflection is to allow ourselves to become aware of them and subject them to critique, including that of others. Examining our feelings and judgements also helps us to locate what for us is the heart of the matter: the issues most at stake, the reason the situation stirs up these particular feelings, the questions we most want to resolve.

Exploration is also the stage at which the pastoral cycle becomes truly interdisciplinary. Often it will involve using frameworks of explanation drawn from disciplines other than theology. Depending on the subject of the reflection, these might include: the psychology of human development, of bereavement, of group behaviour; understandings of leadership styles, teamwork and collaboration, change management, systems theory; adult education; the anthropology of ritual and symbol – and many more. All truth is God's truth, and all these fields of endeavour are attempts to describe and understand the world he has created. But we may need to be careful about the assumptions embedded in these disciplines or espoused by the particular writers we choose to use. For this reason, the pastoral cycle envisages a critical conversation between the perspectives we choose to call on for the Exploration stage and our knowledge of theology.

Up to now we might simply have been describing reflective practice as it is carried out in a number of fields. The key element of distinctively *theological* reflection is the space given at the Reflection stage for the resources of Christian tradition, and especially for the Bible. Some techniques of reflection will ask at this stage: 'What passages from Scripture does this incident/ these feelings bring to mind?' In this way we bring the Bible as an authoritative source for Christian faith and practice directly into contact with the particular incident or situation at the heart of the reflection. Later in this chapter I will be examining in some detail the role the Bible plays in theological reflection, and the reasons it is particularly suited to such a role. But beyond the Bible, the Christian also has the resources of tradition: church history with its many accounts of the lives and struggles of brothers and sisters in Christ; liturgy and hymnody, which may sum up the particular insight we need in an apt phrase; and of course the tradition of formal theology stretching back over the centuries, through which the church has endeavoured to understand God more deeply.

The resources for theological reflection at this stage are so extensive that a choice will need to be made about which are most appropriate. Sometimes the perspectives required are fairly obvious, such as the Christian tradition of hospitality in a reflection on the plight of asylum seekers. At other times the relevance of a particular theological theme may be less obvious but nevertheless powerful, as in 1 Corinthians 9.9 where Paul draws on a provision of the Old Testament law made for the benefit of oxen to make a point about the right of Christian teachers to support from their congregations; or the theme of hospitality may be found to speak to a situation of conflict in a church or other organization. And of course, the Reflection stage also includes a dialogue or 'correlation' between the theological perspectives chosen and the interdisciplinary insights that figured in the Exploration stage.

To provide another example, one of my students chose to write a dissertation on the experience of pastoral reorganization in one particular group of churches.[6] The benefice in question had been brought together a few years before. The rector of the two parishes left suddenly, without explanation. In the ensuing interregnum a decision was taken to carry out a pastoral reorganization involving a merger with a third parish. The benefice was still experiencing dislocation and uncertainty, with a considerable degree of resentment at the changes that had been made, largely without the involvement of the congregations. The interdisciplinary perspectives chosen to examine this situation were bereavement, change management and the experience of blended families; and to accomplish this, the writer had to familiarize herself with each of these. The three theological themes she chose were the Body of Christ, the Good Shepherd and Holy Saturday, the day after the crucifixion, poised between despair at the death of Christ and the hope of resurrection. By carefully outlining the experience of the churches and working with these six themes, it was possible to build up a picture of a benefice struggling with its past while pointing forward to the possibilities for the future that emerge from Christian life and faith.

Exploration and Reflection together lead to 'new insight'. This is the point at which the various insights from the interdisciplinary approaches and the theological tradition crystallize to form a new perspective on the situation at the heart of the reflection. This may take the form of a fuller and clearer understanding of why the action taken at the time was in fact the most appropriate response; or it may provide guidelines for acting differently in future. The outcome of TR may be a holistic, theologically grounded interpretation of the situation or incident, which may itself form a pattern for responding to similar situations that may arise. Equally, the new insight may be a deepened understanding of a passage of Scripture or a theological doctrine, through having seen how it applies in this particular situation. Or it may be an awareness of a new question thrown up by the situation, a challenge to existing beliefs requiring further theological exploration.

All good reflection culminates in the stage of Response. In some cases this will involve concrete proposals for action; or perhaps, as a first step, an outlining of the possibilities. These may be highly creative: who would have thought that flip-flops provided by Street Pastors to young women affected by alcohol would make such an impact? But this is a response that emerged from theological reflection on the potential of enacted love and hope in a situation that appeared a denial of human potential and purpose. Sometimes the response will be less a particular action than a transformed self-understanding or renewed perspective on situations such as the one chosen for reflection, to be taken forward into life and ministry.

I have given a brief outline of a formal process of TR. But most TR is informal and takes place spontaneously, often 'in the moment'. When teaching theological reflection I emphasize that what I see myself doing is like coaching. A tennis or golf coach may systematically take apart a player's forehand or chip to demonstrate where it is going wrong. For the time being the player must concentrate on getting it right, but during the game itself he will forget about the mechanics and simply focus on where he wishes to place the ball. In a similar way, learning how to do TR in a formal way alerts students to the possibilities for reflection in everyday life and ministry, gives them sound models for reflecting effectively and acts as a kind of quality control on their everyday informal reflections.

Now let me introduce the example I wish to use as the basis for the rest of this chapter. It is not an 'exemplary' piece of reflection, which demonstrates just how it should be done. It is, rather, a real example from the experience of Rob Gallagher, a parish priest engaged in the day-to-day work of ministry and mission. It has the further advantage that it is in print, in the book *From Strangers to Neighbours* by David Evans and Mike Fearon. It describes a pastoral encounter of a demanding nature, but not outside the range of experience to be expected in the context of inner-city ministry.

> Originally built by slave-owning white Liverpudlians as an Anglo-Catholic shrine, St Margaret's remarkably is now seen by the local people as being *their* church, where the traumas of births and deaths can be attended to, and where the deep questions of life and death can be asked without fear and ridicule. It is already part of its neighbourhood: a community ready to tell Rob its stories.
>
> The neighbourhood looks to the church to baptize their children, though they don't want to be long-term members. The parents make promises they may not keep – at least not on the church's terms. 'I make the assumption that God is on their

side, and that my role is to work within their understanding of God, and to help them to deal with their own spirituality in their own terms', says Rob.

Rob speaks of a woman who asked him to go round to her flat. When he arrived, he noticed that the armchairs and settee were badly ripped. The woman explained that she had had a serious drug habit. She was a prostitute who sold her body on the streets to pay for her addiction. One day, she looked into the eyes of her eight-year-old daughter, and realized that she couldn't continue this way of life any longer, so she tried diligently to change her life. She found work and began to get her life back in order. But the neighbours came to believe that she must be pushing drugs, to have managed so well, so they called the police. *It was the drug squad who had ruined her only furniture, by slitting it open to search for narcotics.* Rob remembers:

> We were on the torn-up settee and she was in tears. Then she turned to me and said, 'I am determined not to go back to drugs and prostitution, for the sake of my child. But I've got to *mark* this resolution in some way. When I look at my child, all I can think of is having my girl baptized. Will you do her?'
>
> My head was saying: What about church attendance? What about the vows? Does she know what they mean? Has she heard about Jesus? Will the child be confirmed afterwards? But my heart said simply 'Yes!' I'm not sure that the theology would have meant anything to her but, being well-versed in Scripture, the line that was going through my own mind – my 'gut feeling' – was . . . 'You are not far from the kingdom of heaven.'[7]

I have used an exercise based on this incident at least a dozen times to introduce both ordinands and practising clergy to the nature of theological reflection, and although I would not claim that the exercise is all that is needed to help someone understand TR, it has never failed to engage them and throw light on what we mean by it. In this chapter I want to explore six elements of the reflective process that emerge from that exercise, remembering that although the example is drawn from the experience of someone in ordained ministry, these elements apply to all Christians, lay or ordained, and to everyday discipleship as well as ministry.

Critical Incidents

First, Rob's encounter is a classic illustration of what we mean by a 'critical incident'. In this context 'critical' is not being used to suggest that the event was some kind of crisis but rather as a technical term.

> What makes it critical is that it is an event, or series of events, which lie outside one's normal range of usual experiences. It is not a sense of crisis which makes it critical. It is the response it produces. A critical incident is one which produces an emotional reaction in the person who experiences it. It makes an impact. It makes one think. It suggests that there is more to a situation than meets the eye.[8]

In this explanation Charles Chadwick and Phillip Tovey mention both feeling and thinking, and we can already see from the example that in a critical incident there is often a demand for action of some kind: already it is apparent that reflection is intended to integrate thought, feeling and action.

Reflection begins with everyday life, with experience or practice. As we will see, it does call on the resources of formal academic study but essential to its very nature is that it is 'situated' in the flow of life. Life, as we know, does not run on rails. It is not predictable and can be distinctly messy, challenging us in a variety of ways. Life is made up of 'incidents' and 'situations', situations that frequently overlap, so that, for example, an incident that concerned a request for baptism was also about a mother's concern for her daughter, that same mother's relations with her neighbours and the ongoing campaign by the police against drug pushers.

Some of the incidents and situations we encounter are those it is usually possible to treat as 'routine': driving to work on a familiar route, cooking a meal, watching a television serial; or at work, handling a familiar job like making a series of calculations, hanging a door or making a sales enquiry. Others are more demanding: they are situations where it is apparent that we will need to think more deeply. These might include finding an alternative route when our usual journey to work is likely to be delayed by road works; choosing which meal to offer to guests; visiting a friend in hospital; helping our children with their homework; or, at work, undertaking a new or particularly demanding job, getting to know a new colleague or taking part in a planning meeting dealing with a problematic situation. And some incidents and situations we might call 'critical': conflict, whether with a friend or colleague or in church, is likely to generate 'critical' incidents; likewise the surprising or unexpected, any situation that arouses strong feelings or 'makes us think', that leaves us uncertain how to act or, having acted, whether we did the right thing.

It is important to stress that critical incidents are not always negative: they include situations of joy and celebration, such as the time when my family were enjoying our meal out of doors on a particularly warm and balmy evening and a nightingale sang for about a quarter of an hour from a neighbouring tree; or an experience of uplifting worship with a tangible sense of God's presence. Feelings of joy, thankfulness, wonder and awe may also help to make an incident worth the effort of further reflection.

Some critical incidents involve large numbers of people, who may be responding very differently; indeed, those differences may contribute to making the incident critical. An example might be a church or a workplace where something the leadership or management think of as a small adjustment is seen by others as an enormous and challenging change. Other critical incidents involve just one person: it is their particular response, the thoughts and feelings that arise in a situation that is unremarkable for everyone else involved, but which lead them to reflect. An example is given in Chadwick and Tovey's Grove booklet:

> Last week, I called at a home where I am always warmly welcomed. I enjoy going to visit this person. The door opened as usual and I was told, 'I'm sorry but it's not convenient to see you today. The painter's calling to give me a quote for the

guttering', and the door was shut. I felt pretty hurt and rejected by this. 'Surely my visit is more important than the painter's. I've worked really hard to make time to come here today', I thought as I left the property. I was inclined just to put it out of my mind or even not visit this person again. After all, many people said how good and conscientious I was at pastoral work. Reflecting on this incident with members of our Pastoral Team helped me to reconsider my reaction. What had made me so upset? Who might have been benefiting most from my visits? I resolved to spend time thinking about my own assumptions about being a Pastoral Visitor, not least in terms of my own wants and needs. I came to see that in visiting I had a need to be wanted, that this was a shadow side to my helping others and that I had felt rejected because this person was not grateful for my helping. I had to spend time in prayer to re-centre my thoughts and feelings and check through what I was doing. In the end this gave me a greater sense of calling and a more realistic view of ministry.[9]

This incident was critical for just one person; others might not have given it a second thought. But it served to bring to the surface something about the assumptions that sustained and guided this person in pastoral work. In this incident the Pastoral Team played a significant role in enabling reflection. Only a little is said about them, but enough to suggest they provided a context of both support and challenge: challenging the visitor to address difficult feelings and perceptions, and providing support in the process of change. As a result the visitor addressed thoughts, feelings and actions, recognizing that these were all closely tied together. And the outcome was a more 'realistic view' of ministry tied to a 'deeper sense of calling'. The visitor gained a significantly greater understanding of the purpose of pastoral ministry as a result of engaging with this particular pastoral encounter, as well as a greater understanding of their own weaknesses and contribution.

Here is an example of the way something that might have been a 'routine' encounter became a 'critical incident' because of the emotional reaction it prompted, which in its turn enabled the visitor to realize that there was more to it than might have met the eye. He or she was tempted to put it out of mind. And for most of us there will be incidents and situations that we treat as routine, whereas deeper consideration may help us to realize that there is much worth pondering: the potential for wonder daily available to us through the beauty of nature; the precious gift present to us in each person we encounter in daily life; or the suffering, injustice and political upheaval presented to us in nightly news broadcasts.

All these and more are potential situations for reflection, but in theological reflection there is a distinctive added dimension. The purpose of TR is to discover the presence of God in the situations that make up our lives. Its basic question is: 'Where is God in this situation?' Or it may be relevant to frame the question in a way that highlights some particular aspect of God's presence: 'Where are the signs of God's kingdom?', 'What would Jesus have done?' or 'What is God's call?'

Intuition

In a challenging situation, unsure how to act, Rob sought to draw on the resources of Christian tradition, and into his mind came a verse from the Bible: 'You are not far from the kingdom of heaven.' He is thinking of the exchange between Jesus and one of the scribes about the greatest commandment in the Law, in which the scribe concedes that love of God and neighbour is more important than religious ritual (Mark 12.28–34). This verse provides Rob with a framework in which to interpret the woman's situation and in particular her request for baptism for her daughter, a framework that also guides his subsequent actions. There is a likeness between the present-day situation and the situation in the Gospel story. In both, someone without explicit faith in Christ is honestly searching for what is good and right and finding it in the dictates of love. In both, the demands of love take priority over those of religious rectitude. But the connection occurs to Rob spontaneously. He does not first analyse the situation, recognize the priority of love in the woman's request and then find a Bible verse to explain and justify his response. The quotation arises by way of intuition and, having arisen, provides the framework he needs through which to interpret the situation and decide what to do.

Intuition plays a key role in theological reflection. Chadwick and Tovey's description of critical incident analysis includes a stage at which they ask: 'What does this remind you of in the Scriptures?'[10] Patricia O'Connell Killen and John de Beer's 'Education for Ministry' method of reflection includes a stage at which the reflector pauses to ask: 'What is the heart of the matter?' and is then asked to bring to mind an image that sums up the thoughts and feelings that arise.[11] In this respect TR works in a very different way from the method of most accepted approaches to study and learning. These tend to place the emphasis on our ability to analyse explicit concepts, so as to be able to give clear reasons for our conclusions. In most academic contexts, relying on intuition would be dismissed as unscholarly. Intuition appears to be a mysterious, unaccountable and highly dubious way of arriving at the truth. And yet what I hope to show in this section is that it is much closer to *the way our minds actually work*. We really do use intuition to arrive at most of our conclusions – although it is important that we subsequently analyse these conclusions with some rigorous questioning to test out the validity and value of the insights that have arisen intuitively. And that is just what the process of theological reflection, properly conducted, involves.

In what follows I am attempting to present a condensed version of the conclusions I set out in my earlier book, *Divine Revelation and Human Learning*,[12] in which I used elements of the psychology of human learning: the way our minds work when encountering new information and unfamiliar situations, and the way we store information in our memories. I drew on research in a variety of psychological disciplines, including cognitive science and social learning, to build up a picture of human learning and relate it to the way we come to know God himself through the process of revelation. Since the work I carried out for that book, the new science of cognitive neuroscience has begun to further verify its findings. For example, it has demonstrated the importance of bodily mechanisms in the way we perceive and interpret the world, the way memory works and the importance of our emotions in the way we respond to situations. How, then, are we to understand intuition in the broader context of human learning?

1 *Learning is the outcome of a process of interaction*

This interaction takes place between the new information contained in unfamiliar situations, such as the critical incidents we considered in the previous section or in formal educational contexts such as lectures, and the stored information derived from our previous experience. This stored information exists in the form of 'mental models': models of situations, based on past experiences, that tell us what those situations are 'about' and what to expect. In Rob's case, he would have brought a considerable amount of prior knowledge to his encounter with the woman and her daughter, based on his experience of ministry in that parish and including his 'mental models' of prostitution, drugs and the role of the police, as well as of baptism.

Rob will have used these mental models to interpret the situation facing him. They will have provided a framework within which to interpret the facts of his surroundings, such as the torn sofa and the mother's request. Rob's first requirement was to 'make sense' of the situation, to give it some coherent meaning. But it is not only in such challenging situations that we attempt to give meaning to our surroundings. We do this all the time. In the words of Sir Frederic Bartlett, a pioneer in the psychology of memory, there is an 'effort after meaning' in all our processes of perception and attention.[13]

Much of the complex process by which Rob adjusted to his unfamiliar situation will have been entirely unconscious. Our mental models are elements in what the philosopher Michael Polanyi called 'tacit knowledge'. Polanyi is famous for his dictum, 'We know more than we can tell.'[14] His great insight was that tacit knowledge based on past experience makes up by far the greatest proportion of our knowledge, and much of what goes on in our minds when we are attempting to make sense of the present situation takes place without our being able to explain or define what it is we are doing.

In this process of interpretation there is a complex dialectic at work. Without calling on our past experience in the form of mental models, we cannot interpret our day-to-day, moment-by-moment experience. But on the other hand, we must not perceive *only* what our mental models lead us to expect. We must also be open to the new, and ready to incorporate new information into these mental models. The mental map I use to drive to work every day represents my 'working knowledge' of the route and includes the landmarks I need for navigation, though it may omit a good deal of what would be included in a paper map of the area. The cook's knowledge of baking teaches her how to follow each particular recipe. On occasion, these mental models may require updating: a new roundabout or one-way system needs to be incorporated into my mental map; or the cook decides to try a new recipe with an unfamiliar ingredient. For the more challenging situations, like getting to know a new colleague at work, I may need to draw on a wider range of experience, my knowledge of other colleagues and of the workplace, perhaps my knowledge of people in general, in order gradually to develop a set of expectations to cover this particular colleague.

The flow of life, where reflection takes place, is made up not simply of situations but of *interpreted* situations. It is the interpretation that defines the situation, as it did for the pastoral visitor: it was the interpretation of the words encountered on the doorstep that made the situation what it became for the visitor. And the dynamic of knowing is that we *must* interpret before we can understand: it is the expectations that we bring to each situation that define it. This creates what Thomas Kuhn called the 'essential tension': all our perception, comprehension and learning consist of a negotiation between our expectations of what we are likely to encounter in any given situation, based on past experience, and the present experience of what we actually do encounter.[15] As the cognitive psychologist Ulric Neisser puts it, 'There is a dialectical contradiction between these two requirements: we cannot perceive *unless* we anticipate, but we must not see *only* what we anticipate.'[16] With the work of David Kolb on experiential learning, this dialectic became an accepted feature of human cognition.[17] Our concepts or mental models by which we interpret the world are always held tentatively and provisionally. We are aware that they are in continual need of updating. And this process of adjustment and updating is in fact continually taking place: it is the process through which we learn from experience.

2 *Our mental models do not consist of abstract concepts but of* patterns
In his encounter with the woman and her daughter, Rob will have been able to call on his considerable store of information about pastoral visits in general and visits in this parish in particular in the form of a mental model, providing him with the readiness to respond to each new situation. But his mental model for a pastoral visit will not have consisted in a 'general theory' of pastoral visiting. It will rather have consisted in a flexible set of patterns based on his memory of scores or even hundreds of previous visits. These will make Rob alert to the patterns of each subsequent visit: the kinds of need people in his parish are likely to have, the range of attitudes to authority he is likely to encounter, his expectations of people's attitude to the spiritual and religious dimensions of life.

This, I think, is one of the reasons why Jesus, who was obviously a penetrating observer of human life, framed so much of his teaching in the form of parables. A parable is a pattern, a metaphor, inviting us to see something in a particular way: the kingdom of God as like a seed growing secretly or yeast in a loaf or treasure in a field; God's mercy as like that of the father of the prodigal son; his grace as like that of the employer of the workers in the vineyard. Unlike a concept, a parable is open-ended, inviting us to explore further. And also unlike a concept, it invites an emotional as well as an intellectual reaction: we may be drawn to the father's example or scandalized by that of the vineyard owner.

Some of the patterns in Rob's memory will have become *exemplars*. These are the examples of pastoral visits that stand out, perhaps the time when he was able to help resolve a difficult conflict situation or when he led someone to faith in Christ. The pattern of those visits may take central place in Rob's memory. They will be the patterns that organize all the rest, and the ones he is most likely to go to for guidance in new situations.

In the previous chapter we saw that Paul urged his readers to take Jesus as their exemplar, to model their lives on the pattern they found in him, and that Bonhoeffer writes about being 'assimilated to the form of Christ'. To share the 'mind of Christ' will mean that whenever we come to respond to the situations that confront us, especially the 'critical incidents' that challenge us, the mental model we reach for will be the 'form of Christ', as we have come to understand him. And the Holy Spirit is given for precisely this purpose: to be the living presence of Christ in our lives, directing us to his qualities as the 'treasure chest' in which knowledge and understanding for any given situation are to be found.

3 *The relationship between these patterns or mental models is one of likeness or analogy*

As long ago as 1961 the scientist and philosopher of science Norbert Russell Hanson suggested that the 'logic of scientific discovery' might be analogical.[18] In other words, the scientist, looking for a theory to explain his findings, looks for a pattern similar to a theory with which he is already familiar. Later, Thomas Kuhn built on this to trace the progress of scientific discovery in terms of relationships of similarity.[19]

In an unfamiliar and challenging situation, the way we make sense of it is to interpret it in terms of situations we have already encountered, finding likenesses between these and the new situation. This is exactly what Rob was doing: he drew on his knowledge of Scripture for a situation, or in this case some remembered words of Jesus, that helped him to make sense of his encounter and decide how to respond.

But here is the crucial point: there are no hard and fast rules telling us *which particular* likeness or aspect of similarity we should use to interpret the situation. In Rob's case there were several possible mental models open to him to supply the interpretative clue based on his experience of baptism, of the police, of the drugs trade, of prostitution and of motherhood. There were no 'logical' features of the situation dictating that he was led to one rather than the other. Rather it was his *feelings* and his *values* that led him in a particular direction: his feelings of compassion, his stated intention to encourage the people of his parish to find their own way to faith. And what appears to have been most salient or important for him in the situation, unsurprisingly for a Christian minister, was his perception of the woman's relationship with God: 'You are not far from the kingdom of heaven.'

Because our mental models are orientated to action, they *integrate* thoughts, feelings and values. They exist to suggest to us what we should *do* in a given situation. They therefore need to help us to determine not just the facts of the situation but what is important to us, how we feel and what goals we should pursue.

In a later section we will consider the role of the Holy Spirit in this encounter and ask whether we are entitled to see Rob's response as guided by the Spirit. But at this point we simply need to recognize that Rob was faced with an enormously complex situation, a particularly good example of a 'critical incident'. And we need to recognize that *every* situation we encounter is enormously complex. If it does not appear so, it is because we have been able to simplify it for ourselves by the way we have interpreted it. One of the functions of our mental models is to reduce the complexity of our everyday lives to manageable order, bringing to mind the information we need based on our past experience to be able to respond.

The function of theological reflection is to ask the crucial questions: 'Why that particular analogy?', 'Why those assumptions?', 'Why that response?' TR *slows down* the process of interpretation, requiring us to examine our intuitions. It creates the time for us to notice aspects of the complex situation we might otherwise have overlooked, such as the role of the neighbours, and in particular to recognize and analyse the assumptions we bring to any situation. And it focuses on God, using patterns from Scripture and Christian tradition that appear in some way to be 'like' the present situation and so may help us in discerning God's presence.

Theological reflection thus implicitly incorporates Michael Polanyi's insight: 'While tacit knowledge can be possessed by itself, explicit knowledge must rely on being tacitly understood or applied. Hence all knowledge is either tacit or else rooted in tacit knowledge.'[20] Theological reflection examines the roots of our explicit judgements in tacit knowledge, the influence of our existing ways of thinking on our intuitive responses and plans of action. It is thus inherently reflexive, requiring the willingness to open ourselves to judgement, the judgement of ourselves, of others who may share the process, and ultimately of God, in order to see situations more clearly through the lens of Christian faith and thus to learn and grow in discipleship and ministry.

To sum up: the intuition by which the phrase 'You are not far from the kingdom of heaven' came to mind as the key to the situation is entirely in keeping with the way our minds habitually function. It was guided by the values Rob brought to the situation: his assumption that God was on the side of his parishioners, and his desire to work within their understanding of God 'to help them to deal with their own spirituality in their own terms'; and his desire in this particular situation to empathize with the woman, which is itself an enormously complex tacit skill. Consideration as to why this biblical phrase might hold the interpretative key to the situation and the possibility of questioning whether this were the only or the best possible biblical model to use might come later. But first intuition was required in order to create a coherent pattern of meaning for the situation.

Scripture

The phrase that occurred to Rob as the clue to the meaning of the situation he had encountered was taken from the Bible. In theory all sorts of possibilities might have occurred to him: a quotation from Shakespeare, from the novel he had been reading the night before or even from a conversation with a neighbour. But Rob needed authority for any response he made and, as a Christian minister, he turned to the Bible for that authority.

Millions of words have been written about the interpretation and use of the Bible and it is impossible to give a complete account of them here. The aim of this section is to provide an account of the role of the Bible in theological reflection, but to do so against the background of the ongoing debate about the role of Scripture in the life of the church. Perhaps the first and most fundamental observation to make is that the church is the inheritor of a tradition stretching back over more than 2,000 years, which includes the nation of Israel in the centuries before the coming of Christ. Second, that within the church this tradition functions as a source of authority, providing the church with its essential purpose and identity and guiding its ongoing life. Third, although Christian tradition is broader than the Bible, incorporating its worship, its history and the writings of its scholars throughout the ages, the Bible plays a central and definitive role, and indeed the rest of Christian tradition may justly be evaluated according to its faithfulness or otherwise to Scripture.

Having made these observations, however, it is important to recognize that the decision to confer the authority of Scripture on certain books rather than others and discernment of the ways the Bible may rightly be interpreted are both elements of tradition. This complex relationship between Scripture and tradition reflects the fact that the meaning of any particular Bible passage and indeed the 'meaning' of the Bible itself as an authoritative source are not obvious. On the one hand, the meaning of a passage of Scripture is that conferred on it within a community of interpretation. On the other, that community recognizes in the Bible an authority given to it directly by the work of the Holy Spirit, who is also the guide of the community and thus the guarantor of whatever is faithful in Christian tradition. And finally, in the words of Alasdair MacIntyre, any tradition has to be seen as an ongoing conversation or even 'an historically extended, socially embodied argument' about the 'particular point or purpose' of that tradition and the values it expresses.[21]

The Bible as theological reflection

Having acknowledged the place of Scripture within the complex history of Christian tradition, it is necessary to make a decision about the Bible's role and purpose in the light of which to explore its place in theological reflection. My suggestion is that to do this we need to ask why the Bible came into being in the first place: why the various books that make it up and the individual parts of them were originally written down and then preserved, collected, edited and finally put together into the book we know as the Bible. The answer to this question, I suggest, is to be sought along the following lines: underlying every part of the Bible is the question: 'What is the outward form and inward character of a faithful response to God in this particular situation?' In other words, I am suggesting that just as we have seen human knowledge situated in the flow of life and relating to particular interpreted situations, so we see the Bible as arising in particular situations and expressing the desire of those who wrote it, and those who preserved and edited it, sometimes for new situations, to declare, teach or simply explore the form and character of a faithful response to God.

In other words, the Bible itself is to be understood as theological reflection: it is a record of men and women asking such questions as: 'Where is God in this situation?', 'How are we to understand our situation in the light of what we have been taught about the character of God?' or 'What is God's call or demand in our situation?' We can fill out this observation by exploring the way particular texts and in some cases whole books are themselves examples of theological reflection:

- Take for example Psalm 8: 'When I look at your heavens, the work of your fingers, / the moon and the stars that you have established; / what are human beings that you are mindful of them, / mortals that you care for them? / Yet you have made them a little lower than God, / and crowned them with glory and honour' (vv. 3–5). The psalmist considers the wonder and majesty of the night sky and discerns in it an indication of the grandeur and glory of God. Comparing this with the position of human beings, the inhabitants of the world God has created, he nevertheless realizes that humankind has its own grandeur and glory, but that this is ours solely as a gift of the creator. The psalm is a biblical anthropology in miniature, expressed as a theological reflection.
- Sometimes theological reflection in the Bible takes the form of what Elaine Graham, Heather Walton and Frances Ward call 'constructive narrative theology': presenting a reflection in the form of a story, which evokes rather than directly teaches the insights it seeks to convey.[22] One example of this is the book of Ruth, with its theme of God's gracious providence, showing a Moabite woman experiencing the reality of protection under the 'wings' of God, which is a theme of so many of the psalms (Ruth 2.12; Psalm 17.8; 36.7; 63.7 etc.). Another is the source found incorporated into the narrative of 2 Samuel and 1 Kings and often known as the 'succession narrative', telling the story

of the strife in David's household, which eventually led to the succession of Solomon. David Gunn has suggested that this narrative, with its insightful character studies (of David and his sons; Joab, his general; Ahitophel, his erstwhile counsellor), be seen as an extended reflection on the nature of power and leadership, and the interrelation of the personal and the political in the life of a leader.[23] Unlike so many biblical narratives and more in keeping with Israel's wisdom tradition, these chapters make very few references directly to the actions of God. Instead the reader is led by the narrative itself to consider where God may be found and to decide what the lessons of the narrative may be.

- A development of the narrative style of reflection is the parable, the story that draws us in and 'puts us on the spot'. An Old Testament example is the book of Jonah, with its repeated references to Israel's orthodox beliefs about God (Jonah 1.9; 4.2), suggesting that those very beliefs extend the possibility of God's mercy and grace to Israel's hated enemies (Jonah 4.11).

- An example of reflection of a different kind is found in the creation narratives in the early chapters of Genesis. Most of these are attributed in the old theory of sources to the writer 'J', and may well be the work of a group of scholars working together in the court of Solomon. These scholars put together an epic of great sweep, theologizing 'less by formal religious statements than by the linking of the stories and by the more or less direct way that the deity participates in or permeates the action'.[24] The epic begins with the myths of creation and early human history, such as the Creation itself, the Flood and the Tower of Babel. Although drawn from the mythology of the ancient Near East, the J writers have adapted the myths in such a way as to change the portrayal of God. In contrast to the collection of squabbling gods who appear in the pagan versions of these stories, Israel's God is one, and is furthermore portrayed as 'personal but not as mere creature, as parent of all creatures without being sentimental, as respectful of human freedom without being impotent, as moral without being moralistic, as strong-purposed without being dictatorial'.[25] Moreover, the anthropomorphism that records God as fashioning a human creature from the earth, 'walking in the garden in the cool of the day' and later going in person to investigate the crimes of Sodom and Gomorrah, is used in a subtle way to express the relationship of a God who is transcendent and yet personal with his human creatures. In these and a variety of other ways the stories convey a 'feel' for the God whom Israel worshipped, without tying down these observations as doctrine.

- As a fifth example, we may point to the book of Deuteronomy. The book as a whole is a reflection on Israel's tradition of law up to the point of its compilation, probably during the reign of King Josiah of Judah. Conceiving its task as reintroducing God's people to the tradition of the Law and motivating them to keep it, the book's compilers work through collection and arrangement of the material; changes to some provisions to bring them up to date; perhaps also through the inclusion of new material, such as that on the duties of kings in chapter 17; through placing the Law firmly in the historical context of Israel's rescue from slavery in Egypt; but above all through lengthy set-piece exhortations, all to present a picture of Israel's Law as the gracious gift of a benevolent God, which, when it is obeyed 'from the heart', becomes a source of 'life' and 'wisdom'.

- And finally, before leaving the Old Testament it is important to observe that within its pages it reflects the nature of tradition as 'historically extended and socially embodied argument'. Especially is this true of its approach to the mystery of suffering, on which different writers such as the authors of Deuteronomy, the Joseph narrative in Genesis, Ecclesiastes, Lamentations, Job and Second Isaiah present contrasting, balancing and occasionally differing insights on the meaning of this perennial and bewildering feature of human experience.

The observation that the Bible itself has the nature of theological reflection is more than borne out by this survey of some of the writings of the Old Testament. The character of the book itself supports our contention. It is difficult to approach even the legal passages as one might a textbook, clearly setting out the nature of God and his expectations for human life, since the Law is subject to continual revision and extended reflection both within the five books of the Torah and outside them, in the prophetic and wisdom traditions in particular. It is rather the record of a developing awareness of God's nature and Israel's vocation, arrived at through a long process of reflection over hundreds of years, and ultimately incomplete.

Is then the New Testament, in which the source of all grace and truth and the 'image of the invisible God' (Colossians 1.15) is presented in the Person of Jesus Christ, more of a doctrinal exposition than a reflection? Not so: here again theological reflection is very much to the fore in both the material of the New Testament and in the process of its compilation:

- Take first the parables of Jesus: as we saw in the previous section ('Intuition'), a parable is a metaphor, a pattern, offered to us as a way of grasping the truth of God. But few of the parables answer in a transparent way the underlying question: 'In what, exactly, does the likeness consist?' The way the kingdom of heaven is like treasure hidden in a field, or God himself like the father of the prodigal son, or Jesus like the king dividing humanity as a shepherd divides sheep and goats is not necessarily clear and obvious from the parable itself. It has to be explored through reflection and application. And that is exactly what Jesus asks his audience to do, precisely so that the inner meaning of his teaching is revealed to those who receive it with faith and obedience.[26]
- The book of Acts includes within its pages some significant examples of theological reflection. It tells the story of the way Gentiles eventually came to be included within the Christian church. It portrays Peter as clearly foreseeing this development on the Day of Pentecost (Acts 2.39) and yet hesitating when the time came for its implementation. He is eventually convinced by the combination of a dream in which he is invited to 'kill and eat' a variety of unclean animals and an invitation to preach at the home of a Roman centurion, followed by the evident outpouring of the Holy Spirit on those of the centurion's household. Theological reflection runs like a thread through this story. First Peter is puzzled by the meaning of his dream, eventually deciding, in the context of his journey to meet

Cornelius, that he 'should not call anyone profane or unclean' (Acts 10.28). Only the evidence of the gift of Holy Spirit finally leads him, and the believers in Judaea, to the conclusion that 'God has given even to the Gentiles the repentance that leads to life' (Acts 11.18). The terms on which the Gentiles are to be incorporated into the church are only hammered out after long deliberation at the Council of Jerusalem, during which James draws on the book of Amos to explain this surprising development. And the eventual decision of the Council is conveyed to the churches with the words: 'It has seemed good to the Holy Spirit and to us' (Acts 15.28), a sign of the Council's consciousness that, although called on to take responsibility for their decision, it has been arrived at only through reflection with the aid of the Spirit.

- As a third example, we may explore the evidence of his letters for examples of Paul's approach to conflict and controversy in his churches. Habitually Paul uses a clear and consistent approach: he outlines the problem, states the principle he believes holds the solution and explores the way this principle is to be applied. In 1 Corinthians 8—10 the problem is conflict between believers over their attitude to meat sacrificed to pagan idols. The Corinthians appeared to be attempting to resolve the issue on the basis of 'knowledge'. But Paul is clear that the operative principle is rather to be love. Love requires each party to respect and care for the conscience of the other and to adapt their behaviour with this in mind. In the same way love is invoked in chapters 12—14 as the guiding principle for the conduct of their worship. In Philippians there are two principles, *phronesis* and *koinonia*. The church is to 'order its common life' in a way that reflects the 'mind' of Jesus Christ, a disposition to humility, service and sacrifice. Paul offers his own example (twice) and those of Timothy and Epaphroditus as concrete exemplars of the form this disposition might take and then urges the quarrelling Euodia and Syntyche, along with the whole church, to adopt this attitude as the pattern of Christian maturity.
- And finally, the compilation of the Gospels is another obvious example of theological reflection. Scholarship has shown how

each of the Gospel authors structures their book in a richly theological way, each emphasizing different facets of Jesus' character and self-understanding, aiming to present a coherent portrayal not only of Jesus' life but of his identity and significance.

The Bible is thus a resource for theological reflection in the present because it is a record of the theological reflection of previous generations, made up of texts in which God's people in a variety of ways set out to discern the nature of a faithful response to God in their particular situations. Given this understanding of Scripture, biblical scholarship has an important role to play. The scholars can help us to understand in greater depth and detail the historical situations in which the reflections we find in the Bible arose: the nature of the problems and dilemmas facing God's people and the intellectual, historical and religious contexts that form the background to these writings. They can draw out the coherence – or lack of coherence – of the writings and show us the levels of meaning embedded in them. And they can show us the ways the Bible 'talks to itself': one writer drawing on the wisdom of another, such as the way the early Jeremiah draws on Hosea; one writer using another as the context for their own message (in the way Joel 3.10 refers to Isaiah 2.4; Zephaniah looks back to the Flood narrative and the Tower of Babel; Third Isaiah and Daniel build on the prophecies of Second Isaiah); and in particular the way the New Testament takes the Old as its background and responds to it in the light of Jesus.

The Bible in theological reflection

All this means that what Rob was doing in using a particular text to provide a framework of meaning for a given situation was not necessarily simple proof-texting but the bridging of the two 'horizons' of the text and the present day, calling on the insights of God's people as recorded in Scripture to provide patterns for reflection in the present. Viewed in this way, the use of the Bible in theological reflection bears important resemblances to its use in *lectio divina*, in which both mind and heart, intellect and emotions are opened to the message of a particular passage, with the aim of hearing what God might be saying through it in the present. It also echoes the Seven-Step process, originating with the Lumko Institute in South Africa, in which the group listen intently to a passage in order to determine a 'Word of Life' for the coming week or month and decide together how to apply it in action in their own context.[27] In both, the intention is to discover in the text a likeness to the present situation and a pattern of faithful response.

Implicit in all we have said so far is the idea of the 'authority' of Scripture: the idea that in some way the Bible is an authoritative source for the way the Christian life is to be lived and the church conducts itself. Unless the Bible is treated in this way, theological reflection makes no sense. But implicit in the activity of TR is the idea that the Bible is capable of providing a key to answer questions that lie at its heart: 'Where is God in this situation?', 'How is he calling us to respond?' As Tom Wright points out, 'The phrase "the authority of Scripture" can make Christian sense only if it is a shorthand for "the authority of the triune God, exercised somehow *through* Scripture".'[28] This means that if we are to understand the way the Bible exercises authority, and the role it plays in TR, we have to understand the way God exercises authority.

What the Bible shows us is that the authority of God is tied up with the coming of his kingdom. In other words, his authority is not a 'steady state': it is in the process of coming to be. God is at work, through his choice of Israel, the life, death and resurrection, and cosmic enthronement of Jesus and the sending of the Holy Spirit, to restore and renew his broken creation. In this loving process of renewal, God's authority does not impose itself; rather, he invites all who wish to become partners with him in his loving purpose. This is why the Bible is neither a doctrinal manual telling us what we should believe, nor yet a rule book, imposing a certain pattern of life. Rather the Bible is a story: the record of God's gracious action in history. And because so much of the Bible is in itself theological reflection, the record of God's people seeking to respond to God's call in the circumstances of their time, it is ideally suited to be the means through which that process of reflection continues today. But because God's rule is dynamic, still in the process of bringing about the full acknowledgement of his authority, the Bible is far more than a record, far more than simply true information about God's nature and purposes. It is an invitation to join him in the work of the kingdom: to see the world from his point of view and to allow him to take over our lives and use them for his purpose.[29]

Church

At the time of Rob's encounter with the woman who asked him to baptize her child, he was handicapped by the expectation arising from the professional model of ministry that as the vicar, his job was to wrestle with the issues, decide on a course of action and take responsibility for it *on his own*. The record of the story given in *From Strangers to Neighbours* does not make it clear whether anyone else was involved in the ministry that took place on this particular occasion or whether the decision to baptize was Rob's alone.

In this section I want to explore four related aspects of theological reflection:

- First, in New Testament terms, the exercise of Christian ministry by a single person acting alone is not a 'normal' situation. Christian ministry is collaborative by its very nature since it is intended to express the nature of the church as a loving, Christ-centred community.
- Moreover, shared reflection plays a key role in both building up the church and in helping to define the nature of ministry.
- Third, reflection together is usually far more productive and fruitful than reflection alone.
- This is because theological reflection is, by its very nature, a corporate activity. The Christian tradition to which we turn for patterns of faithfulness emerges from the experience of the church in all generations. No one reflects alone: by its very nature reflection connects us with the community of which we are a part.

In the exercise based on the incident, I initially withhold the verse that occurred to Rob, 'You are not far from the kingdom of heaven.' Instead I stop the story at the words 'the line that was going through my own mind – my "gut feeling" – was . . .', and then ask the group what passages of Scripture come to mind for them. As you can imagine, there has been a great variety over the years. They have included:

- The story of the Syro-Phoenician woman and her daughter from Matthew 15.21–28. Like the situation Rob faced, this is a story of a mother and daughter from outside the community, of someone, according to the prevailing understanding the day, strongly voiced on this occasion by his disciples, Jesus should have rejected. And Jesus grants her request for the healing of her daughter, though not without putting her through a rigorous test of her faith.
- 'Let the little children come to me' (Mark 10.14): another account of a situation where Jesus refuses to go along with conventional attitudes, again voiced by his disciples. And Mark's account of the incident tells us Jesus was made indignant by this attitude.
- The story of the woman taken in adultery from John 8.1–11. This is another story of a woman rejected by her community, this time because of obvious sexual sin. And like the other two examples, Jesus rejects and challenges the prevailing assumptions.
- 'Who can withhold water for baptism?' (a paraphrase of Acts 10.47). The link to this passage is obviously baptism, but again it is baptism granted to a surprising group of people, where the gift of the Holy Spirit is an indicator of God's acceptance.
- Isaiah 61.1 – 'The spirit of the Lord GOD . . . has anointed me . . . to bring good news to the oppressed . . .' This passage places the encounter in the context of mission, God's call and anointing to bring good news to the 'poor', the 'oppressed', the 'broken-hearted' and the 'captives'.

Each of the passages suggested has an obvious likeness to Rob's situation. Like the verse 'You are not far from the kingdom of heaven', each potentially provides a framework within which to explore the presence of God in the encounter and his specific call.

Each in its different way recognizes, explicitly or implicitly, the church's call to preach the gospel and to welcome the stranger without judging. And each provides material for further prayerful study.

Had Rob had the opportunity he may well have been able to take his story of the encounter to a supportive group, perhaps of fellow clergy, perhaps of prayer partners, perhaps of co-leaders within the church, in order to open his reflection to others. These and other passages may well have occurred to them. Equally, they may have been able to ask some questions to explore the situation in greater depth: 'What seemed to be the greatest need of the woman and her daughter (or, in other words, what seemed to be the 'heart of the matter')?'; 'Does the little girl have an independent role in this or is she being used simply to mark the mother's resolution?'; 'Might the neighbours have a different narrative of the situation?' And they may have been able to study the Scripture passage where 'You are not far from the kingdom of heaven' occurs, opening a commentary for further enlightenment and prayerfully waiting on the Spirit both in interpreting the passage and for his guidance on how to act in the situation.

At the heart of collaborative ministry lies the commitment to seek the guidance of the Holy Spirit *together*. In the New Testament there is only one single-person leader and that is Jesus, the 'pioneer and perfecter of our faith' (Hebrews 12.2), who is in himself the source of the 'one new humanity' (Ephesians 2.15) in which the whole church shares, and the goal of both individual and corporate Christian maturity (Ephesians 4.13; Philippians 3.15). In the days of his earthly ministry, when he first called his disciples to participate in his mission to the world, Jesus sent them out two by two. When the young church was led to emulate him, they did the same thing, setting apart both Paul and Barnabas, who also took Mark with them as apprentice (Acts 13.1–5). After his break with Barnabas, Paul maintained the same pattern, taking Silas as companion and recruiting Timothy as apprentice (Acts 15.40; 16.1).

In some sections of the church at least, it is commonplace to think of Paul as a single, even 'heroic' leader, but this is very far from the New Testament's portrayal of him and its approach to leadership in general. In the New Testament not even Jesus is called 'leader'; in fact the New Testament writers seem deliberately to avoid the words *archon* (ruler) and *hegemon* (governor) to describe either Jesus or church leaders. The whole framework of understanding seems to derive from Jesus' words: 'it is not so among you' (Mark 10.43). This is not to say that leadership does not take place. As in every group, there must be the exercise of leadership. But in Jesus' community, leadership is not rule but facilitation. The aim is to hear and respond to the voice of the Holy Spirit who, in the words of John Taylor, is the 'chief actor in the historic mission of the Christian church' and 'the director of the whole enterprise'.[30]

Discerning the guidance of the Spirit is therefore a key task for the church, and theological reflection a tool through which to accomplish it. But this process of discernment is a corporate process, in which a group or team reflect together, drawing on the wisdom of Christian tradition, which is our inheritance from the church of previous generations. As Graham Cray puts it: 'In this era, which requires discernment before there can be any strategic planning, leadership is not so much about how leaders discern as about their enabling God's people to discern.'[31]

So in Acts 16 we observe Paul and Silas, having completed the first stage of their missionary journey by visiting the churches established by Paul and Barnabas in Syria and Cilicia, trying to discern the next step. There is clear guidance from the Spirit against preaching in the province of Asia or going further north into Bithynia. Instead Paul has a dream of a man from Macedonia asking for help. This is also the beginning of the first of the 'we' passages in Acts and it is generally assumed that Luke, the book's author, had joined Paul and Silas in Troas, on the Aegean coast. Significantly, in Acts 16.10 it is 'we' who become convinced that God was calling them to Macedonia. There is a clear implication that Paul had shared his dream and that the whole group, including its newest member, had been involved in the final decision.

We misread the New Testament if we read its approach to leadership through the lens of the 'heroic' models of expert leadership current in our individualist society. In the early church, leadership was plural. There are many titles, such as elders, deacons and overseers, but these are always plural. Leadership is a corporate activity. Moreover, the models of our contemporary culture are beginning to change. More and more writers and practitioners in the field are recognizing that one person cannot possibly fulfil all the functions necessary to lead a healthy organization. Leadership is rather a shared activity in which ideally strengths and weaknesses complement one another.[32] And in relation to Christian leadership it has been suggested that one purpose of the fivefold pattern of leadership set out in Ephesians 4.11 is that it brings the very different perspectives of the apostle, the evangelist, the prophet, pastor and teacher to bear on any given situation.[33]

Collaborative theological reflection aiming to discern the guidance of the Holy Spirit plays a key role Christian ministry. Theological reflection is still a tool for the individual disciple, seeking for guidance, help or reassurance, but she will usually find it helpful to share her situation with fellow Christians and invite them to reflect with her. In the groups of ordinands and clergy I have facilitated in theological reflection there have been several occasions when one or other member of the group would bring an incident for reflection, believing that they themselves had already gained a full understanding of God's presence in the situation, only to be amazed at the variety of perspectives opened up by the wisdom of the group. Even without this dimension no Christian reflects alone: as soon as she opens a commentary or Bible study aid to help her understand the Scripture, she will be drawing on the wisdom of tradition.

Finally, reflection plays a key role in building up the church as a loving, nurturing community and, when necessary, bridging the divide between leaders and led, clergy and laity. In his 1983 book *The Reflective Practitioner*, a seminal study of reflective practice, Donald Schön outlines what he sees as the crisis of confidence in the professions, which was then a feature of society in the United States and has since become a feature of our own. He points to the regular occurrence of scandals in which professionals are shown to be incompetent, uncaring or misusing their power, such as we have seen in social work on a regular basis as well as in the mid-Staffordshire NHS Foundation Trust in 2013. He points out that in contemporary culture the power of expertise is coming under suspicion. Rapid change means that it is increasingly difficult for professionals to know everything they need. For example, a doctor may misdiagnose a disease or prescribe the wrong drug simply because he has not been able to keep up with the latest research. And finally, there are the periodic conflicts of value that arise between the professions and the public, as when an architect wants to design a striking and impressive building whereas the client simply wants something that works, and the public may look on the result as an eyesore.

Schön suggests that professionals can rescue themselves from this situation by changing their status from that of expert to reflective practitioner and, moreover, by sharing the task of reflection with the client. When this takes place, instead of trying to sustain the mask of a fount of all knowledge, the professional uses his uncertainties to continue learning. Instead of distancing himself from the client, he actively seeks his co-operation, thereby pursuing real connection instead of status. The client moves from passivity to increasing involvement, from dependency to interdependence, from reliance on the expertise of another to the ability to use that expertise to learn and grow.[34] In the context of a local church used to relying on the professional model of ministry, this approach and the change in status that results represents a transition to a collaborative pattern of ministry, one with the potential to build the confidence of lay disciples and their ownership of the church's ministry.

At the outset of his study of collaborative ministry, Stephen Pickard acknowledges the challenge it poses with a quotation from a colleague: 'To exercise ministry in a collaborative manner requires spiritual maturity.'[35] It requires maturity not only of church leaders, who may have been trained in a hierarchical, one-person pattern of leadership, but also of congregations invited to share responsibility for the church's mission and ministry. But the very tool that lies at the heart of a collaborative approach to ministry, theological reflection, is also a tool that builds maturity, individual and corporate. As Roger Walton points out, shared reflection requires a number of attitudes. 'Courageous openness', 'a faith that is open to God at all times' faces the possibility of change and challenges; 'careful accountability' recognizes the importance of each other and sets aside selfish desires for the outcomes one would prefer; 'conscientious immersion in the tradition' places oneself under the authority of Christian tradition; and 'constant prayerfulness' is open to God's presence in reflection at all times. Each of these both requires and further builds maturity of the congregation willing to take the risk of shared reflection.[36]

The church only becomes a learning organization, capable of adaptation and change in response to challenging circumstances, by engaging in a shared process of theological reflection. Not only does this enable it to recognize the hidden assumptions shaping its life, it does so by calling on the wisdom of all its members committed enough to join the process of shared reflection, rather than that of only a few. And it is this process of shared life through prayerful corporate reflection that enables the church to grow in both unity and maturity, sharing 'the same mind, having the same love, being in full accord and of one mind' (Philippians 2.2).

Holy Spirit

In everything I have written in the previous section about shared reflection I have assumed the presence of the Holy Spirit. The goal of theological reflection is to discern the presence and call of God, and this is precisely the purpose for which we are promised the gift of the Spirit. Comparing the wisdom of the gospel with human wisdom, Paul writes:

> What no eye has seen, nor ear heard, nor the human heart conceived . . . these things God has revealed to us by the Spirit; for the Spirit searches everything, even the depths of God . . . no one comprehends what is truly God's except the Spirit of God. Now we have received not the spirit of the world, but the Spirit that is from God, so that we may understand the gifts bestowed on us by God. (1 Corinthians 2.9–12)

In John's Gospel, Jesus promises that in place of his physical presence his followers will be taught by the Holy Spirit:

> If you love me, you will keep my commandments. And I will ask the Father, and he will give you another Advocate, to be with you for ever. This is the Spirit of truth, whom the world cannot receive . . . But the Advocate, the Holy Spirit, whom the Father will send in my name, will teach you everything, and remind you of all that I have said to you. (John 14.15–17, 26)

In the new era inaugurated by his death and resurrection, Jesus' followers will not be reliant solely on Scripture and tradition. They will have a divine guide who will point them in the right direction, reminding them of Jesus' words, bringing to mind those elements of their heritage most relevant to their situation, providing patterns to help them recognize God's presence. In Jesus the deepest truths of God became incarnate, embodied in his Person. Now this truth is to be available to the disciples through the Spirit dwelling within and among them.

Of course, there is a variety of ways it is possible to exclude the Spirit from the process of reflection: inattention or lack of prayerfulness; the pride or self-confidence that we already understand the situation and know the answer to any problem; the desire for the rest of the group to agree with our point of view; the fear of challenge or change. To acknowledge the Spirit's role in our reflection requires humility, the patience to wait on his timing and the willingness to examine ourselves and to be changed. Indeed, the participation of the Spirit makes theological reflection into an aspect of prayer, through which we seek to know God more deeply, to share his love for the world and discern his will in a particular situation.

The Spirit is an indispensable partner in theological reflection. First, this is because he opens us to the Bible. The Spirit is its author: as the inspiration and guide of those men and women whose reflections are recorded there; and because the church acknowledges the role of the Spirit in the selection of those writings deemed to bear the authority of Scripture. The Spirit is also the interpreter of Scripture, the one who helps us discern the presence of God and the message for us within its pages. Second, the Spirit is indispensable because he opens Christians to one another.

He is the member of the Trinity who binds the Father and the Son in eternal unity, and the one who extends this unity to human beings by drawing us into their loving relationship. The Spirit is the creator of that unity of heart and mind that is the goal of reflection together.

To accomplish this, the Spirit works in and through the normal human processes of perceiving and understanding, valuing and relating. He is not given to us as an added, much less an alien extra. Rather his role is to root our natural abilities in the soil for which they were originally intended: the relationship with God in which all human beings find ultimate fulfilment. The reason this is possible, from the point of view of human cognition, is that, as we have seen in the previous chapter, all learning involves a reconstruction of our sense of identity. As Paul Jarvis puts it, 'In a sense we are constructing our own biography whenever we learn. While we live, our biography is an unfinished product, constantly undergoing change and development . . . People are always *becoming* . . .'[37]

When God draws us into relationship with himself in Christ, the gift of the Spirit, which is the 'pledge' and 'seal' of that new relationship (2 Corinthians 1.22; Ephesians 1.13), creates in us a new identity. It is through the Spirit that we are enabled to cry 'Abba! Father!' (Romans 8.15–16) and to confess 'Jesus is Lord' (1 Corinthians 12.3). Significantly, Paul writes that in the cry of 'Abba! Father!' the Spirit is witnessing 'with our spirit' (Romans 8.16). Our new identity as children of God and companions and followers of Jesus Christ is the gift of the Spirit, who makes the 'form' of Jesus, the exemplar of our new life in restored relationship with the Father, available to us at a deep level of personality. But that identity impacts the rest of our mental world only gradually, as we live it out in the flow of life, interpreting situations and responding to them in new ways. When this takes place we experience the cycle of Colossians 1.9–10. Discerning and living the life pleasing to the Lord, we bear fruit in all kinds of good works and grow further in the knowledge of God.[38]

It is in this way that theological reflection plays an important role in the development of Christian character. Reflection requires of us that we not only focus on the incident or situation but on our own response to it, our feelings, our assumptions and our habitual ways of responding. It invites us to evaluate our actions and attitudes in the light of what we find in the Bible and Christian tradition, guided by the Holy Spirit. It challenges us, implicitly or explicitly, to consider doing things differently. Theological reflection holds the potential for 'deep learning': fundamental changes of perspective and ways of behaving that facilitate growth in virtue.

Here too the Holy Spirit works with the natural processes of human learning and acting. For Aristotle, the virtues were human potentialities, achievable through the exercise of practical wisdom, decision and self-control. The same perspective is shared by the character literature of today. In the educational field, as we have seen, character can be inculcated by a whole-school ethos, the presence of suitable mentors, active pedagogies and direct teaching. In that segment of management literature that concentrates on 'personal mastery', the traits of character helpful to the business leader can be learned through decision and practice.[39] The development of Christian character also requires thought, decision and discipline; but the Holy Spirit is the one who challenges us and enables us to see situations through the eyes of Jesus, who convinces us of the need to change when often we would rather he did not, who teaches us with which virtues we need to 'clothe' ourselves (Colossians 3.12), and who frequently gives us the power to do so when our own inclinations and abilities fall short. We may have to 'work out our own salvation', but true Christlikeness is possible only because 'God is at work in us' through the Holy Spirit, 'both to will and to work for his good pleasure' (Philippians 2.12–13).

Risk

There is one final aspect of theological reflection to which it is important to pay attention at this stage: it is not rule-governed. In TR there are few hard and fast answers. It does not consist in the application of a critically tested general theory to specific situations. Rather it acknowledges there can never be complete certainty about *which* general principles are the ones most relevant and important in a given situation, nor about *how* those principles should be put into practice. Instead, through TR the practitioner seeks to discern an appropriate *pattern* of response: a way of thinking, feeling and acting in the situation that seems to acknowledge the presence of God and the call of Christ in the situation.

In his response to the woman's request for her daughter's baptism, there are several different ways Rob may have 'got it wrong'. There may have been important things about the situation of which he was unaware. He may have chosen the wrong Bible passage as a framework within which to interpret the situation. He may have misinterpreted the passage. He may have been wrong in trusting his 'gut instinct'. Theological reflection opens us up to the possibility of error precisely because it is situated in the flow of life, where every situation comes already interpreted, and many are messy and ambiguous, and often subject to conflict.

In some situations, such as where the safeguarding of children and vulnerable adults is at stake, there are procedures that have to be followed. In most there are principles of good practice. On the other hand, we live in a society that is increasingly risk-averse and in which, as a result, professional practice is becoming subject to ever closer control and accountability. In an article entitled '"Professional Wisdom" in Practice', Joseph Dunne deplores the tendency to organize and regulate even people-centred practices such as nursing and social work according to the dictates of 'technical rationality'. In essence, argues Dunne, this is an attempt to 'disembed' 'the knowledge implicit in the skilful performance of the characteristic tasks of the practice from the immediacy and idiosyncrasy of the particular situations in which it is deployed' and convert it into 'explicit, generalizable formulae, procedures or rules'. The assumption behind this approach is that the only valid knowledge is 'objective' knowledge. The practitioner's tacit knowledge, her 'practical know-how' based on accumulated experience, which she is capable of deploying in a flexible way in a complex variety of situations, is discounted. Holding her accountable is deemed to require a procedural rule book made up of 'objective' standards of practice for which only explicitly codifiable knowledge is allowed to count as relevant. 'The ideal', comments Dunne, 'is a practitioner-proof practice.'[40]

When we put ourselves in the place of Rob Gallagher in his encounter with the reformed prostitute, however, it is comparatively easy to recognize the ways 'technical rationality' fails completely to capture the multi-dimensional complexity of the accumulated experience on which he is drawing:

- In the first place, Rob brings his existing mental models, drawn from his experience of motherhood, prostitution, drug addiction, the police, baptism and the relationship between the church and this particular local community. He needs to deploy all these to help him interpret the situation facing him.
- He also brings with him not simply his existing experience but his values. There is a variety of outcomes in this situation: that this mother experiences acceptance from the representative of the church; that she comes to know God's love; that she joins the church; that she remains free of drugs; that her daughter's future is not blighted by association with drugs and prostitution; that the church is well thought of in the neighbourhood. The relative importance Rob assigns to each of these possible outcomes will depend on the values he brings. For example, in his role of vicar, is it important to him that someone comes to church? He has told us that his approach is to meet members of the community on their own ground and their own terms, which suggests that this may be less important for him than supporting the woman in the pursuit of her own hopes and aspirations.
- In the light of his previous knowledge and his experience, and the values he brings, Rob will be defining and redefining the task in the course of the encounter. Is it simply to ensure that this mother experiences acceptance for herself and her child? That she remains free of drugs? That she understands the baptismal promises? That she is enabled to continue on a spiritual journey? That the relationships between her and her neighbours are restored? That the police are challenged about their approach? As the mother tells her story, Rob will be trying to sort out the important from the less important, looking for clues to help him decide what his response should be.
- At the same time he will also be defining his role in the relationship, both for himself and for the woman. He is the local

vicar: but how does this woman understand that role? What does she expect of him? Is there a possibility of this encounter being transformative for her – or for him?
- Finally, Rob is deploying a repertoire of skills, such as empathetic listening, as he listens and attempts to steer the conversation. His eyes and ears and – perhaps in a house that has recently been used for drug-taking – his sense of smell will provide him with a constant stream of feedback as he seeks to interpret the situation and decide on his best possible course of action.

Donald Schön refers to this process as 'reflection-in-action': the process of reflection that takes place in the immediacy of situations. It is this that reveals most clearly the values, experience, habits of thought and feeling we bring to situations, and this reflection-*in*-action will itself become the subject of reflection-*on*-action, when Rob pauses later to consider the way he handled the encounter. If he does so with the support of others, choosing perhaps to make use of a formal method of TR, a variety of further factors may be taken up in that reflection:

- The meaning of the situation for the actors involved: the mother, the neighbours, the police, the little girl, Rob himself.
- Rob's awareness of his feelings about the police, drugs, prostitution and baptism, based on his experience of these things.
- The possibility of specialist knowledge that either Rob or the members of the reflecting group may have about such things as police methods, the drugs trade or the church's liturgical provision and rules.
- The Christian theological tradition, as found in Scripture and the writings of theologians down the centuries.
- All culminating in a decision about possible courses of action. Might the church seek to act as advocate for the woman, or as mediator between her and her neighbours? Should the baptism go ahead and, if so, who should be invited? What role might the congregation play in befriending and supporting her?

Painting a rich picture of the situation in this way allows us to recognize, with Michael Polanyi, that explicit knowledge, the knowledge that can be 'disembedded' and codified, is dependent on a base of tacit know-how. The issue between the two approaches is: *What counts as valid knowledge?* For technical rationality, only universal, decontextualized theory is allowed to count as 'knowledge' and the legitimacy of situation-specific judgement is denied. For the reflective practitioner, on the other hand, knowledge arises from and is related to the flow of life, made up of interpreted situations.

Thus the principles of good practice consist of shared mental models derived from experience. They are similar to the habits that make up good character: reliable ways of interpreting and responding to similar situations. Moreover, not only are these principles similar to the foundations of good character but, being rooted in judgements of value, good character is required to recognize and apply them. For this reason, a 'good' doctor, 'good' teacher or 'good' social worker must also be a good person. The 'professional wisdom' required for good practice has the nature of a virtue ethic for a given field.[41]

The risk inherent in theological reflection is thus a reflection of the character of knowledge itself. Knowledge is the skill of responding to complex situations on the basis of previous experience. This risky quality is also a reflection of the nature of Christian faith. Jesus was not someone who followed the rule book. He rather sought to discern the presence of God in each individual encounter, responding flexibly to each person he met on the basis of his perfect love. Christian discipleship is not primarily a philosophy but first and foremost the communal practice of following Jesus and participating in the sharing of his love in the world. And the Bible is not presented as an instruction manual but as the record of a community's reflection on their encounter with God and with the truth incarnate in Jesus.

In this chapter I have given a brief introduction to the process of theological reflection and analysed some of its most important elements in order to show that TR is not only a reflection of the way people actually do learn and grow in both competence and maturity but also a means by which, under the authority of Scripture and Christian tradition, in company with fellow believers and empowered by the Holy Spirit, Christians learn to be conformed to the image of Jesus Christ in the way they live and seek to share in his mission. In the next chapter we will look specifically at the church's teaching ministry, whose aim is to enable Christians to grow, individually and corporately, as disciples of Jesus and to equip them for ministry. And what I hope to show is that good practice in Christian teaching not only makes full use of theological reflection but is faithful to the cycle of experiential learning, which itself underlies and gives shape to TR.

Notes

1 Ripon College Cuddesdon student assignment: used with permission.
2 Jane Leach, 'The End of Theological Education: An Analysis of the Contribution of Portfolio Learning to Formation in Ministry within a University Context', *Journal of Adult Theological Education* 7.2, 2010, pp. 117–204; quotation from p. 135.
3 For a full account, see Paul Ballard and John Pritchard, *Practical Theology in Action*, 2nd edn, London: SPCK, 2006; Laurie Green, *Let's Do Theology*, 2nd edn, London: Continuum, 2009.
4 Kolb's learning cycle was, along with liberation theology, one of the two original sources for Green's formulation of the pastoral cycle. See Green, *Let's Do Theology*, pp. 17–18; also Judith Thompson, *The SCM Studyguide to Theological Reflection*, London: SCM Press, 2008, pp. 51f. A fuller account of the learning cycle will be given in Chapter 3.
5 Iris Murdoch, *The Sovereignty of Good*, New York: Schocken Books, 1971, pp. 43, 40, 91; quoted in Charles Wood, *Vision and Discernment*, Eugene, OR: Wipf & Stock, 1985, p. 75.
6 It is hoped that this work might become the subject of a Grove booklet at a future date.
7 David Evans and Mike Fearon, *From Strangers to Neighbours*, London: Hodder & Stoughton, 1998, pp. 134–5. I am grateful to Rob Gallagher for allowing me to use the story of this incident as the basis of this chapter.
8 Charles Chadwick and Phillip Tovey, *Growing in Ministry: Using Critical Incident Analysis*, Cambridge: Grove, 2003, p. 9.
9 Chadwick and Tovey, *Growing in Ministry*, pp. 10–11.
10 Chadwick and Tovey, *Growing in Ministry*, p. 15.
11 P. O'Connell Killen and J. de Beer, *The Art of Theological Reflection*, New York: Crossroad, 2004, pp. 27–43.
12 David Heywood, *Divine Revelation and Human Learning*, Aldershot: Ashgate, 2004.
13 Frederic Bartlett, *Remembering*, Cambridge: Cambridge University Press, 1932, pp. 14–33.
14 Michael Polanyi, *The Tacit Dimension*, London: Routledge & Kegan Paul, 1967, p. 4.

LEARNING TO CONNECT LIFE AND FAITH

15 See Thomas Kuhn, 'The Essential Tension: Tradition and Innovation in Scientific Research', in Kuhn, *The Essential Tension*, Chicago: University of Chicago Press, 1977, pp. 225–39.

16 Ulric Neisser, *Cognition and Reality*, San Francisco: W. H. Freeman & Co., 1976, p. 43.

17 See David Kolb, *Experiential Learning: Experience as the Source of Learning and Development*, Englewood Cliffs, NJ: Prentice-Hall, 1984, pp. 43–51, 106–9.

18 N. R. Hanson, 'Is there a Logic of Scientific Discovery?', in H. Feigl and G. Maxwell (eds), *Current Issues in the Philosophy of Science*, New York: Holt, Rinehart & Winston, 1961, pp. 20–42.

19 Thomas Kuhn, *The Structure of Scientific Revolutions*, 2nd edn, Chicago: University of Chicago Press, 1969, p. 189.

20 Michael Polanyi, 'The Logic of Tacit Inference', *Philosophy* 41, 1966, pp. 1–18; quotation from p. 7; reprinted in *Knowing and Being*, London: Routledge & Kegan Paul, 1969, p. 144.

21 Alasdair MacIntyre, *After Virtue*, 2nd edn, London: Duckworth, 1985, p. 222.

22 Elaine Graham, Heather Walton and Frances Ward, *Theological Reflection: Methods*, London: SCM Press, 2005, pp. 47–77.

23 David M. Gunn, *The Story of King David: Genre and Interpretation*, Sheffield: JSOT Press, 1989.

24 Norman K. Gottwald, *The Hebrew Bible: A Socio-Literary Introduction*, Philadelphia, PA: Fortress Press, 1985, p. 325; see also the comments of Gerhard von Rad in his commentary, *Genesis*, London: SCM Press, 1961.

25 Gottwald, *Hebrew Bible*, pp. 328–9.

26 This I take to be the thrust of Jesus' word to his disciples in Mark 4.10–12 (parallel Matthew 13.10–17).

27 www.fabc.org/offices/olaity/AsIPA docs/Gospel Sharing Methods/1. Seven Steps Method of Gospel Sharing.pdf.

28 Tom Wright, *Scripture and the Authority of God*, London: SPCK, 2005, p. 21.

29 Wright, *Scripture*, pp. 21–32.

30 John V. Taylor, *The Go-Between God*, London: SCM Press, 1972, p. 3.

31 Graham Cray, *Discerning Leadership: Co-operating with the Go-Between God*, Cambridge: Grove, 2010, p. 15.

32 See, for example, David Pendleton and Adrian Furnham, *Leadership: All You Need to Know*, Basingstoke: Macmillan, 2012, pp. 74–96.

33 Alan Frost and Paul Hirsch, *The Shaping of Things to Come*, Peabody, MA: Hendrickson, 2003, pp. 165–81.

34 Donald Schön, *The Reflective Practitioner*, Farnham: Ashgate, 1983, pp. 3–20, 287–307.

35 Stephen Pickard, *Theological Foundations for Collaborative Ministry*, Farnham: Ashgate, 2009, p. 1.

36 Roger Walton, *The Reflective Disciple*, London: Epworth Press, 2009, pp. 104–10.

37 Paul Jarvis, *Adult Education and Lifelong Learning: Theory and Practice*, 4th edn, Abingdon: Routledge, 2010, p. 39.

38 For more detail on the relation between the Holy Spirit and human cognition, see my *Divine Revelation and Human Learning*, pp. 132–44.

39 See, for example, Stephen Covey, *The Seven Habits of Highly Effective People*, London: Simon & Schuster, 1992; and Daniel Goleman, *Emotional Intelligence* and *Working with Emotional Intelligence*, published together, London: Bloomsbury, 2004; original publication 1995 and 1998. By 'habits' Covey means what we have described as *habitus*, settled dispositions translated into habitual actions. The introduction to Goleman's *Emotional Intelligence* is entitled 'Aristotle's Challenge' and refers to the way Aristotle taught that the way to virtue was to handle emotion with intelligence.

40 Joseph Dunne, '"Professional Wisdom" in Practice', in Liz Bondi et al., *Towards Professional Wisdom*, Farnham: Ashgate, 2011, pp. 13–26; quotation from pp. 16–17.

41 See further several essays in Bondi et al., *Towards Professional Wisdom*: Daniel Vokey and Jeannie Kerr, 'Intuition and Professional Wisdom: Can We Teach Moral Discernment?', pp. 63–80; Elizabeth Campbell, 'Teacher Education as a Missed Opportunity in the Professional Preparation of Ethical Practitioners', pp. 81–93; David Carr, 'Virtue, Character and Emotion in People Professions: Towards a Virtue Ethic of Interpersonal Professional Conduct', pp. 97–110.

3

Leading the Learning Community

Learning for Discipleship

All God's people are called to be disciples. In Jesus' day his disciples were 'followers', whose task was to accompany him and share in his ministry. But even in the Gospels the idea of 'following' Jesus 'on the way' begins to develop a deeper, metaphorical meaning: the idea of sharing with him the 'way' of the cross, a commitment to a way of life based on the pattern of God's kingdom. The disciple is a learner, but not one who simply gathers information; rather one whose goal is to become 'like the teacher' (Matthew 10.25), to echo his goals and quality of life.

Thus for Paul and the other New Testament authors, 'discipleship' meant transformation into the 'image' or 'pattern' of Christ: 'to be conformed to the image of [God's] Son' (Romans 8.29); to be 'renewed in the spirit of your minds' putting on the 'new self, created according to the likeness of God in true righteousness and holiness' (Ephesians 4.23–24); to be transformed by the Spirit into the likeness of the Lord 'from one degree of glory to another' (2 Corinthians 3.18); to bear in our lives the 'fruit of the Spirit' (Galatians 5.22–23). The goal is that Christians 'grow up in every way into him who is the head, into Christ' (Ephesians 4.15), that 'Christ is formed in you' (Galatians 4.19). Significantly, each of the last two quotations is addressed to the community as a whole. Christian maturity is a corporate undertaking: the image of Christ is to be seen not so much in the virtuous individual but in the pattern of relationships that develops in the church as Christians learn to love each other and the wider world.

If we think of this as a learning process, what it involves is the transformation of the Christian's mental models, which make up 'tacit knowledge': the way we structure past learning so as to form the lens through which we see the world and respond to present experience. Several New Testament examples make this clear. In Jesus' parable of the unforgiving servant (Matthew 18.21–35), he portrays a man who, despite having received forgiveness himself, is unable or unwilling or unable to extend it to others. Jesus is teaching us that in Christian discipleship the characteristic of mercy, and with it the readiness to forgive, should be part of the Christian's *habitus*: the way we habitually interpret and respond to the world. The same applies in relation to generosity: writing to the Corinthians, Paul reminds them of the example of Jesus' generosity and challenges them to be similarly generous, promising them, in an echo of the Sermon of the Mount, that God has undertaken to supply all their needs (2 Corinthians 8.9; 9.8). In his letter to the Philippians, as we have already seen, he sets before them the pattern of Jesus' self-giving love and asks them to make it their own pattern of thinking, feeling and acting. In Christian discipleship, mercy and generosity become habitual responses because our 'tacit knowledge' is gradually transformed: in the way we interpret situations, whether in our own direct experience or encountered through the media, we become better attuned to the needs of others and thus more ready to respond in a merciful and generous way.

Discipleship is a gradual step-by-step process of transformation with the goal of becoming the people we are called to be. As 'children of God' transferred from the dominion of darkness to the kingdom of God's Son (Colossians 1.13), we inherit the privileges and responsibilities of our status: forgiveness of our sins, the gift of the Holy Spirit, access to God in prayer, understanding of his will and a vocation to live 'to the praise of his glory' (Ephesians 1.12) by demonstrating in our daily lives the quality of his love and extending it to others. The full realization of all we are to become as God's children is our eventual destiny (1 John 3.1–2): in seeing Jesus 'face to face', writes Paul, we will 'know fully, even as [we] have been fully known' (1 Corinthians 13.12). But the period of our earthly lives, during which we are called to 'follow' Jesus 'on the way', is a period of gradual transformation 'by the renewing of [our] minds' (Romans 12.2); that is, in the way that we interpret and respond to situations. It is often painful, a process of death and resurrection, by which the old ways of thinking 'according to the flesh' must be put to death in order to serve God 'according to the Spirit' (see Romans 8.1–8; Colossians 3.1–17).

The transformation of our lives as Christian disciples has a number of dimensions, both 'inward' and 'outward'. Inwardly we are talking about the development of Christian character, the acquisition of habitual qualities or virtues expressed in relatively stable and yet flexible ways of responding in a variety of situations. The effects in our lives may be far-reaching: far more so than we expect. This is beautifully expressed by C. S. Lewis in a passage in *Mere Christianity*:

> Imagine yourself as a living house. God comes in to rebuild that house. At first, perhaps, you can understand what he is doing. He is getting the drains right and stopping the leaks in the roof and so on: you knew that those jobs needed doing so you are not surprised. But presently he starts knocking the house about in a way that hurts abominably and does not seem to make sense. What on earth is he up to? The explanation is that he is building quite a different kind of house from the one you thought of – throwing out a new wing here, putting on an extra floor there, running up towers, making courtyards. You thought you were going to be made into a decent little cottage: but he is building a palace. He intends to come and live in it himself.[1]

The pain arises from the continual requirement of repentance: the realization that a particular tendency in our lives, a way of behaving, a source of motivation, a defence mechanism deeply embedded in us since childhood, is displeasing and dishonouring to God and harmful to ourselves and others. We realize that this pattern of thought or way of behaving is part of our old, 'fleshly' self and needs to be renounced. We may feel remorseful at the effect we can now see it has had in our lives and those of our nearest and dearest. We may feel exposed and alarmed at the possibility of learning to live in a new way. But as Lewis so clearly expresses it, God is not put off: he knows what he is doing and has the power, through the presence of the Spirit in our lives, to accomplish it. He is making us into palaces, fit for him to dwell in.

Another aspect of repentance is that *metanoia*, or change of mind, through which our priorities are reordered. We come to recognize that visible success, material wealth and even the good opinion of others are not necessarily the most important things in life: the coming of God's rule into our families and places of work is. Our social and political opinions and perhaps even our friendships change as we learn to interpret the world in the light of God's coming kingdom. Writing about the ministry of preaching, Walter Brueggemann declares: 'I understand preaching to be the chance to summon and nurture an alternative community with an alternative identity, vision and vocation, preoccupied with praise and obedience towards the God we Christians know fully in Jesus of Nazareth.'[2] This new identity, vision and vocation has the power to transform our priorities and relationships, directing us to 'hunger and thirst for righteousness', to become people of peace, to 'strive first for the kingdom of God' (Matthew 5.6, 9; 6.33) as long as it is learned not simply as information but as 'tacit knowledge' through which we interpret the rest of our experience. But we must see Brueggemann's definition as a summary not solely of the purpose of preaching but of the whole enterprise of Christian learning for discipleship, of which preaching is but one aspect.

The embrace of a distinctive Christian vision has consequences for the 'outward' dimensions of discipleship. It funds the distinctively Christian practices we shall examine in a later section of this chapter: not simply those associated with worship but also those that 'address fundamental human needs in response to and in the light of God's active presence for the life of the world', including keeping Sabbath and hospitality.[3] It requires a commitment to participation in the common life of the church, the call to build ties of friendship and partnership with fellow Christians who may be very different from ourselves. In an age of individualism, the call to Christian *koinonia*, or fellowship, poses the challenge of moving from independence to interdependence, perhaps of accepting the need to sacrifice our own personal preferences for the well-being of others. It also calls us to mission and service in the world, which is itself a powerful source of learning and change.

In this process of both outward and inward transformation, theological reflection offers enormous potential as a tool for learning and change. Anchored in concrete life situations, it takes for granted the 'situatedness' of experience, requiring us to focus on appropriate Christian responses to the challenges of the everyday. It works in the way our minds work – that is, the way we typically understand and respond to situations by drawing on the familiar patterns of the past – and asks us to consider the possibility of new and transformative patterns of responding. It holds together our intellectual grasp of the elements of a situation with our feelings and values. It draws on the resources of Scripture and Christian tradition, honouring the Bible as the means by which God draws us into the ongoing narrative of his people and thereby transforms us. It takes place in fellowship with the church of both past and present. It is located in prayer, both individually and corporately, and relies on the presence and discernment of the Holy Spirit. And it issues in changed perspectives and concrete action.

The learning cycle
One of the reasons that theological reflection works in this way is that it is echoes the recognized cycle of experiential learning, as formulated by David Kolb in the 1980s. In fact Laurie Green, who first proposed the pastoral cycle as a model of reflection in the 1990s, cites Kolb, along with liberation theology, as one of the key factors in the development of the various techniques of reflection.[4] Comparison of the pastoral cycle with Kolb's learning cycle is complicated by the difference in the way the term 'reflection' is used in the two formulations. But broadly speaking, Green's cycle of Experience – Exploration – Reflection – Response, with the Exploration and Reflection stages culminating in 'new insight', echoes the Experience – Reflection – Conceptualization – Action of the learning cycle.

Just as the pastoral cycle begins with a focus on experience, the learning cycle begins either with the challenge of an unfamiliar situation or new information taken in as a result of a formal learning experience. 'Formal' learning may take many different forms, including taking part in a planned learning session, but also reading a book, newspaper or magazine, watching a television documentary or simply reading the instructions for a new household gadget. 'Informal' learning may result from a wide variety of experiences, such as a chat with the neighbours, a walk in the countryside, an argument with a friend or partner, an accident, moving house, bereavement or having a baby.[5] In the learning cycle, 'Reflection' names the internal work that then follows as our minds, almost unbidden, search for connections with our previous experience in order to make sense of the new information. 'Conceptualization' names the stage of crystallization, at which we form conclusions about what we have learned and incorporate these into the mental models by which we structure the world. Finally, 'Action' corresponds to the Response phase: again this may take the form of a definite decision or simply a new and more adequate perspective on the situation from which to act in future.

As we saw in the previous chapter, in the learning that takes place as we grow in Christian discipleship, the Holy Spirit cooperates with the normal mechanisms of human learning. He is given to us to make our identity in Christ as children of God, friends to whom Christ makes known everything he hears from the Father (John 15.15), a reality in our lives. As Paul puts it, we are confirmed in this identity as the Spirit bears 'witness with our spirits' (Romans 8.16). To draw on the example from Ann Morisy given in the Introduction, the desire to devote time and effort to service of the poor reflects a growing awareness of that new identity, and the response to the advertisements for easy credit flows from the reordered scale of values of those gradually coming to understand the mind of the Father. To encapsulate my earlier argument, all learning springs from and contributes to our ability to relate to the world; and at the heart of that relating lies our sense of identity. The gift of a new identity through the work of the Spirit thus begins to reshape and redirect our learning; and conscious dependence on the presence of God's Spirit as our teacher and guide, such as in theological reflection, further enables the process of transformation.

Since the Spirit honours and works through the normal ways people learn, this means that knowledge of good practice in teaching and learning, and the skills that go with it, are essential for those with the responsibility of encouraging and enabling Christian discipleship. The role of the teacher is to *help the learner to learn*. The teacher is the servant of the learning process, whose goal is to see the learner grow and thrive. Sometimes, especially in contexts in which the learner is relatively new to Christian faith, teaching will take the form of instruction, but with the goal of freeing the learner from dependence in order to become a fellow disciple and companion of Christ.

Leadership of the learning process is therefore similar to leadership in collaborative ministry. Just as Christ is the one leader, so he is the one master; no one is the disciple of another but all are disciples of Christ. The goal is corporate Christian maturity, a community capable of discerning God's call together as well as individually. In both collaborative ministry and in Christian learning, the leader and the teacher are enablers, their special talents and greater responsibility gifts through which the Christian community maintains its faithfulness to Christ's call.

Planning a Programme of Christian Learning

As a gifted teacher with a clear sense of how best to address the needs of his hearers, Jesus used a variety of educational approaches. Much of the teaching his disciples received arose in the natural course of their life together, as a result of challenges from those around them, disputes among themselves and tricky situations in the course of their mission, and Jesus was skilled in using these incidents as occasions for reflective learning. But his methods also included formal teaching: sometimes in the form of parables with an explanation attached, often through pithy and memorable sayings; and although the compilations of his teaching we encounter in the Gospels, such as the Sermon on the Mount, may not have been delivered exactly as they are pictured there, it is nevertheless clear that Jesus regularly took his disciples aside to instruct them.

Likewise, in the early church the book of Acts and the New Testament letters convey a picture of a community in which reflective learning from one another arose naturally in the course of a common life. But from its earliest days this community 'devoted themselves to the apostles' teaching' (Acts 2.42), and the epistles show clear evidence of the presence of 'teachers' as a recognized gift within the churches and the outline of a pattern of teaching that would have made up the earliest 'catechesis' to be passed on to new converts.

Thus there is clearly a place for formal instruction as an element in the 'kingdom learning' by which Jesus' followers grow in their ability to love and serve him and one another. This element of planned teaching is especially relevant for those who are new to the faith. Whatever their journey to faith, it is likely that several important elements of Christian belief, much of the Bible and, crucially, that sense of the Bible's overall narrative sweep, which is so central to Christian life and faith, will be unknown to them. They may yet be unaware of how fundamentally the basic tenets of Christian faith and expectations for Christian behaviour differ from those of the culture with which they are familiar.

All this argues for a greater emphasis on catechesis, or basic instruction in Christian faith, than the contemporary Church, still largely shaped by a past in which the outline of Christian faith was widely known and the culture of the wider society owed much to Christian tradition, has been used to. In 1993, Steven Croft remarked that the Church of England had no 'National Curriculum . . . no guidelines for what adult Christians should be taught at the outset of their Christian lives', although he was able to list 12 possible Christian nurture courses from a variety of sources. His book *Growing New Christians* went on to describe the Christians for Life course then in use at St George's Halifax, where he was vicar, and which later became the basis for the Emmaus Nurture course.[6]

The Church of England's response to this challenge currently takes the form of the Pilgrim course. According to its website, the Pilgrim course aims to 'help every local church to create a place where people can explore the Christian faith together and see how it can be lived out each day'. Its approach is based on 'participation in a pattern of contemplation and discussion with a group of fellow travellers'. Assuming very little knowledge of Christian faith, it 'aims to equip people to follow Jesus Christ as disciples in the whole of their lives'.[7]

Pilgrim's method is seen as an echo of that of the early church, centring on 'the transmission of key texts' that sum up the heart of the Christian message. The key texts on which the course is based include the Lord's Prayer, the Ten Commandments, the Beatitudes and the Apostles' Creed, but the course also includes sections on the Eucharist, the Bible, Church and Kingdom, as well as an introductory course on basic Christian belief. In its approach, Pilgrim largely honours the learning cycle: groups are encouraged to link the content of the course with their own prior experience, and given plenty of opportunity to reflect on it both individually and through group discussion. Thus, in a session on God as Father, group members are invited to reflect on what they see as the qualities of a great parent and, if they wish, to share their own experience of parenthood. A biblical passage on God's fatherhood is introduced, with periods of silence for each person to reflect on what strikes them most in the passage. A reflection is then introduced with plenty of opportunity for discussion and questions, and the potential difficulty associated with the portrayal of God in the Old Testament as angry and apparently vindictive is faced head on. The possible weakness of the course appears to be at the Action phase of the learning cycle, which would be the Response stage of the cycle of theological reflection, since the session lacks a focus on how group members might respond to the idea of God's fatherhood in the course of their daily lives.

Early indications are that Pilgrim is proving a fruitful approach to basic Christian nurture, although it has to be acknowledged that no course is likely to be accessible to the full cultural spectrum represented in the Britain of today. In particular, it is doubtful whether anything taking the form of a 'course' has the potential to reach members of the 'non-book' culture, whose experience of and approach to learning tends to focus far more on action and reflection in a much less systematic way. It is also important to recognize the stage at which Christian disciples, increasingly informed about the basics of the faith and growing in confidence as learners, begin to want to apply their faith to specific areas of life and mission. A church that aims to produce well-instructed Christian disciples also needs to be a church ready to engage with the issues of the day and equip its members for ministry and mission. In the American context, Thomas Hawkins quotes research that suggests that a church with a 'thinking climate' contributes more effectively to Christian maturity than does the church's traditionally most important asset – pastoral care.[8]

Churches in areas where their congregations generally enjoy a high level of education need to challenge themselves by asking whether they are providing opportunities for their members to think through issues of Christian faith at a level even as demanding as that expected of 16- to 18-year-olds in the UK school system. Churches in areas of lower educational attainment have a different challenge: that of discovering ways of helping people to learn and grow in their faith who may not be less intelligent but have been less successful in traditional schooling. As we have seen, methods of teaching and learning based around action and reflection have potential in both these areas. Not long ago I received an email from one of our former students, now ordained, in which he shared the way he had been able to help a group from his parish to think about a particularly difficult and yet vitally important issue:

> Just wanted to share the following with you. Last night a small group from St James got together to reflect on the issue of human trafficking. We used Laurie Green's spiral of theological reflection (pastoral cycle): Experience – Exploration – Reflection – Response. One clear thing to come out of this for me was how empowering using theological reflection with a small church study group is. For me this empowerment was expressed in two ways – the group's realization that they do and can do theology and reflect theologically; and second, the clear drive that such processes have to concrete action.

In this case my friend Andrew used a structured method of theological reflection as the approach to learning. In many cases this may be the ideal approach. The group began by watching a video from the Stop the Traffick organization as an introduction and starting point. They then shared together their own knowledge, experience, reactions and questions. The theology they would have drawn on for the Reflection stage would have been the 'ordinary' theology of the members of the group. Some if not all may have benefited from instruction over the years through sermons, group studies and perhaps even formal teaching, but few, if any, would have experienced the formal theology of the university. But those resources were enough to give the group members confidence that they 'do and can do' theology: that a distinctive Christian approach to problems of national and international importance is possible and beneficial.

The Action phase of this particular reflection demonstrates how much is possible as a result of a simple exercise such as this. The group put on a display as a way of alerting the other members of their church to the issue. They then formed a social justice group, which went on to meet regularly to consider and respond to issues of homelessness, Fairtrade and modern slavery. Before long they were asked to develop and deliver a diocesan response to issues of human trafficking and modern slavery, the issue that began the process. Their experience is a particularly powerful example of the potential of theological reflection to bring together issues of life and faith.

A structured method of reflection may be ideal but it is not always necessary. The close relationship between TR and the learning cycle means that well-structured learning that honours the learning cycle *is*, in effect, theological reflection. It is learning that brings Christian belief and everyday experience together in a way that enables the learner to apply theology to experience, to respond with feeling as well as with the intellect, to see the world through the lens of Christian faith and to put their new learning into practice.

How then can churches provide such learning opportunities and so nurture a 'thinking' congregation confident in living out Christian discipleship in every area of their lives? I want to suggest and briefly survey six key elements of an effective teaching and learning programme.

1 Deciding on the scope of the programme
The first question is deciding on the extent of your teaching programme and weighing up all the factors involved, which might include the needs of different age groups, the rhythm of

the church's year, the extent of inter-church and ecumenical co-operation and the church's goals in mission. For example:

- How will you provide for the needs of children and young people? Do you think in terms of separate children's activities during times of worship or do you consider that children should be taking their place as part of the worshipping community; or do you try to balance these two priorities? How do you plan to nurture teenagers in their faith? Is this something your church can cope with on its own or do you need to co-operate with other churches to provide an appropriate setting for young people? Is there a case for specific learning activities for other age groups, such as older people? Or men's groups? Or for women's groups?
- Does your church have a seasonal rhythm, with an expectation of special activities in Lent, for example, or at other seasons of the year? How then can you make the best use of those opportunities? Are you able to place the question 'What shall we do for Lent this year?' into a bigger picture of planned learning for the whole church?
- Is your church part of a group or team and if so what difference will this make to your provision? Are you planning for the group as a whole or for each individual church? And how comfortable are members of the congregations likely to be engaging in inter-church activities? Are you able to make the most of the resources available to bring together interested learners with gifted teachers? Do you have ecumenical links that offer further potential?
- What are the training needs of the church? Is there an opportunity to provide appropriate training and nurture for those who lead intercessions in worship, so as to build their own lives of prayer and enhance the church's corporate prayer life? Is there a need for specific training for a particular mission initiative, such as the Alpha course? Or is there a need to equip the church as a caring community, perhaps through a focus on listening skills? Or to enable church members to identify their gifts and passions for God's service through a course like SHAPE?[9] What training is available, or even required, outside the church, from

dioceses and other Christian agencies, to enable people to train in areas such as pastoral counselling or participate in mission programmes such as Street Pastors?
- What role is the regular Sunday preaching to play in your overall approach to developing discipleship? How will you honour the parts played by preaching in worship, pastoral care and leadership as well as education?[10]
- How will you sort through the variety of 'off-the-shelf' courses for training and nurture to identify the ones that are right for your situation?

The extent of these questions suggests that even before trying to respond to them all, it will be helpful to ask another: 'Who is going to take responsibility for this?' Is it to be the clergy alone? Or a committee of the church council? Or a specially chosen group? And if so, who is to be a member of that group? Are the members to be chosen because they hold a particular office, such as churchwarden, for their gifts and enthusiasm or for a combination of these? Liz Varley, discussing the make-up of a group like this, draws attention to the potential value of the 'gritty non-expert' who will constructively criticize from the outsider's point of view and contribute the user's viewpoint to the planning process.[11]

Many churches have regular and often long-established home groups, which are traditionally seen as the place where learning for discipleship takes place. However, as we saw in Chapter 1, research suggests that what small-group members tend to value most about their groups is 'belonging' or 'community', with the Bible or Christian teaching generally figuring as less important. Small groups are good at providing places for people to belong and build relationships, and at reinforcing the values of the church of which they are part, but less effective as places of teaching and learning unless they are specifically set up for this purpose. And while they are good at strengthening the relationships within the church and between Christians, they are much less good at encouraging their members to build relationships outside the Christian community and so facilitating mission.[12] To plan the church's teaching and learning programme around larger groups might appear to downplay the element of belonging, but it is perfectly possible to include opportunities for building relationships by planning the teaching sessions in such a way as to alternate between periods of whole-group instruction and activities in smaller groups.

The existence of a planning group with a recognized brief provides the opportunity for the pros and cons of the different approaches to be thoroughly discussed and prayed over, drawing on the variety of experience and preferences represented by the members. It should also identify and bear in mind some basic questions of philosophy:

- Is Christian education mainly about helping individuals on their spiritual journey or about building up the whole church as a loving and serving community?
- Is it simply about passing on the riches of Christian inheritance, the Bible and tradition, or should it include helping people to discover God in just relationships, risk-taking and caring community?
- What should be the relationship between the learning programme and the needs of the church's mission: is the programme all about mission, or does it include space for contemplation, Sabbath and areas of individual interest?
- Are there any elements of the programme that might be open and relevant to not-yet-Christians? And if so, might there be a benefit in seeking to run courses of Christian instruction in 'secular' venues, perhaps even as part of the local adult education provision?

One church responded to a course on the occult run as part of the local adult education programme by offering a course on 'Christian spirituality'. In these days of increasing interest in 'spirituality', a simple course on the Lord's Prayer offers the opportunity to tackle some of those areas of huge interest and importance to many in society: the nature of God; the commitment to justice and community embodied in God's kingdom; the importance of just provision for material needs; the importance of forgiveness; the nature of evil – to name just a few!

And finally, in planning a programme of education for Christian discipleship, it is important not to neglect to check on what people are expecting. Questionnaires to discover areas of interest and concern can be backed up by personal contact with those who sign up for a particular course or series, perhaps with a series of telephone calls to find out why people have responded to the invitation, what they hope to gain and the kind of learning activities they find most helpful.

2 Creating a learning environment

The learning programme lovingly planned by a group of committed enthusiasts may fall disappointingly flat because in the church as a whole, learning for discipleship is not seen as a priority. It is therefore important to take steps to 'prime' expectations: to convey the importance you wish to place on discipleship before issuing the invitation to a specific learning event. Here there are three areas to consider in particular:

- Does the church's physical environment speak of a commitment to learning? Are the venues comfortable and well equipped, with adequate toilet and kitchen facilities? Is the church willing to invest in the equipment that might be necessary for a well-run educational programme, such as flip-charts and data projector; and are these up to date and well maintained? Are you expecting to meet in a corner of a draughty church hall in January or in a warm, brightly lit, comfortable and well-equipped venue?
- Consideration of the physical environment is largely a question of identifying and removing barriers to participation. The second area is about how to encourage it actively. This is done most effectively, perhaps, by providing news of previous events in the form of displays in places people gather, items in a magazine or news-sheet, via social media or a news spot in a service, complete with appreciative quotes from participants who don't mind sharing their enjoyment. Even more effective is the factor that is most difficult to organize: word of mouth; but even here it may be possible to enlist key people to gossip the message.
- And third, what does the church have in place to support and encourage learning? The possibilities here include a bookstall, with regular reviews appearing in the magazine; or perhaps a

'think spot' for the weekly notices: a cartoon, a Bible verse, a striking quotation, a piece from the local newspaper, a set of telling statistics, a poem or verse from an unfamiliar hymn, each conveyed in a way that invites and helps people to reflect, raises questions, and so perhaps whets the appetite for further learning.

3 Deciding on aims and objectives

The subject of aims and objectives can be a controversial one when discussing the goals of an educational programme. Some people will argue that since everyone comes to learning with different needs, it is unwise or even wrong to specify too tightly what it is you expect people to learn, and that it is important to leave open the possibility of the unexpected insight. Others will argue that unless there is a clear aim, it is unlikely the learning programme will achieve very much: 'Aim at nothing and you are sure to hit it!' My own view embraces both sides of the argument. We can never legislate for all the benefit people derive from learning activities or plan in advance for everything that is to be learned, but aims and objectives are nevertheless vital as an element in planning not only the programme as a whole but individual learning sessions. Without knowing what we were hoping for, whether on a large or smaller scale, it will be impossible to evaluate whether we have in fact achieved anything worthwhile. It is important *both* to plan as carefully as possible *and* to leave space for the unexpected. God's Holy Spirit can be expected to be at work in both areas: helping us to discern the needs and to create really effective and enjoyable teaching sessions, while still encountering people in unexpected places and using our carefully designed programmes for purposes of his own that only he could have predicted.

In educational parlance our goals, or what we hope to achieve, are described in two ways: 'aims' and 'objectives'. Aims are big picture: our global aspirations for a programme as a whole. Thus the aims for a programme of Christian nurture might be to provide:

- everyone with a basic understanding of the Christian faith;
- opportunities for an experiential encounter with God through worship, prayer and the presence of the Holy Spirit;

- an experience of Christian community that helps people to begin building loving relationships;
- an opportunity to make a considered decision about Christian commitment.

The aims for a Lent course on some parables of Jesus might include:

- growing in understanding of the way Jesus' parables speak to their context;
- understanding and being able to discuss the reasons Jesus used parables in his teaching ministry;
- identifying some of the ways the parables speak to us as individuals, as churches and to our society;
- becoming more open to be challenged by Jesus' teaching and identifying ways we may be called to respond to these challenges.

You will notice that each of these lists, while referring to the content of the course in each case, is framed in a way that puts the *outcome for the learners* at the centre. In other words, the first list does *not* say 'To provide an account of the basics of the Christian faith' but talks about the understanding the learners should have by the end of the course. It is a crucial aspect of aims and objectives that they must state not what is to be *taught* but what is to be *learned*. The teacher may teach, and so fulfil a goal expressed in terms of content, but the question is: 'Has anyone learned anything?' Framing aims and objectives from the point of view of the learner is far more demanding, but is a continual reminder of the calling of the teacher not to 'lord it' over the learners but to serve them. In the church we are all disciples together, called to serve each other with our different gifts.

'Objectives' are much more specific and refer to the outcomes of a particular learning session – at least as far as it is possible to plan for them. Thus for a learning session on Christian giving, such as the one that appears as part of the third section of the Emmaus Nurture course, Living the Christian Life, the objectives might be expressed as follows:

As a result of this session we hope that all the participants will:

- understand the principles of Christian stewardship;
- understand the way the church's finances work;
- be motivated to take the first steps towards sacrificial giving.[13]

You will notice at least two things about these objectives. First, they include not only understanding but attitude. It is a well-recognized feature of all education that its goals embrace not only intellectual understanding but also attitude or disposition. And this is especially important for Christian discipleship, where the overall goal is to help people deepen their love for God and for one another, and their desire to serve. Two of these objectives cover areas of understanding and one looks for a change in disposition. It would also have been possible, depending on the purpose of the session, to include an objective focusing on skills. If, in addition to providing basic learning about the Christian approach to money, we had also been training people in the principles of sound budgeting, then the objectives would have had to include the ability to draw up a budget, as well as the desire to live within it – another objective directed towards attitude.

Second, it would be possible in principle to measure how successfully these objectives have been achieved. We could include an exercise as part of the session that would demonstrate whether or not the participants had really grasped the principles of Christian stewardship. We could have asked them to put together a presentation for others on the way the church is financed. We could also have tested the possible change in attitude towards giving by means of a questionnaire. You might choose, for perfectly good reasons, not to do any of these things. In many churches the culture of Christian discipleship is not so well established as to enable us to do this without appearing threatening or overbearing. But it is perfectly possible to envisage a situation in which the learners would be sufficiently motivated to welcome a session that demanded these things of them. To recognize your own progress is one of the key motivators in adult education, and the fact that churches routinely avoid challenging their members in this way, even in situations where it might be acceptable, may be a factor that tends to make learning for discipleship less effective.

To talk about aims and objectives in this way gives rise to an obvious and very important question: What gives you, as the teacher, or ideally as the planning group, the right to frame expectations of the learners in this way? Is it not more appropriate for us to offer the learning session and allow the outcome to remain between God and the participants? There are several answers to this question:

- You are the leaders of the church, responsible before God for the church's growth together as a community, for the fruitfulness of its mission and at least for providing opportunities and encouragement for the growth in discipleship of its members. As part of your stewardship, it is important that you are in a position to evaluate the effectiveness of the activities designed to achieve these goals.
- As teachers you bring knowledge of the subject areas and knowledge of good practice in teaching and learning. You are in a better position than the participants to judge what the outcome of the learning ought to be.
- It is to be hoped that you are acting out of love for each of the participants. You desire their growth in faith. You want them to experience the love of God in ever deeper ways. You want the church to grow as a loving and supportive community. You therefore want them to change, even though some steps along the road of discipleship may be costly; and you want them to know and rejoice in the fact that they are changing.
- And finally, you have a source of authority in the participants' agreement to attend the course you have planned, especially if, as I suggested earlier, you have also checked with at least some of them what they are expecting and hoping for.

But the last two bullet points also point to the importance of the participants' own goals: the reason they have chosen to attend the group or course; the outcomes they themselves are hoping for. It is a fundamental principle of adult education that adults are independent learners. They learn best when they see the relevance of the learning to their own lives and when the learning offered meets their own goals and aspirations. This is the reason why the planning of the programme as a whole should take careful account of the needs and desires for learning being expressed in the congregation; and why it is good practice at an early stage to allow every member of the group to explain what they are hoping for from a course; and even better practice to remember the goals the learners have brought with them and check that they are being addressed, making adjustments in the course content and objectives if necessary.

Having spent some considerable time examining the concept of aims and objectives, it is now important to restate a principle that cannot be sufficiently emphasized: the teachers' ability and willingness to frame the objectives *from the point of view of the learners* is one of the most important factors in the success or otherwise of any programme of learning. Without the willingness to express what it is you hope will be *learned*, programmes of learning will never advance beyond mediocrity. Here are some of the reasons why:

- The more clearly goals are defined, the more effective recruitment is. Being able to state clearly the purpose of a course and what you hope the outcomes will be for the participants helps you to 'sell' the course to the right people and helps them in their decision whether or not to attend.
- The more clearly the goals are defined, the greater the learning that takes place. This is because clear aims and objectives help you in your preparation to design the session to meet those objectives, and helps you when deciding what to include and what to miss out. Understanding the intended outcomes also tells the learners what it is they are supposed to be learning and thus enables them to focus.
- The more clearly goals are defined, the better the teacher can choose appropriate teaching/learning strategies, materials and methods. Having decided on the objectives, the next logical question is always: 'How best can I help the participants to achieve these outcomes?' Once you begin to master the

various learning methods available, clarity about the objectives helps you choose the methods that best suit the outcomes you are hoping for, as well as the ability and expectations of the group.
- The more clearly goals are defined, the easier it will be for both teacher and students to evaluate progress.[14]

And finally, clear aims and objectives are a challenge to reflection. Alongside the practical goal of planning and delivering a programme for discipleship, the planning group will also need to take time regularly to reflect on the reasons for what they are doing. Effectively, this means they will need to engage in theological reflection, reminding themselves and expanding their vision of the role the task entrusted to them plays in the coming of God's kingdom. Framing aims and objectives takes an effort: it is hard work. At every point there is a question, often unexpressed: 'Why this aim?' 'Are the goals we are seeking to achieve still the ones God is calling us to?'

At the point that the group decides it is time to address this question again, any one of the aims chosen can become a jumping-off point for reflection. Imagine a church that has decided to run a Lent course on some parables of Jesus and has framed the aims for the course in the way I have suggested above. The group then takes these aims, one at a time, and begins to ask: 'Why?' 'Why do we want to people to understand the way Jesus' parables speak to their context?' The answer may be along the lines of the benefits of understanding Jesus' life and teaching more clearly. 'Why, then, do we want people to understand this?' Because in understanding Jesus against the background of his own time, we come to appreciate better his message for us today. 'And why is that a good thing?' Because as a church we need a clear and correct understanding of just who Jesus was and the impact he made on his own society, so that we resist the temptation to make him in our own image. By this time the group is touching on some of the major issues in Christian learning, identifying some of the other key questions on which it would be fruitful to reflect, and growing in their own discipleship as well as their ability to participate in this ministry. And there are still three more aims for that particular session of the course to work with, should they choose!

4 Designing the courses

The variety of methods that can be used in planning a course or learning session is vast, and it is disappointing that the typical church-based course uses such a small selection of them. However, help is available from a variety of books full of practical ideas, and having experienced some of these it is not too difficult to adapt them to the needs of any particular group.[15] Here are a few brief guidelines:

- The course and sessions must be designed to meet the objectives! Aims and objectives act as a guide for what should be included and what methods are most likely to be fruitful. By forcing you to focus on the learning outcomes, objectives also force you to focus on the methods best adapted to achieve them. For example, to return to the session on Christian giving, if you have included an objective that looks for a change in attitude or disposition (such as greater willingness to give generously), you will need to include an activity that allows or encourages the participants to make this response. You might include: a value exercise, using keys and other objects as symbols of what we most value, to help them recognize and express their priorities in life; a time of silence to reflect on a particular question; the opportunity to reflect with a trusted neighbour on the way they spend their money; and so on. If you design the session only around the factual content without building in time for one or more of these activities, your attitude objective – the most important of the three – is unlikely to be achieved.
- The design should honour the learning cycle. It should include opportunities for the learners to make links between the subject content of the sessions and their existing experience. It should provide plenty of space for reflection on the new information you wish to teach. It should give everyone a chance to recognize and express their conclusions. Sometimes these will involve a powerful new insight or some other profound change, and you need to make space for this and for the learners to recognize

and affirm the new insights they are taking away from the session. It should also include some guidelines for action: suggestions as to how the new insights from the session might affect our everyday lives. It is not necessary to include all four aspects of the learning cycle in every session. You might design a course so that one session is an all-action experience but the following one provides plenty of space for reflection. You might major on input one week and provide time for reflection and discussion the next. Or you might devote the whole of the final session to the Action phase of the cycle, asking how we might respond, individually, as a group or as a church, to all that has been learned.
- By doing this you will also be honouring the different 'learning styles' within the group. This is an aspect of education I have not addressed, a vast subject in itself, but worth further study.[16]
- You will also want to tailor your choice of methods to the participants' level of ability and confidence. One exercise I use every year with our ordinands begins by asking them to draw a picture to represent their idea of the church. Even for these highly motivated men and women, I always take time to reassure them that they are not going to be judged on the standard of their artwork! And it is an exercise they typically remember throughout the course.
- Be as creative as possible! The sessions people most remember and through which they learn the most are those that most engage them. Don't be gimmicky, so that people remember the exercise but not the point, but do use variety.

5 *Presentation*

Learning, as we will see in the following sections, takes place in relationships. This means that the character of the teacher is one of the most important elements in fruitful learning. We can all recall the teachers who had the greatest impact on us, and in almost every case this will be to do with an element of their character. Top of the list are likely to be the twin attributes of justice and love. In childhood we appreciate teachers who are firm but fair: who thereby create a safe space for learning. In adulthood, learning is still a risky undertaking, and we still look for safe spaces created by teachers who care enough to set clear boundaries and firm expectations, the right combination of support and challenge, enabling learners both to feel affirmed and to grow.

One of our commitments as teachers, then, will be continually to improve our facilitation skills, through reading, practice and reflection.[17] Another will be to improve our skills of preparation and delivery. But it is in the area of character that the greatest challenges arise. Growing in the ability to teach well and growing in personal and spiritual maturity go hand in hand. In many ways it is about achieving a balance: confidence in the value of one's own perspective balanced by the humility to accept the contributions of others; willingness to value the learners' insights but without allowing the talkative members of the group to take over; encouraging the timid while deflating the over-confident; keeping one's eye on the goal (and the clock) while making space to explore in unexpected directions. All summed up in the one overriding attitude: 'It's not about me!' Rather it is about seeing Jesus glorified in the lives of others.

6 Evaluating the programme
And finally, it is crucial to know whether the educational programme we have spent so much time and prayer in planning and delivering is achieving what we hoped. General impressions are not good enough: you need concrete information, and this is most likely to come from the participants themselves. So you will need to encourage a culture in the church whereby it is normal for a teaching programme to be followed by a request for feedback, possibly using a questionnaire. Here are some general guidelines on what such a questionnaire might contain:

- One of the most important pieces of information you are looking for is the extent to which the aims and objectives were achieved. Here you will have to think very hard to avoid giving the questionnaire the flavour of a test. Open-ended questions, such as 'What are the most important things you think you have learned?', will go some way towards this. But you may have to think carefully about how to frame the questions to get the answers you want. A multiple-choice question might be the way to go about it. So for the first aim of our Lent course on parables, you might ask: 'If you were asked to explain to a friend in the church what Jesus intended to say to the crowd through the parable of the sower, would you feel a) baffled, b) confident, c) enthusiastic?'

- You will need to know such things as: whether the venue was convenient and comfortable for people; whether the atmosphere of the course was welcoming; whether the teaching given was interesting and clear; whether the learning activities were enjoyable; whether people thought there was the right balance between input and discussion or other response activities. A multiple-choice format with space for people to add comments is again likely to be fruitful here. It allows people to finish the questionnaire in a few minutes if they wish; or to take more time and give their opinions at length. It is important to frame your questions in such a way as to encourage people to tell you about their *experience* rather than offer you their *judgements*. 'It was a very good course' is only valuable if the person is qualified to make that judgement. 'I really enjoyed the course' is a piece of hard evidence. It is even more helpful if you can find out *why* they enjoyed it!
- A programme in Christian discipleship is intended to encourage and enable people to make changes in their lives, in response to Scripture and in the power of the Holy Spirit. This means that the most important outcomes are those that stand the test of time. While immediate feedback can provide valuable information, the most vital aspect is likely to be the difference it is still making in people's lives some months later. So it may be worthwhile bearing in mind the possibility of a follow-up questionnaire. Six months after the event you might ask the participants what they still remember about the course, framing the wording of the questionnaire to prompt them appropriately. Using our example of the Lent course once again, the crucial questions to ask in this case would be about the challenges they identified in the parables they studied and the differences they are noticing in their lives as a result.

Well-designed feedback is likely to help in two particular ways: it will suggest ways you could improve things next time round;

it may also give you an indication of the areas of interest that could form the subject of the next course – especially if you have included this as part of the questionnaire!

The Learning Church

In the previous section we concentrated on the church's programme of planned learning, seeking to provide the outline of a twenty-first-century equivalent of the church's tradition of catechesis, or formal instruction in the faith, and Jesus' and the apostles' practice of formal teaching. But we saw that for Jesus' disciples and the earliest Christians, this element of formal instruction took place against the background of a committed community, learning in informal ways from one another in response to the challenges and opportunities of everyday life and ministry. We also know from our study of both theological reflection and the learning cycle that while formal learning may be planned and episodic, informal learning is taking place all the time and in manifold ways in response to our need to make sense of and respond to the various situations in which we find ourselves. In this section, then, it is time to explore the significant part played by informal learning in the life of the Christian community.

Let us begin by looking at some examples:

- Every few miles, and in our big cities much more frequently, we find church buildings. In Britain, most though by no means all are ancient. These ancient buildings speak to all and sundry of continuity: they are a constant reminder of our Christian past. They bear witness to the spiritual dimension of life and are often valued for this even in an age of secularism and doubt. But in some cases they also speak of decline, especially when the building exudes a faint mustiness due to infrequent use. Of course, these messages are ambivalent: as with all informal learning, they strike people in different ways depending on their own previous experience. One of the churches where I was vicar was a multi-purpose building, where the sanctuary was protected by a screen during the week; and despite the presence of a large cross and the name of the church prominently displayed on the

LEADING THE LEARNING COMMUNITY

exterior, we discovered that several of our weekday users had failed to recognize it as a church! On the other hand, many cathedrals have a regular 'congregation' of people who visit the building in order simply to 'be': to spend time in an atmosphere redolent of the transcendence of God, speaking so powerfully of the significance of the spiritual dimension of life. In other places people will encounter churches with multiple uses: the building may contain a shop, a café or even a Post Office – signs of the way the national Church is searching for a new and more appropriate relationship with contemporary society, which may be understood in a variety of ways in this period of uncertainty and transition.

- Inside the church, the seating pattern and arrangement of the church furniture also makes a statement. The size of the building and the presence of so many seats speak of gathering, but what kind of gathering? Gathering for an event controlled from the front, the direction the seats all face? Or is there a central space surrounded by seating on three sides, suggesting a communal point of focus? Or perhaps the seats are arranged café-style, suggesting more intensive interaction?[18]
- Once the service begins, there is more for the interested participant to pick up informally, although the character of the service as a formal ritual may mean that not all the meanings are immediately obvious. But where there are intercessions, the range of concerns offered for prayer may fairly be taken as an indication of the scope this community's concern; as well as expressing the faith that God is involved with the world and that our prayers make a difference. If the intercessions are led from the body of the church, an implicit statement is being made about the shared nature of these prayers.
- The tone of voice in which the person who leads the intercessions addresses God also conveys a powerful message. Most people are accustomed to picking up messages from gesture, facial expression and tone of voice even more readily than from the words spoken. A distant and formal tone will convey something very different from a warm and reverent tone.
- And to use one more example, a host of impressions are to be gained from the church's weekly notice sheet. Is it well or

cheaply produced? Is it well designed or haphazard? Are the Scripture readings included, thus drawing attention to their importance? What activities does the church engage in or support? What links does it have with the local community?

'Participation' and 'reification'

A casual enquirer or occasional visitor will have learned a huge amount about Christian faith and practice, and about this church in particular, simply as a result of one visit. For the regular churchgoer, the kind of messages I have mentioned here and many more besides are continually being reinforced. Of course, the messages that are actually taken away will differ from person to person. We learn through the interaction of what Etienne Wenger calls 'participation' and 'reification'. And in this interaction there is a continual 'negotiation' between the shared meanings embedded in such things as buildings, seating, prayers and notice sheets, and the meaning the individual worshipper may take from them.

To explain this in more detail: 'reification' means to make something into a 'thing' (from the Latin *res*, meaning 'thing'). Wenger uses reification 'to refer to the process of giving form to our experience by producing objects that congeal our experience in "thingness"'.[19] Church buildings, seats or pews and notice sheets are 'things' that express meanings built up over time. The intercessions represent the desire of the church to pray for the world put into a form for a particular occasion. Although multiple meanings are embedded in each of these, the worshipper's participation involves a particular response; and that participation may have the power to influence the shared meanings of the whole community. So, for example, the intercession leader's tone of voice is an aspect of his own participation in the shared worship event, with the potential to influence the meaning of the event for everyone taking part.

The shared singing of a hymn is a classic example of this interaction of reification and participation. The words 'All hail, redeemer hail / for thou has died for me. / Thy praise and glory shall not fail / throughout eternity' are a particular expression of the church's faith in the atonement through Jesus' death on the cross. But the worshipper makes these words her own in her own particular way, bringing her understanding of the atonement, her experience of faith and her relationship to Jesus to the singing of the hymn. Depending on the congregation, the shared singing of this hymn has the power to inspire the worshippers to deeper devotion; or at the other end of the scale, proves an embarrassing anti-climax devoid of shared meaning.

What is true for hymns is true for the liturgy as a whole, whether that liturgy follows a formal structure or a much less formal but nevertheless well-understood pattern. Potential shared meaning is embedded in both language and posture, but each worshipper responds in their own way. Prayers of confession invite the worshipper to become conscious of his sins, and serve as a continual reminder of the Christian belief in the need for salvation through Christ. The formal recitation of the creed stands as a reminder of the shared faith that brings the church together, and the worshippers participate with varying degrees of understanding and consent. Songs of praise express the majesty of God and invite the worshipper to share in rejoicing, awe and perhaps excitement. And what is true for liturgy is true for every aspect of the church's shared life together. The church's values and beliefs are embedded in shared practices and learned through participation in those practices. As we shall see in the following section, this is a feature not just of Christian worship but of every aspect of life.

It follows from all this that regular participation in Christian life and worship is a powerful source of learning. And simply because it is informal – because it is learning that comes about as a person attempts to make sense of and respond to the situation they find themselves in – it is potentially much *more* powerful than the church's programme of planned learning. In fact the planned learning programme will only be truly effective if what is taught through the preaching, Bible study groups and planned courses is actually reflected in the life of the Christian community: if the practice of forgiveness, taught perhaps in a Lent course on parables and embodied in the use of the confession at most services, is actually experienced through life in a forgiving congregation; if teaching about generous giving is backed up by practices of generosity experienced in all facets of the community's life; and if the encouragement to share one's faith is enabled through opportunities for involvement in mission together. In the light of the power and pervasiveness of the informal learning continually taking place through the life of the congregation, it would be an error to view the planned learning programme as *the* place where learning is happening. Rather it is best seen as one facet of a church seeking to live out the gospel in every aspect of its life together. Its task is to make explicit – and enable people to explore and think through – the distinctively Christian world view that gives shape to the community's life.

Maintaining the faithfulness of the church
The other main task of the church's educational ministry is directed to the life of the community itself. This is a hugely important issue. If it is true that the church's common life is a powerful source of learning for discipleship, questions immediately arise: How do we make sure that what people are experiencing in and through the church's life is actually faithful to the gospel? How do we seek to develop the quality of our shared life, so that what people encounter on a day-to-day and week-to-week basis is a faithful reflection of Christian faith capable of pointing people to Jesus?

The most powerful tool we have for achieving this is theological reflection. Reflection enables us to name and describe our actual experience of the church's life, or some particular aspect of it, to explore that experience in greater depth and then to bring to bear the resources of Scripture and the Christian heritage precisely in order to judge how faithful our practice has been to the call of God in the gospel, the extent to which it reflects the values of God's kingdom or contributes to God's mission in our particular context.

One of our students, now ordained, had previously been a volunteer at a Midlands cathedral. In an email he described to me how the cathedral had used a very informal process of reflection to enhance not only the regular worship but its whole community life:

> We would meet after large services or major seasons to review worship, just the key players, focusing on what had worked and what hadn't. This was widened out to include more people, such as sidespeople, servers, choir members – anyone

who wanted to be there would be welcome. We still did some of the 'What was good?', 'What could have been better?', but questions now included 'What were we trying to say?' and 'Did we say it?' 'What are we communicating about Christian faith in what we do?' 'If I were a first time visitor, what would I have thought/felt/seen/come away with?' This led to far more discussion of what we were doing and why, and a growing understanding of how our faith, our own worship, the liturgy and importantly God's/our mission are all interconnected. Asking the questions led to people being able to share and reflect together and gave the opportunity to learn and grow in both individual faith and our worshipping life together, while also improving our liturgical practice.

Interestingly, this was a conversation that had not been planned as TR from the start but gradually developed in that direction. It arose from a shared concern for the quality of worship, which lies at the heart of any cathedral's life. It developed to include both aspects of that worship: 'reification' in terms of the liturgy and 'participation' in terms of 'our own worship' and the experience of the visitor. At no point was a formal technique of reflection introduced, but the natural tendency was to move in the direction of informal reflection. The conversation began to link the shape of the worship with the faith that inspires it, and as happens in most such conversations, the questions got deeper as the process continued. It enriched not only the shared worshipping life of the cathedral but the individual discipleship of those taking part. Learning arose naturally from reflection on a particular aspect of the church's mission.

Examples abound of renewal in the life of local congregations as a result of what is in effect TR, even if not recognized as such. Here are just two:

- Alison Gilchrist's Grove Booklet *Creating a Culture of Welcome in the Local Church* begins with a comparison of her experience in the outpatients' department of her local hospital and in her local church, backed up by the accounts of several others whose experience of the lack of welcome from a local congregation is equally depressing. She then sets out a brief theology of welcome, drawing on Scripture, before going back to the Exploration stage, looking at the problem of 'introversion' in the life of the church. Finally there is an exploration of possible action in the light of her theological understanding, culminating in a brief summary of good practice. The booklet includes in its appendices a number of resources to enable local churches to do the reflecting for themselves: a hospitality audit, a Bible study and several suggestions for group exercises and reflection. Alison doesn't just tell us how we ought to do it and why, she leads us through a process of reflection and then encourages us to do the further work of reflection together.[20]

- Robert Warren's book *The Healthy Churches Handbook* is an account of a theological reflection.[21] He and Janet Hodges, the Adviser in Local Mission for the Diocese of Durham from 1994 to 2002, discovered a significant discrepancy in attendance figures between churches in the diocese that were growing and those that were declining. They set out to explore the characteristics of the churches that were growing, eventually settling on the 'seven marks of a healthy church'. The book itself sets out to provide a theological explanation for these marks.

The Action phase that arises from *The Healthy Churches Handbook* is the healthy church audit, which churches are encouraged to carry out. The potential disadvantage here, though, is that the work of reflection has already been done: churches are asked to evaluate themselves in terms of an already existing framework. In contrast, the leaflet 'Growing Healthy Churches', originally produced as part of the 'Springboard' initiative, provides plenty of examples of churches doing the reflection for themselves:[22]

- A church did a survey of their members to find out how far their faith was nourished and how far public worship connected with their lives (Experience stage).
- Study of Scripture caused one church to set up a support group for single mothers and another to launch a recreational club for the elderly (Reflection stage leading to Action).

- Some churches have met with representatives of their local communities in order to help them identify ways they can best serve the needs of the community (Exploration).
- A church took over a year to identify itself as 'called to hospitality': this was first explored as God's hospitality to them in the Eucharist, then as to how it could be expressed in the local community and daily living (Exploration and Reflection leading to Action).
- One church completely rethought its theology as a result of engaging with the local 'benefit culture' (Experience and Exploration leading to Reflection and consequent 'new insight').

What I am suggesting here is that while the seven marks provide a useful benchmark to enable churches to audit their common life, it may be that the *process* of reflection that emerges from this has the greater potential for renewal and deepening of discipleship together.

The adaptive congregation
Embedding the discipline of reflection in the life of the church, whether through recognized methods or in more informal ways, enables a local church to become a 'learning organization', a church capable of adaptive change in response to the pressures and challenges of a fast-changing world, guided by its core purpose and identity. This is precisely what TR offers: a means of continually evaluating our practice in the light of the gospel.

Why is this necessary? Because, as Thomas Hawkins points out, the speed of change in society is now so rapid as to have become bewildering.[23] New possibilities for communication – the internet, emails, texting and social media – have become available within less than a generation. Computerization and the vastly increased capability of the communication media have led to industrial change on a global scale, a development that has had huge knock-on effects on the role of national governments. Not only is the world available to us at the touch of a button or a few clicks on the computer keyboard but the world is arriving on our doorstep in the form of vastly increased international mobility. Many of the things our grandparents' and even our parents' generation took for granted are no longer true, and one of the most important of these is that we would learn everything important that we need for life by the age of 18. In order to cope with this rapidly changing world, learning needs to become a lifelong process.

It is not only individuals but also churches that need to learn, not for the naïve and simplistic reason of 'So as not to be left behind' but because the messages and meanings embedded in ancient buildings, rows of seats, photocopied news-sheets, monologue sermons and traditional Christian language all change as society changes. The conditions of everyday life in which all Christian believers are called to live as disciples of Christ change, and the potential and possibilities for mission, the outflow of God's love for the world, come and go with bewildering speed. In this rapidly changing world, fewer and fewer of the problems we encounter are 'technical' problems, capable of solution by means of what we already know; more and more are 'adaptive' problems, requiring us actively to search for the knowledge we need to respond to them.

All this requires churches willing and able to go on learning, through bringing to bear the wisdom of the past on the problems and opportunities of the present. As Hawkins expresses it:

> Tomorrow's church requires leaders who are educators skilled in developing people and their gifts. The leader's basic work becomes shaping and reshaping meaning in a community where people engage together in the shared practice of ministry. Church leaders traditionally gave attention to teaching Christians the proper doctrines and beliefs. In the emerging information era, they equip Christians with tools and strategies that allow them to learn continuously by reflecting on their everyday ministry experiences.[24]

The key to achieving this, Hawkins suggests, is to bring learning and ministry together. In other words, the church's planned learning programme needs to be integrated with the whole mission and ministry of the church, recognizing where opportunities for learning emerge naturally from the church's ministries, and flexible enough to respond to the needs and challenges of the moment. The task of the learning programme will be governed by questions such as:

- Is this aspect of our church's life faithfully expressing the gospel?
- Are we losing sight of God's call in this area of the church's mission?
- Where is the Holy Spirit calling us as a church at this present moment?

And these are all echoing the fundamental question of theological reflection:

- Where is God, and what would be a faithful response to him in this particular situation?

If this sounds complex and demanding, the way it works out is remarkably simple. It involves using the tool of TR in flexible and appropriate ways to continually monitor the faithfulness of our church's life and discern the areas into which God is calling us to mission. Each year I ask a group of ordinands at Ripon College Cuddesdon, as part of their course in ministry and leadership, to think of ways this might work in a church with which they are familiar. Here are just a few of the suggestions one group came up with, many drawing on actual experience in their placement or sending parishes. Many reading this will recognize things already taking place in their own churches:

- A Bible study or reflection on an item on the church council's agenda.
- Discussion with the choir about the way singing expresses our response to God, or on the words of a particular hymn or anthem.
- Leading a group in a structured TR on a crisis in the locality.
- A Sunday Gospel-type group as part of sermon planning, which reflects on the lectionary readings before the following Sunday service and what they may be saying to us as a congregation.
- Gather all those who lead intercessions to reflect together on the importance of intercession as part of worship and to explore different ways of praying.
- Regular supervision meetings for people involved in lay ministry, providing a space for them to reflect on the situations and people they have encountered and where God has been at work.

- Do active practical things like making a community garden, but link it to Scripture and prayer and reflect on why we are doing this, using the 'I wonder . . .' style of questions from Godly Play.
- 'Table talk' using cards to prompt discussion on an issue, topic or theme.

. . . and so the list goes on. I am not suggesting that a church should be looking to do *all* of these things, or that they should be always engaging in this process of reflection on some aspect of their common life. Several of these suggestions have the character of 'interventions': a planned process by which people are made aware of their assumptions in some area of experience and helped or encouraged to change. A very simple intervention, such as the opportunity for a choir to reflect together on the meaning of Christian worship or a whole-church reflection and response to a local crisis, has the potential to transform the church's life and relationships in far-reaching ways. Such interventions may be carefully planned in advance or may arise spontaneously in response to circumstances. Several of the examples of reflection from the 'Growing Healthy Churches' leaflet given above are illustrations of this: a one-off event or planned process, which had a significant effect in the life of the church.

Are there any areas of the church's life too unimportant to include in this process of reflection? In his chapter on discerning and implementing vision in the life of the church, James Lawrence puts forward the following 'supposal':

Imagine visiting a church building on a Saturday morning. As you enter, you spot an elderly lady arranging flowers at the front. She smiles and continues with her work until you draw alongside her on your tour of the building. After various pleasantries you enquire if she always does the flowers. She replies, 'Oh yes, I do them to help people feel warm and welcomed when they come to the service, especially the guests. It can be such a strange experience if you haven't been before. And we take them to the housebound and elderly on Monday to show them a little love and care. It gives us a lovely opportunity to talk and pray with them.' Somewhat surprised by her response, you ask her if she has always seen flower arranging that way. 'Oh no, I used to be on the rota. I didn't mind doing it once in a while, I quite enjoy flowers. But a few years ago our minister got us to think about the church, what we're here for, what God might be asking us to do, and I began to realize . . .'[25]

That lady had responded to a call from God that arose as a result of a process of reflection in which the flower arrangers were invited to 'think about the church, what we're here for, what God might be asking us to do'. Perhaps the vicar who asked her to do this had been using the 'Evening Conference for Flower Arrangers' suggested by Liz Varley in her book *Catching Fire*.

> 7.15: Arrival. Coffee. Create a name badge with a picture of a flower on it.
> 7.40: Introductions in small groups. Everyone says a little about who they are, their interest in flower arranging and why they chose the particular flower to draw on their label.
> 7.50: Groups discuss what good flower arrangements contribute to an act of worship and report their observations.
> 8.20: A practical session by an experienced flower arranger, perhaps teaching an advanced technique, included to give the group members a sense that they have learned something worthwhile.
> 8.40: Bible study on Mark 14.1–9, the woman who anointed Jesus' feet. Groups are invited to note and share anything in the passage that seems to be saying something about their ministry of flower arranging.
> 8.55: Guided meditation, incorporating several of the insights that might emerge from the Bible study.[26]

Flower arrangers, choir and music group, magazine editor, website designer, children's and young people's group leaders, Alpha or Emmaus team, church council finance subcommittee – there is no area of ministry in which TR cannot play a role in maintaining the church's focus on its call and faithfulness. The same is true when it comes to discerning the potential and becoming equipped for mission:

- Umoja is a programme designed to equip churches and Christian groups for community engagement. *Umoja* is a Swahili word that means a spirit of unity and togetherness. The programme has already been widely used throughout the world under the auspices of Tear Fund and has been adopted more recently by the Mothers' Union for use in the UK. Incorporating a variety of creative activities, Umoja has a clear reflective structure, devoting considerable time to meditation on Scripture and placing it at the heart of each session. For example, the second session, designed to enable the church to assess the resources at its disposal, includes an introductory game requiring the group to make the most effective use of the resources available to it in the room. It then moves on to in-depth reflection and meditation on the stories of Elijah and the widow's jar of oil and Jesus' feeding of the 5,000, in order to place at the centre of the group's thought the way God sees and uses human resources. Only in this light is the group then encouraged to engage in a comprehensive survey of the resources available to it in the church and in the local community. Exploration of the practical problems and opportunities, and meditation on the message of Scripture, are held together in shaping the group's response.[27]
- After Sunday is an organization dedicated to enabling all God's people to become effective disciples in their places of work and daily life by breaking down the sacred/secular divide that infects the minds of many if not most Christians. According to their website: 'After Sunday's vision is of Christian disciples who, by integrating their faith with their daily life and work, become more effective partners in God's mission to the world, so enabling their communities to flourish.' One of the key tools they offer is the Faith Life Conversation. This is a way of bringing a group together to discuss an issue of shared concern arising in the course of their day-by-day experience. Gathering around a table and using a paper tablecloth, the group are asked to follow the steps of the pastoral cycle, defining the issue clearly and noting the definition on the tablecloth, before each sharing their own experience of the issue, exploring it together, drawing in the resources of the Christian tradition and exploring possible responses, using the tablecloth to record their shared insights. Access to sources

of information to help with both the Exploration and Reflection stages is noted as one of the requirements of the conversation.[28]

What happens when people refuse to reflect together? Some years ago I cared for a church during an interregnum. The church building was so full of pews that there was very little room even for the congregation to chat to one another over coffee after a service; and yet apart from at the largest funerals, most of the pews were never used. One of the churchwardens said to me: 'You'll only take any pews out of here over my dead body!' On the surface he was completely closed to the idea of reflecting on the place of the pews in the church's life. His attitude was an example of what Peter Senge calls 'defensive routines'.[29] However, if I had been able to listen attentively while he explained to me why he was so attached to the pews, I might have gained some valuable insights not only into his particular attitudes but into the past history of the church, which would have guided me in my leadership of it. Defensive routines like this may appear merely obstructive but they may equally provide the key that unlocks the door to significant learning.

Learning and ministering together
Everything we have said so far about learning for discipleship, whether by means of a planned learning programme or through shared reflection on the church's ministry and mission, has profound implications for the nature of relationships within the church and the styles of leadership best adapted to nurturing a community of disciples. The first and perhaps most important observation to make is that you cannot expect to treat adults as dependent learners. As we saw in Chapter 1, in the 'secular' sphere it is recognized as best practice to treat adults as independent learners who learn best:

- when their existing experience is respected and they have the chance to connect any new information with this existing experience;
- when they can see the direct relevance of any new information to their personal learning goals;
- in peer groups, where they are able to share insights and listen to those of others;

- where they are able to evaluate their own learning and see progress for their efforts.

Traditionally the church has fallen into the trap of treating adults as dependent learners, expecting them to learn information chosen for them by others, whether through sermons, study groups or teaching programmes, submitting to the authority of a hierarchical leadership. Theological reflection, by its very nature, honours the experience of each member of the group, invites the group to work together and moves towards clearly identifiable outcomes directly relevant to the situation. But it also does something else: it takes independent adults and invites them to become interdependent learners. The very nature of the learning event contributes to Christian *koinonia*, or partnership, in which the search for God's presence and calling lies at the heart of the learning process.

In fact hierarchical leadership stifles the life and creativity of the group. Learning through TR requires skilled facilitation, but the facilitator is the servant of the group rather than its director. Her task is to facilitate the sharing of experience and exchange of insights brought by each member of the group, to support and perhaps to challenge the group as together it seeks to discern, through the reflective process, the wisdom of God for the given situation. As Thomas Hawkins notes:

> When congregations become learning organizations, church leaders reframe their basic tasks and responsibilities. Pastors cease to perform ministry on the congregation's behalf. They instead foster learning environments where the whole people of God can shape and reshape meaning within a community of shared practice, continually clarifying those meanings in the light of a deeper understanding of the revelation made known in Jesus Christ.[30]

This style of enabling leadership not only encourages and provides opportunities for every church member's growth in discipleship, it also reflects the style of collaborative leadership clearly taught by Jesus, modelled by the early church and recognized in the best contemporary literature on leadership as being the style best suited to allow an organization to change and adapt.[31] In hierarchical leadership decisions are made by a few people, who are likely to be limited in their capacity to understand and weigh up all the factors to be taken into consideration. Wherever a hierarchical leader is present, moreover, the ability and willingness of the ordinary members to share their observations freely may be stifled out of concern about challenging the leader's authority or courting his disapproval.

In contrast, shared reflection in a non-hierarchical context has the potential to make available the full wisdom of the group. The contributions of the 'little ones', whom nobody previously thought of as sources of wisdom, are allowed to be heard. As Alan Roxburgh and Fred Romanuk remark:

> Leadership is about cultivating an environment that innovates and releases the missional imagination present in a community of God's people . . . an environment in which the Spirit-given presence of God's future may emerge among the people of God . . . Missional leadership cultivates an environment in which the people of God imagine a new future rather than one already determined by the leader.[32]

Thus as I remarked in the introduction to this chapter, the relationship of the Christian teacher to the learners is similar to that of the collaborative leader, who honours the wisdom and insight the Holy Spirit may be giving to the members of the church or team. Laurie Green identifies the potential role of the 'people's theologian': someone who plays a bridge-building role between those whose calling it is to immerse themselves in the Christian tradition through disciplined study, and the ordinary Christian congregation. The task of these bridge-builders, Green suggests, is fourfold:

- To work within the group or congregation as an 'animator', drawing on a variety of methods of teaching and learning. This, writes Green, 'will call for all the skills of the adult educator'.
- To be themselves experts in the Christian tradition, so as to be able to 'draw on it liberally' and know what the scholars are saying about it (but as 'servants of the Christian faith tradition and not controllers of it'), so as to make it available

to the 'ordinary theologians' of the learning group. And just as Stephen Pickard remarks about collaborative leadership, this is a role requiring 'spiritual maturity'.[33]
- In working with the marginalized, it is vital that the people's theologian has integrity with that group. This may call for the deliberate choice of downward social mobility and the willingness to adopt the perspective of the poor.
- The people's theologians must always affirm the responsibility of the group: she must never 'take over' or allow the group to defer to her expertise. Learning and reflecting is something the group must do together.[34]

In a provocative quote, Green links the perspective of the poor and marginalized, such as the base communities of South America, the pioneers of shared theological reflection, with the situation of the church in this country, afflicted by clericalism:

> It is in the nature of oppression that the oppressed begin to think in the same categories as the oppressors, and so group members will themselves believe what they have been told for so long – that they are not academic enough to handle theology nor 'ordained enough' to be theologians.[35]

My friend Andrew, by facilitating the group in his congregation in the process of TR, led them to see themselves as capable of 'doing theology' as well as realizing that theology might lead to practice. This is the challenge to all of us who are called to lead the learning congregation: do we have the spiritual maturity to forsake the role of expert in order to become servants of the learning of others?

The Congregation as a Community of Practice

In the previous section I showed that discipleship is learned through participation in the life of the Christian community. Although planned learning programmes such as the Pilgrim course play their part, the life of the community itself is likely to be the most powerful source of learning. The local church's shared understanding of what it means to be a Christian is embodied in shared practices of worship, service and witness, and learning how to participate in these practices is an important aspect of learning Christian faith.

One of the tasks of the church's learning programme is thus to make explicit the implicit understanding of what it means to live the Christian life embodied in these shared practices in order to equip all Christians, but especially those relatively new to faith, to participate with understanding. Theological reflection is one of the most powerful tools for accomplishing this, bringing together the Christian disciple's lived experience and the tradition of Christian faith, our story and God's story, so that the pattern of God's love as revealed in Jesus Christ and shared among us by the Holy Spirit becomes the lens through which we learn to view not just our religious practice but the whole of our experience. Reflection not only helps us to understand better what it means to participate in the Christian community, it also offers disciples opportunities to reflect on the whole of their life in order to see it through the lens of Christian faith. Theological reflection also enables corporate learning: reflection on the church's pattern of that shared life helps to ensure that it remains faithful to God's call and that the church is equipped to adapt to the rapid changes in society and discern the possibilities for mission in its own particular context.

In this section I will be further exploring the crucial insight that Christian faith is embodied in shared practices. How extensive are these shared practices? Is there a pattern for Christian life that we can describe in terms of 'Christian practices'? What do we mean by a 'practice'? And what does it mean to describe a local congregation, and the church as a whole, as a 'community of practice'? I will begin by looking at a proposal from the United States that the Christian life can indeed be described in terms of a set of recognizable shared practices. Having glanced at this approach to discipleship, I want then to begin to examine the more complex underlying questions as to how we are to understand the concept of a 'practice' and a 'community of practice'. The reason for doing so is that both practices and communities of practice are structures of relationship, action and knowing within which learning takes place. This examination therefore takes our study of learning to a new level and lays the foundation for the exploration of learning for ministry, the subject of Chapter 4.

'Christian practices'

Anyone who undertakes a basic course in Christian discipleship, such as Pilgrim or the Emmaus Nurture course, will learn that there are certain spiritual disciplines through which Christians express and grow in their faith: Bible study; personal prayer; corporate worship; regular participation in the Eucharist or Holy Communion. They may also learn – and those following the third phase of Emmaus Nurture, 'Living the Christian Life', certainly will learn – that Christian discipleship also includes the practice of stewardship, including regular sacrificial giving, and of informal witness to their faith among friends and colleagues.

Two of the most influential writers on Christian education in the United States, Craig Dykstra and Dorothy Bass, have proposed that it is possible to define a number of 'Christian practices', which together give shape to the Christian life. One important aspect of this proposal is that it mediates between two alternatives, neither of which provides a satisfactory account of the way Christians should be expected to grow in discipleship. On the one hand, if the Christian life is learned through participation in one particular Christian community, perhaps a local church, or conceivably a grouping of local churches, such as the New Wine, Proclamation Trust or On Fire networks, there is the risk that the individual may simply be expected to adopt a standard set of attitudes and pattern of life in conformity with their own particular church or network. On the other hand, to limit the expected pattern of Christian living to the spiritual disciplines, such as prayer and Bible reading, leaves each individual to work out for themselves a pattern of discipleship in the most challenging area of experience: engagement with the life of the wider community in their places of work, leisure and family life.

In place of these alternatives, Dykstra and Bass suggest that the Christian life is in fact structured by a set of practices deeply rooted in Christian tradition. Christian practices are ways of living out fundamental areas of human life. They are 'things people do together over time to address fundamental human needs in response to and in the light of God's active presence for the life of the world'.[36] Or to put it more simply, we might say that they are 'ordinary things done differently because of Christian faith'. To give some examples:

- Everyone needs to engage in relationships, and the Christian practice of hospitality proposes a pattern for relationships with Christians and non-Christians, structured both by sacrificial love and appropriate boundaries. The practice of Christian hospitality is rooted deeply in Christian tradition, beginning in the Old Testament but expressed most especially in Jesus' distinctive approach as both host and guest, and the sharp criticism he made of the cultures of his day. The purpose of Christian hospitality is to create a welcoming space in which guests can experience love and acceptance. One of its key features is that there is no expectation of reciprocation. Christian hospitality is offered freely as a gift of grace.[37]
- Everyone needs to order their household economically: to earn their income legitimately, budget appropriately and live within their budget. The practice of Christian stewardship orientates and guides these ordinary activities in the light of:
  o the call to all human beings to govern the world in accordance with God's purposes, with an eye to the flourishing of all creatures;
  o Jesus' admonition to trust God for our basic needs and his command to make them an object of daily prayer;
  o the New Testament's encouragement to reflect God's grace towards us in our financial dealings with others.
- Everyone needs rhythms and balance in the way they order their lives; periods of rest and recuperation to balance periods of activity. In addition, we need deliverance from the potential tyranny of work as the means by which we earn our living and define our identities. The discipline of Sabbath-keeping places a limit on work, providing not only a space for rest but an opportunity to rediscover our true identity in relation to God through worshipping and honouring him.[38]
- Everyone experiences conflict and broken relationships. The practice of forgiveness, firmly rooted in Christian belief in the

grace of God and trust in the reconciliation achieved through Jesus' death on the cross, limits the potential damage of conflict and offers the possibility of restored relationships.
- Everyone lives under the shadow of mortality, the knowledge that there is a limit on all we strive for, the inarticulate sense that it is only possible to assess the significance of our lives in the light of an eternity we do not fully understand. The appropriate Christian response, suggest Dykstra and Bass, is the Christian practice of 'dying well', rooted in the hope of resurrection in Christ.

In my view, a particular strength of this approach is that the practices outline by Dykstra and Bass relate to what Ann Morisy has named the 'foundational' and 'vocational' domains of spirituality.[39] They provide the shape of a Christian approach to areas of life we share with people of all faiths and none, setting out clear patterns for discipleship in each of these areas. They enable Christians to address some of the most fundamental questions of life and provide the pattern of a credible and distinctive pattern for living. Moreover, each of the practices is rooted in Scripture and Christian tradition, so that it provides a way of living out the tradition we share, providing Christian orientation and guidance in areas where it is all too easy to adopt the mentality of the prevailing culture. Finally, each practice embodies not only Christian beliefs but affections, skills, virtues, relationships and symbols. It is far more than a 'rule for living' applied in practice; rather it is a complex whole in which all the different dimensions of life come together.

By learning to live out clearly defined Christian practices, twenty-first-century disciples are not being left to work out a pattern of Christian life from scratch. They take their places in a community guided by centuries of tradition. But neither are the practices to be understood as a given; like the example of intercessions in worship we encountered in the previous section, the precise shape they will take in the life of each particular person or family is subject to negotiation through participation. Moreover, this process of negotiation through which the practices take shape enables us to understand the Christian tradition more deeply: taking Jesus as the exemplar for Christian hospitality helps us to understand how radical he was in his own day; reflection on the practice of Sabbath-keeping teaches us both why we need Sabbath and why God gave it. It is also possible for the practices to become corrupted: hospitality by the desire for luxury; household economics by the allure of wealth and fear of insecurity; forgiveness by the deep wounds we may be carrying in our lives or through the influence of the surrounding culture. Like every other aspect of Christian tradition, the practices are subject to a dynamic of sin and redemption, and yet this very fact opens up further possibilities of encountering God afresh in reflection and renewal.

What is a 'practice'?
The idea of Christian practices as proposed by Dykstra and Bass is an idea still in its infancy, yet to be extensively explored. It may well prove attractive, offering as it does a structured and yet flexible approach to Christian nurture for the whole of life. It represents a particular expression of the theme I developed in the previous section: that the pattern of Christian faith is embodied in the practices of the Christian community; and that Christian faith is learned most effectively by reflection on practice in the context of participation in the life of the community.

This approach to Christian learning draws on the increasingly influential work of the philosopher and ethicist Alasdair MacIntyre, which I briefly mentioned in Chapter 1. MacIntyre argues that one of the effects of the Enlightenment is the loss of the concepts of virtue and character: that the Enlightenment introduced a way of thinking within which these concepts no longer made sense. One of the reasons for this is the insistence that all valid knowledge can be codified in rules and generalizations. The effect is to place the emphasis on abstract theory and to downplay the importance of concrete human experience. In order to recover the idea of a virtue and make it comprehensible once again, it is necessary to reinvent ways of talking about the concrete reality of everyday human life. One of these is the concept of a practice.

What, then, is a practice? MacIntyre defines it as:

- a coherent, complex and co-operative human activity;
- which has both a social context and a history;

- and a goal, recognized both by those engaged in the practice and those outside;
- whose standards of excellence are 'internal' to the practice itself; that is, they are defined in relation to the goal, history and context of the practice;
- and these standards of excellence can be, and frequently are, systematically extended.[40]

This is a very compressed definition, so it would be as well to try to unpack it a little before explaining the significance of the idea of a practice for our study of learning. First, then, to qualify as a practice, an activity must display a degree of complexity. A simple activity like planting turnips is not a practice but agriculture as a whole is; kicking a football is not a practice but the game of football is; bricklaying is not a practice but architecture is. Practices include games such as chess or cricket; professions such as teaching or nursing; artistic endeavour, including painting and music; scientific research; running a business; raising a family. Practices embrace the whole of life. And they include, for our purposes, Christian discipleship and ministry; or rather, each of these involves a variety of practices, each with its history, context and purpose.

Practices also display both continuity and change: they have a history and a social context and develop over time. The history of farming, for example, is one of almost continuous development in order to meet the needs of society for food. Partly this consists of technological developments, such as techniques of selective breeding, new kinds of machinery and, more recently, the science of genetic modification. Partly the developments reflect the interaction of farming with its wider social context, such as changing patterns of land ownership and the pressure for greater efficiency exerted by rising population. The game of cricket has changed radically in the past two or three decades in response to changing patterns of leisure and entertainment in society. In a similar way the practice of Christian worship has developed over time in ways that reflect both social and cultural developments: such as changes in technology, in the way language is used in society, in the styles of music available and in the way emotions are expressed.

Integral to a practice is the idea of its inherent goal or purpose: to feed the population, to provide a leisure activity or source of entertainment or to glorify God. And yet these goals arise through a complex process of negotiation between those involved in the practice and the wider society. Over the past two or three generations the relative importance of economic efficiency and protection of the environment has been in a state of almost continuous negotiation between the farming community and society as a whole. Thus standards of good practice are likewise in a continual state of development and negotiation. The game of football, and sport in general, has begun to play a much more important role in the nation's psyche, reflecting both technological advances and cultural changes. Along with this development, the expectations of society have led to a much greater emphasis on player safety, while the question of 'fair play' in a number sports is a standing subject for debate. Here too standards of excellence and of good practice continually evolve. Christian worship is not exempt from this process of negotiation: the role of worship in national life has also radically changed, with patterns of church attendance no longer driven by 'obligation' but far more by 'consumption'.[41]

Thus MacIntyre suggests that human life and relationships are structured by participation in shared practices. It is here that their significance lies for our study of learning. A practice represents a complex interweaving of action and relationships, affections and commitments, knowledge and skills, values and qualities of character. Participation in a practice requires the possession of a certain amount of background knowledge, the deployment of a range of skills and the exercise of certain virtues or qualities of character. Farming, as well as requiring the understanding of crops, livestock, soils and farm machinery, and skills of husbandry and agriculture, also requires qualities such as patience in working with the rhythms of the climate and care for the land and environment. Sports such as cricket involve basic knowledge and a considerable degree of skill but also require virtues such as courage, humility and sportsmanship. Scientific research requires the skills and what Michael Polanyi called 'connoisseurship' to interpret the outcome of an experiment and to plan further experiments, and the commitment and passion required for the patient search for truth.[42] Academic research requires the intellectual virtues of 'certain types of attentiveness, of patience, of intellectual humility, and of seasoned judgement'.[43]

Now it is time to spell out the implications of the concept of a practice for our study of learning for both discipleship and ministry. In brief it is this: participation in shared practices is the context within which learning takes place. The goal of learning is to become more proficient in a valued practice, whether in the field of one's employment, in leisure activities such as learning chess, cricket or a musical instrument, in the pursuit of academic or scientific research, or growth in Christian discipleship. And in that process of learning, the 'knowledge' one seeks to gain is inextricably linked with the practical skills, goals, commitments and virtues required for participation in the practice.

Theoretical knowledge in the form of rules and generalizations abstracted from the context of a specific practice is thus always a secondary form of knowledge. The primary form of knowledge is the practical know-how – consisting of a complex interweaving of knowledge, skills, goals and values – required for the pursuit of a particular practice. And much of this is shared 'tacit' knowledge, consisting of all those things we simply take for granted in order to participate in the practice, many of them irreducible to definition. As Etienne Wenger writes, communities of practice call on a shared repertoire, which includes: 'routines, words, tools, ways of doing things, stories, gestures, symbols, genres, actions or concepts that the community has produced and adopted in the course of its existence, and which have become part of its practice'.[44] The role of 'theory' is to make the meanings implicit in the various elements of this tacit knowledge explicit, so as to enable us to reflect on the shared practice.

Practices provide a framework for interpreting the problems of everyday life, as they did when Rob Gallagher called on his knowledge of the practices of pastoral care, baptism, motherhood and Christian mission to make sense of his encounter with the woman asking for baptism for her daughter (see Chapter 2). They guide us towards those elements of the situation on which we can profitably reflect: the love of a mother for her daughter; the effects of prostitution on those caught up in it; the response of the police to drugs in society; the requirements of Christian commitment; the scope of God's love. Practices give shape to everyday reality, and structure the tacit know-how that forms the base level of our knowledge.

Communities of practice

Practices never exist in the abstract: they are located in communities. They consist of people doing things together. In fact practices take relationships for granted: to recognize that life is made up of communities of practice is to acknowledge that we grow and learn and find our identities in community. A local congregation is an example of a community of practice, and organizations like denominations and indeed the wider church as a whole consist of networks of interrelated communities of practice. The shared knowledge of the community is simply one aspect of its common life. As Wenger writes: 'Communities of practice . . . are about knowing, but also about being together, living meaningfully, developing a satisfying identity, and altogether being human.'[45]

What, then, is a community of practice? How are we to describe a local church as a 'community of practice'? It is, first, a group of people united by participation in a number of shared activities. We have mentioned some of these in earlier sections of this chapter. A local church usually has a building in which it meets for worship and perhaps for other purposes. The building has a certain seating pattern, designed with a view to facilitating a gathering for worship. The worship follows a familiar pattern and is supplemented by a variety of other activities, which together make up the community's shared life.

I have constructed the description above purposefully to omit the most important element about these activities: each one has a *meaning* for the people who take part in them. In fact it is the meaning of these activities for the participants that turns them into shared practices. The meaning may not be the same for everyone who takes part. The church building may speak to one person of inheritance and continuity, to another of stale tradition. As we have seen, there takes place a continual interaction of 'participation' and 'reification' in which each individual participant derives meaning from the shared form of the practice and contributes meaning through their participation.

Ideally the meaning of each of these elements in the life of the community is related to the whole community's shared sense of purpose. This purpose may be multi-faceted. The purpose of agriculture may be seen as providing the food the community needs for survival, but there are other possible purposes: to provide employment for those who work in it; to preserve a particular way of life; to care for the rural environment. Is the purpose of the game of cricket to provide a leisure activity in which players employ their skills and build their character? Or is it to provide entertainment for others? And what is the purpose of the church? Our whole study takes for granted the present period of transition in which the purpose of the church is in the process of negotiation, moving from the provision of opportunities for worship and a network of pastoral care for those who value religious practice towards a clearer sense of participation in the mission of God.

Another feature of any community of practice is the relationships it facilitates. Here again, we have already considered the scope of these. I have suggested that, as a community of practice, a local church should facilitate relationships in each of four 'spaces'. It will engage in shared activities and shared learning in social space. It provides a context in which members may get to know one another well and form personal relationships. For some it will provide the opportunity for relationships in 'intimate space', where matters of deep concern may be discussed in a safe environment, such as in spiritual direction or the ministry of confession. Finally, the church will have a public face: its leaders often, and its members from time to time, will relate as public figures, playing a role in the life of the wider community.

The meaning of the church's shared practices and the relationships generated by these come together to help form identity. Participation in communities of practice is identity-forming. Through it, each member is giving meaning not only to the practices but to themselves. Implicit in their participation are identity statements such as 'I am a person who worships God', perhaps even 'I am a person who worships God in certain ways'; 'I see

Jesus Christ as a significant figure for my life'; and perhaps 'I am called to share in God's mission.' The Christian practices I listed earlier in this section are themselves identity-forming. To keep the Sabbath, to practise hospitality in a certain way, to give generously and to face death in a certain way all help to define the people we wish to be and become. Christian discipleship is a process of personal transformation in which God through his Holy Spirit forms our identity after the pattern of Jesus Christ.

In common with everyone else in our complex society, Christians are participants in multiple communities. Family, workplace, leisure activities, political party, nation are all communities of practice and all help to form our identity. If our identity is to be formed in the way God himself intends, the Christian community ought ideally to be our primary community of practice, the one that plays the greatest role in personal formation. Communities of practice have boundaries, which are fuzzy at the edges depending on the extent of a person's commitment to and participation in the particular community. Christians live and work alongside others for whom the church has a very different meaning, and one element of their relationships involves seeing the church through the eyes of their non-Christian friends. Christians also have the task of assigning meaning to the other communities of which they are part.

Knowing in community

Knowledge for the individual Wenger defines as 'competence with respect to valued enterprises'.[46] The implications of this simple statement are far-reaching. It means that knowledge is relative to communities of practice: to call on one of Wenger's examples, an office building is known differently by its architect, its builders, the office workers, the cleaners and the postman. 'Knowing' is the skill of participating in the communities of practice to which we belong, and it is always a shared knowing. The aspiring Christian disciple learns in company with her community what it is to follow Christ. She participates in the church's shared knowledge of Christian tradition as it has come to be embodied in the community's life and worship. As Wenger remarks: 'Our knowing . . . is always too big, too rich, too ancient, and too connected for us to be the source of it individually.'[47]

And yet the Christian disciple is not trapped by the knowledge of her particular community. Through her participation she may contribute to the community's shared knowledge, such as when someone asked to lead the intercessions in worship expands the scope of the community's prayers and challenges them all perhaps to recognize God's concern for an unfamiliar area of experience, or to pray in unfamiliar ways. Nor is the community trapped by its shared knowledge: the tool of reflection is always available to enable it to make explicit the tacit knowledge it shares and together grow in its understanding of Christian tradition or competence in ministry and service.

The idea that 'knowledge' consists in rules and generalizations rather than the skills of belonging and participating in communities has blinded the church to the fact that in the context of society it is merely one community among many, and that the skills required for participation in the Christian community do not automatically transfer to other communities. In my view this is one of the most important reasons why, over the past two or three generations, the churches have become progressively more marginal in society.

Local churches must continually be negotiating on the boundary between themselves and other communities: perhaps with the users of the church hall; when using a local school for an event; when sending a group to lead assembly in that school. They are also continually welcoming individuals at the boundary of the community: for nurture courses; Messy Church; weddings; civic services; or in the case of some denominations, baptism (which theoretically requires a much higher degree of commitment than is realistic for most people encountering the Christian community at the boundary). Many churches are skilled at providing the right kind of hospitable space in each of these situations, enabling those who are not members of the community to experience its shared life and with it the beliefs and commitments embodied in its practices.

Where local churches are typically less competent is in helping their members to negotiate the boundaries they experience between the church and the other communities of practice to which they belong. Church members are also members of families, workplaces, leisure groups, political parties and nations. For most of the week they will be participating in these communities, negotiating with and influenced by their norms and assumptions. By failing to recognize the influence on their own members of the beliefs and commitments embodied in the various communities of practice that make up the wider society, and failing to provide significant help to their members in negotiating the boundaries between communities, the church has, in effect, acquiesced in its own relegation to becoming a niche activity for the few.

The way to avoid this fate is for churches to equip their members with the tools to reflect on the *other* communities of practice of which they are a part; in other words to relate Christian faith to the whole of their daily lives and places of work. I have already mentioned the organization After Sunday, which invites participants to use the pastoral cycle to reflect on issues encountered in the course of their everyday life in order to bring a Christian perspective to those areas. Another striking example is the programme What If Learning, reported by Trevor Cooling in his Grove booklet *Distinctively Christian Learning?*[48] This began with the insights of the language teacher David Smith. Reflecting on the programmes he was using to teach children foreign languages, Smith realized that their aim was to equip the students as 'effective tourists': in Cooling's words, 'to put it crudely, to get what they needed from the awkward people who did not speak English in order to have a successful holiday in their country'. Dissatisfied with this approach, Smith undertook some Bible study and designed a programme whose underlying aim was to equip students to offer hospitality to strangers in their own country. The programme replaced functional transactions, such as purchases in shops and asking directions, with activities requiring communication about relational matters with spiritual or moral significance.

At the heart of Smith's programme was the ability to reimagine both the students and the situations in which the learning of a language might play a part. Other examples from What If Learning include a maths teacher who wanted to focus on the importance of serving others. She introduced the story of Florence Nightingale, who used a form of pie chart to communicate to the powers that be the significance of what she had learned in the Crimea. The teacher asked her pupils to construct pie charts to communicate the need for clean water using statistics from the Water Aid website. A science teacher wanted to include in his lessons the experience of wonder at the order, beauty and complexity of creation, so when analysing flower structure he had fresh flowers on the desks and at the end of the session showed stunning photographic images of flowers.

What If Learning is clearly a significant contribution to a kingdom-focused approach in teaching. But in an earlier booklet, Cooling laments the failure of many Christian teachers to perceive the kingdom dimension in their daily work:

> Far too many of them assume Christian ministry and mission are what I call Christian empire building, which they know raises many issues in educational contexts. Therefore, they shy away from thinking of their professional work as kingdom work. We need to build their theological competence before they will be confident to be distinctively Christian in their professional role.[49]

In an Anglican team ministry in South London where I served as a team vicar, a substantial number of the church members worked in various capacities in the worlds of business and commerce in the City of London. When the team rector had been appointed some years before, he had been asked if he would create time to help the members of the business community in the church think through some of the issues they faced in their working lives. In reply he had said that he did not think he would be able to help them, as he himself knew very little about the business world. His idea of teaching was that his role was to be the expert who passed on to the members of the congregation his knowledge and understanding of the Christian tradition – and he was in fact very good at this! Had he been aware of the tool of reflection, and willing to adopt the role of facilitator and 'people's theologian', he might well have answered differently.

When Jesus commissioned his disciples for their worldwide mission, he claimed all authority in heaven and on earth (Matthew 28.18). There is no area of human experience over which the kingdom of God does not exercise a claim to authority. It is therefore a legitimate aim of Christian learning to enable disciples to apply the perspectives, practices and qualities of character learned through participation in the Christian community to all the other communities of which they are a part. In fact not to do so is a denial of Jesus' claim to universal authority and thus a denial of the gospel. No wonder a church ill-equipped to achieve this has become progressively more marginal to society!

Conclusion
'It is surely a fact of inexhaustible significance', wrote Lesslie Newbigin, 'that what our Lord left behind him was not a book, nor a creed, nor a system of thought, nor a rule of life, but a visible community.' And he goes on:

> It was not that a community developed around an idea, so that the idea was primary and the community secondary. It was that a community called together by the deliberate choice of the Lord himself, and recreated in him, gradually sought – and is seeking – to make explicit who he is and what he has done. The actual community is primary: the understanding of what it is comes second.[50]

Newbigin thus neatly sums up the theological basis for the approach to discipleship I have been developing in this chapter: 'The actual community is primary.' That community seeks to embody its understanding of God and his call in its shared life. It continually seeks to test the fidelity of its shared life by reference to the Scriptures and the church's developing tradition under the guidance of the Holy Spirit. Theology emerges in the process, as the community seeks to make explicit who Jesus is and all that he has done. It is not simply by learning that theology but by sharing the life of the community and its ongoing reflection on it that individual men and women grow as disciples of Christ.

The goal of discipleship is conformity to Christ. It is not simply theology or Christian world view that is embodied in the community's life, but its love for and commitment to Christ. The church is a community of value, consciously existing for a purpose: to glorify Jesus and to make him known in its life and through its witness. The primary focuses of discipleship learning are attitudes and dispositions. The goal is the transformation of character, so that Christ is displayed in renewed and transformed relationships. The virtues learned through participation and reflection in Christian community are to affect every area of a Christian's life. In every area of life, he is called to discern the signs and work for the coming of God's kingdom. The purpose of his daily work is to become co-operation with God's Holy Spirit in bringing about the transformation of creation.[51] But this leads us into the theme of ministry, and it is to learning for ministry that we now turn.

Notes

1 C. S. Lewis, *Mere Christianity*, London: Collins, 1952, p. 171.
2 Walter Brueggemann, *The Word Militant: Preaching a Decentering Word*, Minneapolis, MN: Fortress Press, 2007, p. 56.
3 Craig Dykstra and Dorothy C. Bass, 'A Theological Understanding of Christian Practices', in Miroslav Volf and Dorothy C. Bass (eds), *Practicing Theology*, Grand Rapids, MI: Eerdmans, 2002, pp. 18–19. We will be exploring Christian practices in greater depth in the fourth section of this chapter.
4 Laurie Green, *Let's Do Theology*, 2nd edn, London: Continuum, 2009, pp. 17–18; see also Judith Thompson, *The SCM Studyguide to Theological Reflection*, London: SCM Press, 2008, pp. 51f.
5 Anton Baumohl, *Making Adult Disciples*, London: Scripture Union, 1984, p. 26.
6 Steven Croft, *Growing New Christians*, London: Marshall Pickering, 1993, pp. 100–15; *Emmaus: The Way of Faith, Stage Two: Nurture*, 2nd edn, London: Church House Publishing, 1996, 2003.
7 www.pilgrimcourse.org/the-course; the Church of England's 2015 General Synod paper 'Developing Discipleship' specifically recommends the Pilgrim course as material developed by the House of Bishops to encourage discipleship. General Synod Miscellaneous Paper 1977, 'Developing Discipleship', § 18.
8 Thomas Hawkins, *The Learning Congregation*, Louisville, KY: Westminster John Knox Press, 1997, p. 26.
9 'Your Shape for God's Service', originally developed by Amiel Osmaston for the Diocese of Carlisle and now available online from several places, including Carlisle Diocese, CPAS and the Arthur Rank Centre.
10 I have not included a great deal in this chapter about the specific role of preaching in Christian learning. For a much fuller treatment of the sermon as a learning event and the role of preaching generally, see my earlier book, *Transforming Preaching*, London: SPCK, 2013.
11 Liz Varley, *Catching Fire*, Swindon: Bible Society, 1993, p. 15.
12 Roger Walton, *Disciples Together*, London: SCM Press, 2014, pp. 108–22.
13 In fact neither the Emmaus nor the Pilgrim courses use aims in this way. Instead the course material for both includes short sections summarizing the content. There is a perfectly good argument to say that framing objectives in the way I am recommending *for the participants* may in fact be too threatening in the environment

of adult Christian learning, although young people are increasingly accustomed to this as a result of their schooling. What I would say, however, is that the course leaders should be able to express *to themselves* what the objectives are in terms of learning rather than simply content.

14 These points are taken from Alan Rogers and Naomi Horrocks, *Teaching Adults*, 4th edn, Maidenhead: Open University Press, 2010, pp. 162–3; with additions to each of the first three bullet points.

15 Some good places to begin are Yvonne Craig, *Learning for Life*, London: Mowbray, 1994, especially ch. 4 on the varieties of methods suitable for people with different learning styles; Margaret Cooling, *Creating a Learning Church*, Oxford: Bible Reading Fellowship, 2005; Nigel Pimlott, *Participative Processes*, Cambridge: Grove Books, 2009; Sally and Paul Nash, *Tools for Reflective Ministry*, London: SPCK, 2009.

16 The classic place to go for this is *The Learning Styles Questionnaire*, by Peter Honey and Alan Mumford, available at www.talentlens.co.uk/develop/peter-honey-learning-style-series. There are hundreds of sites online providing brief explanations.

17 A good place to begin is the chapter entitled 'Facilitation Skills' in Sally Nash, Jo Pimlott and Paul Nash, *Skills for Collaborative Ministry*, London: SPCK, 2008, followed by *Facilitation Skills in Ministry* by Jo Whitehead, Sally Nash and Simon Sutcliffe, London: SPCK, 2013. The 'bible' for this area is Jenny Roger, *Facilitating Groups*, Maidenhead, Open University Press, 2010. And see Stephen Brookfield, *Understanding and Facilitating Adult Learning*, Milton Keynes, Open University Press, 1986; and from a Christian point of view, Parker Palmer, *The Courage to Teach*, New York: Wiley, 1997.

18 See Richard Giles, *Re-pitching the Tent: The Definitive Guide to Reordering Your Church*, 3rd edn, Norwich: Canterbury Press, 2004, for more on the influence of church architecture on worship and Christian life.

19 Etienne Wenger, *Communities of Practice*, Cambridge: Cambridge University Press, 1998, p. 58. I will examine the significance of Wenger's approach to 'communities of practice' in the next section.

20 Alison Gilchrist, *Creating a Culture of Welcome in the Local Church*, Cambridge: Grove Books, 2004. For a complete training course on providing a welcome in the local church, see Bob Jackson and George Fisher, *Everybody Welcome*, London: Church House Publishing, 2009.

21 Robert Warren, *The Healthy Churches Handbook*, London: Church House Publishing, 2004.

22 This leaflet is now available from ReSource at www.resource-arm.net.

23 Hawkins, *Learning Congregation*, pp. 3–38.

24 Hawkins, *Learning Congregation*, p. 11.

25 James Lawrence, *Growing Leaders*, Abingdon: Bible Reading Fellowship, 2004, p. 212.

26 Varley, *Catching Fire*, pp. 55–8.

27 More information about Umoja is available from Mosaic Creative at www.mosaiccreative.co.uk.

28 An overview of the conversation process is to be found at www.aftersunday.org.uk/reflectiveliving/overview.

29 Peter Senge, *The Fifth Discipline: The Art and Practice of the Learning Organisation*, 2nd edn, New York: Random House, 2006, pp. 232–40.

30 Hawkins, *Learning Congregation*, p. 11.
31 Senge, *Fifth Discipline*, pp. 171–4, 228–9.
32 Alan Roxburgh and Fred Romanuk, *The Missional Leader*, San Francisco: Jossey-Bass, 2006, pp. 5, 9, 42.
33 Stephen Pickard, *Theological Foundations for Collaborative Ministry*, Farnham: Ashgate, 2009, p. 1.
34 Green, *Let's Do Theology*, pp. 134–5.
35 Green, *Let's Do Theology*, p. 135.
36 Dykstra and Bass, 'Theological Understanding of Christian Practices', pp. 13–32; quotation from p. 18.
37 For an exploration of Christian hospitality, see Christine Pohl, *Making Room: Recovering Hospitality as a Christian Tradition*, Grand Rapids, MI: Eerdmans, 1999; also Henri Nouwen, *Reaching Out*, London: Collins, 1976.
38 For an outline of a Christian approach to the Sabbath, see Marva Dawn, *Keeping the Sabbath Wholly*, Grand Rapids, MI: Eerdmans, 1989.
39 See Ann Morisy, *Journeying Out*, London: Continuum, 2004, pp. 139–82; and for a brief summary her article 'Mapping the Mixed Economy', in Steven Croft (ed.), *The Future of the Parish System*, London: Church House Publishing, 2006, pp. 125–37.
40 Alasdair MacIntyre, *After Virtue*, 2nd edn, London: Duckworth, 1985, pp. 187f.
41 See Grace Davie, *Religion in Britain Since 1945: Believing Without Belonging*, Oxford: Blackwell, 1994; and her short article 'From Obligation to Consumption: Understanding the Patterns of Religion in Northern Europe', in Croft (ed.) *Future of the Parish System*, pp. 33–45.
42 Michael Polanyi, *Personal Knowledge*, London: Routledge & Kegan Paul, 1958, pp. 49–65, 132–202.
43 Mike Higton, 'Theological Education Between the University and the Church: Durham University and the Common Awards in Theology, Ministry and Mission', *Journal of Adult Theological Education* 10.1, 2013, p. 31.
44 Wenger, *Communities of Practice*, p. 83.
45 Wenger, *Communities of Practice*, p. 134.
46 Wenger, *Communities of Practice*, p. 4.
47 Wenger, *Communities of Practice*, p. 141.
48 Trevor Cooling, *Distinctively Christian Learning?*, Cambridge: Grove, 2013. See further www.whatiflearning.co.uk; and for more detail and reflection, David I. Smith and James K. A. Smith, *Teaching and Christian Practices: Reshaping Faith and Learning*, Grand Rapids, MI: Eerdmans, 2011.
49 Trevor Cooling, *Called to Teach: Teaching as a Missional Vocation*, Cambridge: Grove, 2010, p. 10.
50 Lesslie Newbigin, *The Household of God*, London: SCM Press, 1953, p. 32.
51 See Miroslav Volf, *Work in the Spirit: Toward a Theology of Work*, Eugene, OR: Wipf & Stock, 2001.

4

Learning for Ministry Together

Learning Ministry as a Practice

Ministry is a practice, or rather a family of related practices, and learning for ministry is initiation into those practices. Some of the practices involved are required for several different forms of ministry, while others are more specialized. The practice of pastoral care, which lies at the heart of the specialist ministry of pastoral care and counselling, is also an important element in ordained parish ministry, chaplaincy, work with families, children and young people, and for those working with the elderly. Small-group leadership is likewise an important element in all these forms of ministry and several more. Coaching, often undervalued as an element of ministry, is another practice that plays an important part in a variety of ministry contexts. The care of ancient buildings is very much a specialist field, though many of those involved in the leadership of congregations need an acquaintance with it.

A practice is a corporate activity, and the knowledge required to become a participant, achieve competence and then excellence is held in common. Sometimes it is possible to point to particular repositories of this knowledge. In relation to supervision, for example, the book *Supervision in the Helping Professions* by Peter Hawkins and Robin Shohet has been widely acknowledged since its publication as the most important and comprehensive source.[1] The lack of a study of supervision specifically for ministry contexts was partly addressed by Frances Ward's *Lifelong Learning* and then by Jane Leach and Michael Paterson in *Pastoral Supervision: A Handbook*.[2] As we shall see, the internet plays an increasingly important role in the sharing of such knowledge. What is significant about books like these, and many others, such as a large number in the field of leadership, is that they are not simply books of theory but represent a distillation of the writers' practical wisdom in these fields; and they are written in such a way as to pass on that practical wisdom. We shall have more to say about the nature of practical wisdom later in this section, but at this stage it is important to note that it resides primarily in people. Books and websites may be a secondary and derivative source, but practical wisdom is a personal quality. People learn primarily from other people, and it is from people that wisdom is learned.

Mention of practical wisdom draws attention to the fact that the shared knowledge of a practice is multi-dimensional: it embraces far more than facts, theories and principles. It also involves skills, dispositions and qualities of character. The 'skill' of attentive listening, for example, involves technical know-how such as adopting an open posture and techniques of reflecting back what has been said. But genuinely attentive listening requires that these techniques are firmly embedded in a set of attitudes and dispositions: the love required to create a hospitable space and to listen without judgement; the humility rightly to value a person's confidence and to hold back on proffering 'good advice' until the right time.

Practices also develop: agreed standards of excellence are a vitally important component of shared knowledge and are continually under review within the practising community. The nature and purpose of Christian pastoral care, for example, has been almost continuously under discussion for the past 40 or 50 years. One of the key issues has been the relative importance of individual counselling over building supportive community; another the proper influence of the variety of 'secular' approaches. The nature and importance of teamwork and collaborative practice in congregational leadership is another live issue.

Learning practices

In an article of 1985 the brothers Hubert and Stuart Dreyfus examined the stages by which a person advances in the learning of a practice, from beginner, through proficiency, to expertise, and which I will illustrate from the games of cricket and chess, both of which Alasdair MacIntyre defines as practices.[3]

- At the very start of the process, the 'novice' is taught a limited number of context-free variables and simple rules. The cricket player is taught to 'watch the ball on to the bat' and learns the techniques of the different strokes; the chess player the numerical value of the chess pieces and the rules governing their moves.
- The advanced beginner builds on these simple rules the ability to recognize situational variables, such as the way to play against a variety of bowlers or, for the chess player, recognizing when one's position has become overextended.
- Up to this stage the developing player is learning by following rules and recognizing their application in an increasing variety of situations. 'Competence' arrives only when these rules are integrated and subsumed in a plan or goal, such as the need to play for the tea interval or an opportunity to attack the opponent's king. In each case rules and variables have become part of a 'game situation' with features that stand out as more or less important. The adoption of these plans organize the different aspects of the game or skill into a model of whole situations, in which some features stand out as more significant than others, and contribute to the decisions about which moves to make and which strokes to attempt.
- Further progress is made by gaining experience in a variety of game situations, and learning to recognize the similarities and differences between them. At the same time the practitioner is building up a repertoire of possible plans and responses. At the stage of 'proficiency' he is able to devise plans for an increasing number of situations with an increasingly developed ability to judge the likelihood of success.
- Until at the stage of 'expertise' the best response in each game situation becomes as much a part of his store of experience as the ability to recognize those situations. 'The expert performer . . . understands, acts, and learns from results without any conscious awareness of the process. What transparently *must* be done *is* done.'[4]

By this stage it is estimated that the chess master can distinguish anything up to 50,000 types of situations without conscious reflection. His store of knowledge has advanced well beyond the learning of rules and generalization. The title of the Dreyfus article, 'From Socrates to Expert Systems', is of considerable significance. The development of modern computer software shares with the ancient philosopher the assumption that it must be possible to reduce the knowledge of an expert to clearly defined decontextualized generalizations and universal procedural rules. Not so, claim the Dreyfus brothers: that is not the kind of thing knowledge is. Our knowledge is stored as remembered multi-faceted situations connected in complex ways by relationships of similarity and dissimilarity.

Learning how to practise ministry
Let us now look at two examples of the way the practices of ministry are learned, both from spheres of ministry involving lay and ordained people: first, the practice of taking a funeral; second, of planting and leading a fresh expression of church.

Most people licensed to take funerals in the Church of England, whether they are lay or ordained ministers, will have received some form of initial training. The training required of ordinands at Ripon College Cuddesdon includes a week-long course on funeral ministry. The week covers three areas of basic instruction: the process of bereavement; the Christian understanding of death, resurrection and future hope; the requirements of the service itself and the liturgical resources available from the Church of England. In another context we also offer training in the basic listening skills required at a funeral visit; and the course includes a detailed step-by-step description of all that is involved in a funeral, from initial contact to the service itself and what comes afterwards.

In relation to funeral ministry, most of the ordinands are novices. Nor will they have the opportunity to practise until they leave college and are ordained. Our task is to equip them with some basic rules and generalizations to give them confidence as they take their first steps. But taking a funeral is far more complex than applying a set of theoretical generalizations to a specific situation. From her first funeral visit, each of these students, now ordained, will be doing several things:

- She will be interpreting the situation and helping the family members to interpret their bereavement: talking perhaps about

the feelings they are experiencing, encouraging them to recall their memories of their loved one and helping them to prepare for the funeral itself.
- As she builds a relationship with the family members, by listening with empathy to their experience and asking sensitive questions, a complex, if unstated, negotiation of role is taking place. Some will view her as an authority figure, others as a hired functionary, whereas she probably sees herself as a minister of the gospel offering pastoral care.
- At the same time, she will be defining and redefining the immediate task – to offer comfort and reassurance, provide information, prepare for the funeral service, encourage faith and hope – in light of her 'reading' of the situation.
- To achieve these things she will be drawing on a repertoire of actions and responses embedded in habitual practice, sometimes using the same words as on previous visits to ask questions, sometimes varying the words to meet the demands of the situation.
- She will be doing this from the standpoint of a consistent set of values: openness to and love for the family and the decision to serve them; commitment to the Christian faith and the hope of resurrection in Christ.
- Her knowledge of Christian faith, of the process of bereavement, of the possibilities for the funeral service, of the way the needs of the family for pastoral care might be met are not, therefore, 'theories' she is applying in a particular situation. They are areas of expertise she is 'indwelling' and through which she skilfully responds to the situation.

As she gains in experience our ordinand, now an ordained minister, will move through certain stages of competence. At first she will be remembering all she has learned in college, consciously relying on the outline for funeral ministry she was given there. However, she will quickly come to recognize certain patterns – the difficulty people have expressing their feelings; their reluctance to share unhappy memories; the possibility of anger, expressed or unexpressed; anxiety about the content of the service – and will develop a repertoire of ways of responding. With further experience her deployment of this repertoire becomes unconscious and intuitive: she is picking up familiar patterns and responding to them without the need of conscious thought. She is learning to recognize when the response she encounters with a family is familiar and predictable and when it is not, and when there are particular factors in the situation that need further exploration. The patterns of events surrounding ministry at funerals and the variations on these stored in her memory gradually grow and she becomes adept at recognizing and responding to them in flexible ways. Step by step she becomes an expert practitioner, capable of instructing others.

The means of this learning is reflection. Ideally this will take place with a more experienced practitioner – in the case of Anglican clergy, their training incumbent – but it may take place with a peer group or simply on her own. Ideally it will take place consciously: she will set aside time to think through the events of a particular funeral, asking herself what was familiar about it and what was strange; what were the feelings she encountered and what were the feelings stirred up in her; what could have been done better; where God was present in her encounter with the family, her preparation, the service and follow-up; and so on. But even when this process of reflection does not take place consciously, perhaps because she thinks herself too busy to set aside the time required, it will still take place. She will still act differently in response to previous experience: perhaps avoiding saying certain things that caused misunderstanding on a previous occasion, but without thinking through why that misunderstanding occurred; perhaps developing the habit of using a certain prayer because it seemed to go well on a particular occasion. We learn a practice through reflection on experience, ideally in company with fellow practitioners, and the more thoughtful and conscious that reflection, the more effectively we are likely to learn.

My second example is the relatively recent creation of a community of practice for those involved in planting and leading fresh expressions of church. In the early days, several pioneer ministers, such as those interviewed in 2006 for *Expressions: The DVD*,[4] would describe their work with phrases like: 'We're making it up as we go along.' Already, however, stories and testimonies from leaders of fresh expressions were being made available, some through the DVD and others in books, such as those collected by Chris Stoddard and Nick Cuthbert in *Church on the Edge*.[6] And as early as 1999, George Lings of the Church Army's Research Unit had begun his quarterly series of booklets under the title of 'Encounters on the Edge', each booklet telling the story of a new approach to church planting and reflecting on the lessons to be drawn from it.[7]

And 2006 also saw the publication of an article by Michael Moynagh entitled 'Good Practice is Not What it Used to Be: Accumulating Wisdom in Fresh Expressions of Church', in which he drew on his experience of new forms of business organization to explain the processes necessary to gather and share the dispersed wisdom gradually building up as a result of experience of developing new forms of church throughout the country and abroad. Under the headings 'connecting', 'collecting' and 'reflecting', Moynagh highlighted the importance of sharing stories and drawing out the important principles, theological and otherwise, being learned within the practitioner community – principles such as pioneers' personal formation; 'cultural exegesis' of the location or network where the fresh expression is to be planted; 'building-in reproduction', or thinking from the start about how the newly created church will reproduce itself.[8]

All this was brought together in the Fresh Expressions website, a place where stories could be shared and through which experienced practitioners with a knowledge of Christian theology could reflect and draw out the lessons for the community as a whole. This very quickly led to an agreed definition of a 'fresh expression', with the purpose of distinguishing genuinely new forms of church rooted in a particular context from rebranded youth groups or lunch clubs. And over time the 'Guide' section of the site gradually grew to provide a source of accumulated wisdom, rooting fresh expressions of church in church history and theology and also providing practical advice to those involved.[9] One of the features of the Guide is to communicate the theological reflections provided by those with expertise in formal academic theology in a way accessible to those without formal training. For example, the traditional understanding of the church as 'one, holy, catholic and apostolic' is 'translated' for the benefit of practitioners as consisting in four relationships: In, Up, Of and Out.

Through the website, as well as a series of learning events throughout the country, the constituency of pioneer ministers, people who by nature tend to be independent and impatient of control, especially by the traditional church, were drawn together into a community of practice within which accumulated wisdom could be shared. By 2012, Moynagh was able to write that there was no longer the need for pioneer ministers to 'make it up as they go along'. Principles of good practice were becoming firmly established and increasingly well known. A framework was being developed within which new stories could be interpreted. Most importantly, because of the way the network had been framed as a community of practice, 'principles of good practice' were being worked out in a collaborative way. Rather than governing the practice, they emerged as a result of mutual learning.[10]

There is still room for people to try genuinely new things, but when they do they have the accumulated wisdom of the community behind them to guide them. Significantly, around 40 per cent of the leaders of fresh expressions are what have been called 'lay lay' people: people with no formal training for ministry.[11] They have learned through participation in the community of practice.

Practical wisdom

What I have emphasized through these examples is that the outcome of learning a practice is 'practical wisdom': the accumulation of the knowledge, skills and dispositions required to become a competent practitioner in a form that makes the lessons of experience flexibly available in the infinite variety of situations that occur in the course of the practice. We have already seen that the 'mind of Christ' Paul desires for his churches consists of a practical wisdom. We have also seen that the way we hold our knowledge, as flexible patterns based on remembered and interpreted situations, serves as the basis for practical wisdom. Moreover, I am claiming that the way we learn practical wisdom is through theological reflection in its many and various forms. It is now time to enquire more closely into exactly what is meant by 'practical wisdom': what is its essence and how is it learned? Let us first remind ourselves of some of the key features of theological reflection:

- It involves focused attention on the specifics of a given situation: the ability to describe an incident or situation in detail, drawing out the features that appear to be most significant but without overlooking the small details that give it its unique character; recognizing the features it shares with other similar situations but also how it differs from these. It requires the ability to comprehend and describe life in all its complexity and particularity.
- It draws on a variety of non-theological resources: principles of effective leadership; the characteristics of children or of older people; the process of bereavement; tools for 'exegeting' or reading local culture; and so on. It also requires the ability to place these in a dialogue with theology: for example, to recognize those approaches to leadership that echo a Christian understanding of the purpose of human life and those that fail to do so; to correlate the understanding of identity in child development with theological approaches to personal identity; to recognize in bereavement the importance of relationships for human life generally; and so on.
- It draws on the resources of Christian tradition: it requires the ability to interpret Scripture intelligently; knowledge of the doctrines of the Christian faith; experience as a member of the Christian community.
- It is integrative: it involves considering situations from a variety of different points of view; it makes connections between the various divisions of theology – interpretation of the Bible, church history, systematic theology and so on, which in a formal academic context are usually studied separately; it also makes links between theology and other disciplines.
- It looks for patterns of continuity and discontinuity: it aims to provide theologically grounded interpretations of situations or, alternatively, to take note of where situations challenge conventional theological interpretations.
- It is geared to application: it asks how the insights gained from the process of reflection may be taken forward in concrete ways.

- It is reflexive or self-involving: not only does theological reflection challenge the practitioner to evaluate his existing interpretation of the situation, it asks him to become aware of his feelings, values, motives, assumptions and dispositions. It points to future learning needs, such as unanswered questions and inadequate responses.

Through disciplined reflection on their gradually increasing store of experienced situations, our funeral minister or pioneer missioner is acquiring and developing the ability to discern the salient features of a given situation and respond in a flexible way on the basis of plans and goals that express a relatively stable set of dispositions. And it is precisely the ability to hold together the particular and the general, to see both the big picture and the unique features of a situation, that lies at the heart of practical wisdom. As Joseph Dunne puts it:

> To be practically wise or a person of good judgement is to be able to recognise situations, cases or problems as perhaps standard or typical – that is to say, of a type that has been met previously and for which there is already an established and well-rehearsed rule, recipe or formula – or as deviating from the standard and conventional, and in either case, to be capable of dealing with them adequately and appropriately.[12]

This capacity to discern the nature of a particular situation, the way it corresponds to other similar situations and the ways it is unique, and to interpret that situation by placing it in an appropriate framework of understanding, is a description of the Aristotelian virtue of *phronesis*, the intellectual virtue that enables us to apply the virtues of character to specific situations. We may be courageous, generous or compassionate, but we need to be able to discern in any given situation just what courage, generosity or compassion requires of us. *Phronesis* is, therefore, the capacity of 'right seeing' or 'virtuous perception'.

The problem at the heart of practical wisdom is its dialectical character. In Aristotle, *phronesis* is both an expression of good character and also an educator of character. In order to exercise *phronesis* one must desire the good, both for oneself and for others. But in order to achieve the good, one must have practical wisdom. Or as Aristotle puts it: 'We cannot really be good without practical wisdom, or practically wise without virtue of character.'[13]

As we saw in Chapter 2, this dialectic between the particular and the general, the specifics of a situation and the experience we bring to bear in understanding it, is a characteristic of *all* perception. At the heart of cognition is the continuous interaction between the world of shared experience and the world 'in our heads', the mental models based on our previous experience. Without the deployment of these mental models we have no framework for interpretation. But we are intuitively aware that these mental models may need to change if we are to understand situations aright. Indeed, we may find ourselves needing to substitute completely different frameworks of interpretation – see the situation in a whole new light – if we are rightly to understand it.

Practical wisdom names our capacity to do this both rightly and virtuously: the extent to which we are genuinely open to each new situation; the ability to grasp its significant features; the flexibility we bring to judgements about it; our ability to foresee the consequences of a variety of possible responses. And each of these facets of our perception will be influenced by the virtues that make up our character. A settled disposition to act compassionately, courageously or generously will influence the way we perceive a situation, the features of it we take to be significant, the possible responses we envisage.

This capacity for practical reasoning, combining thinking, feeling and acting, proceeding from the virtues and educating the virtues, is the capacity that both enables us to engage in theological reflection and is educated by theological reflection. Theological reflection, requiring us to pay attention to the specific features of situations, to use our theological understanding as a lens through which to interpret them, to consider possible practical responses and to choose the best, guided by our perception of the good, acts continually not only to increase our intellectual grasp of such situations but to create in us greater flexibility in both interpreting and responding to situations and to build the capacity for 'virtuous perception' and for discerning good and right action. It is a tool through which virtuous and godly habit of life is continually being shaped and reinforced.

The Challenges Ahead

The ideas of ministry as a practice, the key role of practical wisdom in the way ministry is exercised, and the place of theological reflection in the learning of practical wisdom, especially when these ideas are taken together, have enormous implications for the way people are most effectively trained for ministry. In the final section of this book I want to look specifically at the training for ministry that needs to take place in the context of the local church. Before I do that, however, it is necessary to look critically at the assumptions that have dominated the way people have been trained at national level for licensed ministry, whether lay or ordained, since these have exercised enormous influence over every aspect of the church's life. I asked in Chapter 1 why the church had been allowed to become so dysfunctional that many of its members failed to see the need for transformation and service; that is, for discipleship and ministry. In this section I will attempt to answer that question, drawing on all I have tried to explain about the nature of learning and of knowledge.

'New insights', writes Peter Senge, 'fail to get put into practice because they conflict with deeply held internal images of how the world works, images that limit us to familiar ways of thinking and acting.'[14] Over the past generation or so, the internal images that have governed the way the church has traditionally operated have been changing. We have made significant progress in our understanding of God's mission and towards the aspiration to become a missional church. The Church of England has embraced a collaborative understanding of ministry, in which all are encouraged and equipped to play their part in mission. Its criteria for the selection and formation of its ordained ministers recognize the central place of reflective practice and express the aspiration that all clergy are equipped to be teachers of others.[15] Despite these encouraging changes, however, there still exist some powerful 'internal images' or 'assumptive frameworks'[16] that hold us back – about the nature of leadership, the nature of learning and knowledge and about the nature of theology. These assumptive frameworks are embedded in the way most Churches approach ministerial training, and the result is that, despite the encouraging recent developments, people training for ordination are not being effectively equipped for the challenges of a fast-changing world. My aim is to examine these corporately held frameworks of understanding and suggest how they need to change.

The nature of leadership
Traditionally, the task of leadership has been seen as planning, directing, controlling and evaluating an organization's activities. Leaders set the direction for the organization, take decisions about the tasks to be accomplished and those who will be responsible for them, monitor their progress and provide feedback. In times of crisis and difficulty they are looked to for solutions. In order to accomplish these tasks, leaders are expected to have more knowledge and greater skill than their subordinates. In most organizations it is expected that they will have been carefully selected and have had specific training for their role.[17]

This model of 'heroic leadership', in which leaders occupy the top level of a hierarchical pyramid, is dysfunctional in several ways. In the first place, decision-making is in the hands of a small number of people. To make good decisions, the leaders at the top of the organization need access to the best information. But information travels slowly: frequently the leaders are out of touch with what is happening. It is the subordinates, the ordinary members of the organization, who see most clearly where things are going wrong and are in the best place to offer solutions. In a hierarchy, the welfare of the organization depends on the knowledge and skills of the relatively small number of leaders. The much larger reservoir of experience and expertise in the lives of the membership as a whole is relegated to a less important, sometimes insignificant role.

Second, in a hierarchical organization the leaders take sole responsibility for the organization's performance. Others are free to concentrate on their own narrowly defined tasks. They are not encouraged to think about the well-being of the organization as a whole and are in constant danger of losing sight of the vision that animates the life of the organization in favour of their own particular areas of interest. The possibility of conflict between personalities and departments is ever-present.

Third, because heroic leaders take all the responsibility, make all the key decisions and are expected to have greater knowledge and skill than anyone else, they are continuously kept busy with routine work. Minor problems, such as conflict over relatively trivial matters, arrive on their desks and eat up the time that should be devoted to building a shared vision and helping people to grasp it.

In the heroic leadership model the leaders overperform while the ordinary members are allowed to become passive, relieved of the responsibility for the organization's direction and well-being. In the short term, heroic leadership has its satisfactions: a problem solved, a person helped, the feeling of being important and valuable. But heroic leadership can also be a way leaders fulfil their own needs, such as the need to be needed, to be significant, to be in control, to be a 'messiah figure' on whom others depend.

When the organization is a church, and the leaders are surrounded by the mystique either of priesthood or of a particular ideology of 'leadership', the situation can become even more entrenched. Both leaders and members can point to accepted theological justifications of why things should be so. Both can take refuge in the deference due to a person of special status. The answer is not to do away with priests or leaders but to redefine their role in the church as representatives, enablers and 'animators' of the ministry of the whole church. In the case of the Church of England, this is the understanding of priesthood already set out in the report 'Education for the Church's Ministry' in 1987. This sees the central task of the ordained as, 'bringing the [ministry of the whole church] to be in the way God's mission in the world requires', a task that can only be achieved when the whole church, in its turn, 'recognises, trusts and sustains the ordained minister' in her own ministry of enabling and equipping.[18]

We saw above in Chapter 2 how shared reflection is capable of breaking down the divide between 'expert' leader and non-expert led, empowering all those who take part and creating a sense of genuine partnership and shared ownership. Shared reflection acknowledges the wisdom and expertise that exist in the whole community, draws on them and encourages shared responsibility. As Thomas Hawkins expresses it:

> In the future, the ability to 'grow' people becomes the key characteristic of effective and faithful leaders . . . When congregations become learning organizations, church leaders reframe their basic tasks and responsibilities. Pastors cease to perform ministry on the congregation's behalf. They instead foster learning environments where the whole people God can shape and reshape meaning within a community of shared practice, continually clarifying those meanings in light of a deeper understanding of the revelation made known in Jesus Christ.[19]

The first 'internal image' that requires challenge, therefore, is the model of heroic leadership still embraced by a sizeable proportion of the church's leaders.[20] In its place is required a model of adaptive leadership, which can often mean challenging expectations. According to Ron Heifetz:

> Rather than fulfilling the expectation for answers, [the leader] provides questions; rather than protecting people from outside threat, one lets people feel the threat in order to stimulate adaptation; instead of orientating people to their current roles, one disorientates people so that new role relationships develop; rather than quelling conflict, one generates it; instead of maintaining norms, one challenges them.[21]

These characteristics of an adaptive leader, Thomas Hawkins points out, were characteristics of Jesus' ministry, and in particular his teaching methods. He answered challenges with questions, selected people for unfamiliar roles, challenged social norms, created unexpected roles and relationships and deliberately stretched his disciples by pulling them out of their 'comfort zones'.[22] Yet at the same time he also provided that other necessary element in adaptive leadership: a 'holding environment'. He combined challenge with support, creating 'safe spaces' of acceptance for the journeys of self-discovery on which he wished his disciples to embark. To 'reimagine' ministry includes reimagining the church as an adaptive organization in which leadership is offered by a wide variety of the members rather than a few specially 'set apart'. It means reimagining the role of the ordained as servants and enablers of God's mission, part of whose role is to represent this to the whole church, to call and equip each member of the church to play its proper part.

The nature of knowledge

A second area in which we need to examine our 'internal image' concerns the nature of learning, and in particular the nature of knowledge itself. I have already noted several times in the course of this book that we do not hold our knowledge in the form of a general decontextualized theory. In Chapter 2, I noted the contrasting approaches to helping relationships of 'technical rationality' and reflective practice and suggested that the difference between them boils down to a different understanding of what constitutes valid knowledge. In this section I want to address this point directly.

The differences between the two reflect a profound shift at the heart of contemporary Western culture. In the previous section I drew on an article by the brothers Hubert and Stuart Dreyfus setting out the stages by which people learn to participate in a practice. The full title of the article is 'From Socrates to Expert Systems: The Limits of Calculative Rationality'. The modern designers of computer programmes share with the ancient philosopher the assumption that all valid knowledge is reducible to rules and generalizations. The Dreyfus brothers describe the way Socrates 'stalked around Athens looking for experts in order to draw out and test their rules'. In the case of Euthyphro, a prophet and expert on religious piety, he challenges him to articulate the rules by which he recognizes pious behaviour. Euthyphro can supply plenty of examples but no rules. His judgement has been trained by experience to recognize the pattern of pious behaviour but he cannot explain the rules he uses to make such judgements. The expert is not using generalized theory to arrive at his judgements. He is drawing on the patterns created by his experience of many concrete examples, perhaps running into the hundreds. Nevertheless, Plato insists that he must be using rules and generalizations, even though he himself fails to recognize this, and it is the philosopher's task to draw these out and make them explicit.[23]

The assumption of the modern age, which was given definitive form for modern Western culture by the European Enlightenment, was that valid knowledge takes the form of a general theory located in our minds, which corresponds to the way the world is. Being essentially theoretical, this knowledge is reducible to rules and generalizations and capable of formulation by means of abstract concepts. In other words, our knowledge is like a library or computer memory, neatly arranged according to rational criteria, and sits passively waiting for us to call for it when needed. The success of science in explaining the world by means of theoretical generalizations appears to justify this view of what knowledge essentially is.

Our exploration of how learning takes place, however, suggests that the Enlightenment view of knowledge is in fact a simplification. Our knowledge does not consist of a grand general theory but of situationally based and actively organized mental models, comprising a set of flexible expectations for any given situation. These expectations take the form of patterns, related to one another in complex, multi-faceted ways. The expert practitioner is drawing on these patterns to achieve particular goals and purposes, in a pattern of action that unites understanding with values and feelings. We thus arrive at Etienne Wenger's formulation: knowledge is 'competence in valued enterprises'.[24] Far from illustrating the Enlightenment model of knowledge, science and technology are examples of 'valued enterprises' in which, as writers like Michael Polanyi and Thomas Kuhn have pointed out, expertise consists of far more than the knowledge of theories, but includes shared tacit know-how, values and commitments.[25]

In the Enlightenment version of the 'grand theory' approach to knowledge, the validity of our knowledge is guaranteed by 'critical reason'. Moreover, the foundation of critical reason is the potential of the human mind. Valid knowledge arises from a combination of empirical observation and rational deduction, both of which are purely human possibilities. The period of the

Enlightenment thus witnessed the final and decisive dethroning of theology as the unifying discipline of higher study. Christian revelation was no longer to be understood as the key to those basic principles of human life. Rather these are to be discovered by the principles of rational thought, free from the dictates of religious or any other authority. Furthermore, as the guarantor of valid knowledge, critical reason was held to be 'value-free'. In fact the solid core of rationally guaranteed knowledge was carefully distinguished from the less reliable and potentially misleading penumbra of values, feelings and commitments. In this conception of knowledge there is no room for a faculty such as practical wisdom, which brings together knowledge, feeling, disposition and action. And finally, the effect of this erroneous model has been to create an artificial division between theory and practice. 'Real' knowledge, it is held, consists of theory, and practice is merely the application of theory.

All that we have learned about knowledge in the course of this book demonstrates the falsity of this idea. There is in fact no distinction between theory and practice in the way we actually hold and deploy our knowledge: all knowledge is geared to practice and held in the form of interpreted situations in which the possibilities for responding are embedded. However, the effect of this artificial distinction has been to exalt the position of abstract concepts and decontextualized theory in strategies for learning. It has also exalted the status of capacities of abstract conceptualization, logical thought and verbal reasoning and those naturally gifted in these areas at the expense of those more adept at using practical know-how. In relation to training for ministry, it has led in the past to a strategy in which people are taught theory – in the form of academic theology – in isolation from practice, on the assumption that application of the theory can safely be left to a later stage.

The nature of theology

Over the centuries, the church's understanding of the nature of theology has changed in ways that echo the way knowledge has been understood in the wider culture. As practised in the early church, writes Edward Farley, theology was seen as transformative knowledge: a 'cognitive disposition and orientation of the soul', 'a *practical*, not theoretical, habit having the primary characteristic of wisdom'. In the medieval university, however, theology became a specialist study, the subject of discussion and debate. Without losing its earlier sense, theology became 'a cognitive enterprise using appropriate methods and issuing in a body of teachings'. Against the background of Enlightenment thought, it became 'one technical and scholarly undertaking among others'.[26] Rather than the process by which people are transformed in their encounter with God, theology became the product of a scholarly enterprise. And rather than the shared experience of the whole church, it became the specialist pursuit of a tiny elite, while the vast majority of God's people were content to remain in ignorance of it.

At the present time, echoing the profound cultural shift taking place in our understanding of the nature of knowledge, the church's understanding of theology is changing back in the direction of 'a disposition of the soul'. Mark McIntosh writes of the study of theology as the way 'theologians are formed in their encounter with God'. He goes on to describe the goal of theological study as:

> someone whose life has begun to partake of Christ's way of being in the world; . . . someone whose way of thinking, and acting, and desiring is being inspired by the same Spirit who led Jesus towards the truth of himself and his relationship with the one he called Abba. . . . Theology is constantly in danger of getting carried away – from a respectable discipline managed by theologians to a mysterious sharing in God's way of life.[27]

In a similar way Peter Groves, in a contribution to a volume of reflections on the dual calling of priesthood and scholarship, defines Christian doctrine not so much as a critical account of the church's beliefs but as a 'practice'. He recalls how, in the opening chapter of Mark's Gospel, when Jesus was said to be bringing a 'new teaching' he had in fact done nothing other than 'demonstrated authority, power and control' and 'liberated a person from suffering'. His 'teaching' was displayed in his actions; and in the present day, the church's 'doctrine' is simply its life:

'This practice – doctrine – is not something preconceived which is then dropped into an existing context. Rather the life of the Church is both context and practice where Christian theology is concerned.'[28]

What, then, are we to say about the role of 'academic theology', the work of those pursuing theology as a specialist enterprise, usually though not exclusively in the context of the university? Kathryn Tanner makes the following observation:

> Theology is often identified with the productions of educated elites such as clergy and academics. When that identification is made, theology is equated with writings in which conceptual precision and logical coherence are at a premium. These writings are produced in primary conversation with other writings of a similar sort, and they tend to be read only by people with the same educational background and institutional support for sustained intellectual pursuits as their authors.[29]

To put it another way: academic theologians form a community of practice. Academic theology is practised in a distinctive institutional context by people with a certain set of shared interests and agreed working methods. Church and academy form two distinct though related communities of practice. What Tanner calls 'everyday' theology and Helen Cameron 'operant' theology – the theology embodied in the church's shared practices – is necessarily less precise and coherent than the theology that is practised by scholars. Tanner writes:

> Theology as a specialized intellectual activity raises the same sort of questions but often in a more general and abstract way. It investigates them, moreover, in a sustained fashion according to criteria less attuned to the urgencies of everyday life.[30]

It is important, Tanner insists, for the specialized theology of the academic community of practice to keep in touch with 'everyday' theology. In a similar way Jeff Astley has argued for the importance of what he calls 'ordinary' theology, the theological beliefs of 'ordinary' believers without formal theological training.

Comparing ordinary theology with the 'more literate, verbal and conceptually sophisticated approach' of the trained theologian, Astley draws attention to the danger that this may 'blind us to the value of what is without a special status; so that we do not see the worth of the everyday, the usual and the ordinary'.[31] In other words, the 'ordinary' and the 'everyday' have a value of their own. It is in the ordinary and the everyday that discipleship and ministry take place and God's people are transformed; and those whose call is to equip and enable this process of transformation and the ministry that flows from it must avoid becoming locked into a specialized understanding of the church's life and calling that is removed from the everyday.

The journey of Christian discipleship, the exercise of Christian ministry and the pursuit of 'academic' theology each take place in the context of different though related communities of practice. From the point of view of each community, what counts as 'knowledge' is 'competence with respect to valued enterprises'.[32] Thus the academy maintains and monitors the criteria for scholarly excellence, which, as well as the requisite skills and knowledge, also involve distinctive virtues, such as 'attentiveness, patience, intellectual humility, and seasoned judgement'.[33] But discipleship, ministry and academic study are separate though related enterprises. The very meaning of 'theology' is different in each of these communities. The list of virtues required, though closely related, is not the same in each case. Though the theologian may be a member of all three of these communities of practice, his identity, formed in the course of participation in the shared practice, will be subtly different in relation to each community. In one context he is a disciple, in another a minister of the gospel and in a third a theological scholar, and his task is to maintain the coherence of these three sets of roles and sources of self-understanding.

One of the theological scholar's greatest challenges is that in the context of the university, the pursuit of theology takes place in uneasy tension with the dictates of critical reason. According to the Enlightenment's definition, the validity of knowledge as a general theory is guaranteed by the exercise of unaided human reason. Critical reason, it was believed, held the key to the discovery of the fundamental nature of human society and was capable of uniting the pursuit of knowledge in each and every area of human endeavour in a single, universally valid framework through the use of a universally valid method. Authority no longer resided in religious or any other traditions but in the exercise of 'critical reason', which is taken to be value-neutral. One does not need to be a theologian to fall foul of the dominance of what is in effect a culturally specific and flawed understanding of human reason. When the philosopher of science Thomas Kuhn proposed that values play a crucial role in the progress of science, he was attacked as 'irrational'.[34] This fundamental orientation is an example of what the philosopher Charles Taylor has called a 'closed world structure': an assumption that appears so obvious to those who hold it that it blinds them to the possibilities that lie beyond. Its effect is to trap the modern world within an 'immanent frame', in which it no longer makes sense to believe in the possibility of the transcendent.[35]

In contrast, Christian faith proposes another foundation for truth. Truth, it claims, is discovered in a Person: Jesus Christ, the incarnate Son of God. In the light of our exploration of the nature of knowledge, it is possible to see why this should be so. Our knowledge does not take the form of a grand theory whose validity is guaranteed by 'critical reason'. It takes for granted and arises from human purposes in community. Its deepest underlying question, therefore, is the question of human flourishing: what does it mean to be a human being sharing the world with others? Because he embodies in his Person and displays in his words and actions the relationships with God and others that God desires for all his children, Jesus holds the answer to this foundational question. It is this deepest of all truths, carrying with it the promise and power of transformation, that the Christian community is called to explore and live out in its common life, guided and empowered by the Holy Spirit who, Jesus promised, would lead his followers into all truth.[36]

It is quite possible to approach the enterprise of theological study as a Christian disciple as well as a scholar. Many theological scholars not only acknowledge the authority of Scripture and Christian tradition but work successfully within a definition of theology as integrally related to the transformative knowledge embedded in the practices of Christian life, and the discipline of theology is being transformed as a result. But this is accomplished through a process of negotiation at the boundary between communities.

Theology for ministry
All three of the 'internal images' or 'assumptive frameworks' I have named, about the nature of leadership, the nature of knowledge and the nature of theology, are in the process of change. Nevertheless, their combined effect has been seriously to distort the church's understanding and practice in the areas of discipleship and ministry. The New Testament picture is of a universal call to discipleship and ministry. It was to 'present *everyone* mature in Christ' that Paul 'toiled' and 'struggled' with all the strength God inspired in him (Colossians 1.28–29). In stark contrast, the contemporary church currently devotes enormous effort and expenditure to providing theological learning for a tiny minority of its members. The related ideas that leadership is the province of a specially trained elite, that the knowledge required by this elite takes the form of a general theory, and that therefore academic theology provides the appropriate training for the church's ministers still exercise a firm hold on the church's understanding and practice when it comes to ministry and ministerial training. These ideas are so embedded in our thinking and language that 'theological education' has become the accepted term for training for ordained ministry. Moreover, training for lay ministry has also been drawn into this pattern, so that lay ministers typically receive a cut-down version of the training deemed appropriate for those training for ordination.

In contrast, I want to argue in the following paragraphs that academic theology per se provides the wrong kind of training for ministry. It is certainly important that ministry should be resourced by the riches of the church's tradition. But the way theology is pursued and taught in the universities is not the way this is best accomplished. In particular, it is a style of teaching and learning that distances theology from the vast majority of members of the church. Its result is that those entrusted with the leadership of the church understand its faith and tradition from the point of view of one particular set of conventions and modes of thought, while the vast majority of believers understand their heritage of faith in a different way and from a different point of view. In a church committed to a collaborative pattern of ministry, shared by ordained and lay alike, this difference in the way the Christian heritage of faith is made available to resource the church's life and ministry is little short of a disaster.

People tend to teach in the way they themselves were taught, and the fundamental images that we have inherited from the past of what knowledge consists of and the kind of enterprise theology is may continue to influence those of us whose training for ministry took place some years ago, making it difficult to adjust to a changing world and changing church. In the case of the Church of England, we are gradually finding our way towards a renewed form of training incorporating a renewed theology for mission and ministry, but the process is slow and stumbling, and we are still held back by the dominant images of the past.

In the first place, academic theology as traditionally practised tends to be subject- rather than life-centred. Its method is to initiate students into the ways of thinking attendant on theology as a specialist discipline, taking very little account of their existing 'ordinary theology'. As well as being predominantly content-centred, the approach to teaching and learning in academic settings has traditionally been one of transmission, by which I mean that the learner is expected to take over information predigested for her by established experts. The student is a novice, who comes to be initiated into the new world of theology. She learns to read the Bible in its original languages, to apply the methods of biblical criticism recognized as valid by the academic community; she is given an overview of the divisions of doctrine or systematic theology and taught how to carry out deeper enquiry into selected topics; she encounters certain phases in the history of the church and is introduced to the history and principles of its liturgy; and so on through all the subdivisions that make up the study of academic theology. The method of her initiation is to sit at the feet of established experts, either by hearing lectures or reading the books recommended to her, and in this way soak up the required knowledge.

The student of academic theology is thus dependent on the expertise of others. All the goals and purposes of her learning, other than the initial choice to study theology, are dictated by others. She has not attained, and is unable to attain, the status of the adult learner, with a role in shaping the goals and methods of her own learning. In contrast, when people approach training for ministry they come with well-defined goals and purposes of their own, arising from their previous experience and developing sense of vocation. It is a fundamental element in adult education that the learner's own goals and purposes be acknowledged and the learning experience appropriately tailored to meet these goals. The theology encountered as preparation for ministry needs to be theology *for* ministry.

A related point has to do with the structure of theology as an academic discipline. The defining character of the academic paradigm is that its content and methods are defined by the internal structure of the discipline as it has developed over the course of its history. A problem in biblical exegesis is just that: a problem whose significance as well as its solution is defined by the subdiscipline of biblical studies. The differences between one theologian and another in their interpretation of the doctrine of the Trinity or the nature of the atonement are framed as problems within the subdiscipline of systematic theology. As a community of practice, academic theology constitutes a world of its own, with a tendency towards ever greater specialization and increasingly abstract conceptualization. In this specialized world, the goal for the student is to become a competent biblical scholar or theologian. But if this knowledge is to become useful for ministry, the student has to learn how to apply it in the messy and conflicted situations of the real world: to discern which parts of the Bible studied in depth in an academic context might apply to the complex ethical problem with which a particular church member is wrestling, or what the doctrines of atonement and incarnation might have to say in the context of a PCC discussion on the church's mission action plan.

And finally, the way academic theology is taught reflects the history and trajectory of the particular subdiscipline under study. The community's aim is to initiate the novice into the practices of academic study. For this to be successful, she must learn the issues at stake and the big names involved in the most significant controversies within the discipline; build a picture of how the discipline has been shaped by these, and what are its present interests and the most important issues at stake. All this is very different from the requirement of the Christian minister to be resourced by the key methods and insights of the discipline for the practice of ministry or of the disciple to draw on its resources for the practice of faith in everyday life.

A change is therefore required in the way the church relates to and makes use of the insights of academic theology. A few years ago, Ripon College was asked to develop a Masters in Ministry course for serving clergy who were to become leaders of 'ministry areas' in the Diocese of Monmouth. The one thing these experienced clergy made it quite clear they did not want was exposure to 'academic' theology. For them, the word 'academic' meant 'irrelevant' and 'out of touch'. In the event, it proved possible to base the course around several key theological themes, including the Trinity, incarnation, atonement and resurrection, but only because we were able to integrate the study of these themes with the skills they needed to apply theological insights to the considerable problems they were tackling on a daily basis. We had successfully transferred the learning of theology from one community of practice to another, from the academic context to the context of ministry. Our experience bears out a recent American study, which concluded that ministers develop the wisdom they need for ministry most effectively in contexts in which they are enabled to integrate their knowledge of the separate subdisciplines of theology and apply it to concrete situations and relationships.[37]

One cannot 'disinvent' academic theology and, even more important, the church cannot lightly discard the tradition that has been the subject of centuries of theological study. As the pursuit of Christian disciples, the study of theology in the academy continues to yield insights of great depth and fruitfulness for Christian life and practice. Moreover, the way theology is taught in the church's training institutions is also changing. In the case of the Church of England, the Common Awards programme offers a qualification in 'Theology, Mission and Ministry', in which it is intended that reflective practice plays a key role.

The key to making the riches of academic theology available in usable form to the whole church is to incorporate them in an approach to learning through reflective practice. For all its analytical rigour, the way theology is learned in the academy represents only a small slice of the learning process. In relation to the cycle of experiential learning discussed in Chapter 3, it comprehends only the stages of Reflection and Conceptualization, leaving the Experience and Action phases to the realm of practice. Its focus is on theoretical generalization which, as we have seen, is the level of expertise required of the comparative beginner. On the other hand, incorporating the insights of theology into the cycle of theological reflection makes its insights, along with the whole Christian tradition, available to those training for ministry. This is the approach we were able to take with the Monmouth course, an approach successfully used in many other training institutions and one equally applicable in the local church context. It turns academic theology from dominating master into flexible servant in the service of God's mission through the church.

Learning for Ministry in the Local Church

In this final section I will attempt to draw together the strands of the book as a whole and apply them specifically to the task of equipping the local church for ministry. 'Ministry' is not the province of a few specially trained people; it is the vocation of the whole church. The Church of England, and to a varying degree the other denominations that make up the church in this country, have been used to thinking of full-time stipendiary ordained ministry as the standard form of ministry, with every other form, voluntary or part-time, pioneer, lay or ordained, as auxiliary optional extras. Biblically and theologically, however, the standard form of ministry is local ministry, lay or ordained, full- or part-time. The man or woman called either to play a role in serving and building up the Body of Christ as a loving, worshipping community, or to join with others in proclaiming the gospel or serving the wider community on behalf of Christ, embodies the standard form of ministry in a church called to be a foretaste, sign and agent of God's kingdom. However, because the ministry is the ministry of the whole church, it requires in addition a ministry of oversight exercised by those whose calling is to 'bring [the ministry of the whole church] to be' by 'representing and co-ordinating' it.[38]

The church's ministry therefore requires teamwork, but with a deeper dimension reflecting its character as a foretaste of God's kingdom. This deeper dimension is the *koinonia* of the Holy Spirit, the loving unity brought about through participation in the life of God the Trinity made possible by the indwelling Spirit. At the heart of *koinonia* is 'friendship with a purpose'. God's people are to be united in their desire to worship and serve him, their shared commitment to mission and ministry. But beyond their shared purpose, they are to be united in friendship. As Jesus said to the apostles on the night before he died, 'I have called you friends, because I have made known to you everything that I have heard from my Father' (John 15.15). In teamwork, it is easy to value colleagues according to the gifts they bring and the contribution they make to the shared task. In friendship, however, people are valued for themselves, loved unconditionally in their uniqueness. Christian ministry, therefore, draws together people with a variety of gifts, sharing responsibility for the task in hand. But it also draws them together as fellow disciples, companions on a journey of transformation. On this journey the leaders are also disciples, whose part in the shared ministry transforms them as much as it does their fellow servants in Christ.[39]

Learning for ministry in the local church takes for granted the learning for discipleship I dealt with in earlier chapters. Indeed, it is through courses such as Pilgrim, Bishop's Certificates and other formal teaching opportunities that much of the knowledge of the Christian faith essential to informed discipleship will be gained. In my experience, not only is the knowledge gained in such courses essential for ministry, it also inspires many people for ministry. The confidence gained in their understanding of the faith and in their capacity to learn, and the experience of learning in small groups in which their own insights are both affirmed and corrected, build confidence in the possibility of further training.

Learning for ministry also takes for granted opportunities for reflection on discipleship and ministry in places of daily life and work. It requires a church actively equipping its members to live as husbands, wives and parents, to think through issues of care for elderly parents, making a place for single people in the Christian community and extending a loving welcome to those whose lifestyles challenge our presuppositions. It involves opportunities to reflect together on the issues encountered in the challenging environments in which many people work; or like the group that began by reflecting on human trafficking and ended up spearheading the diocesan response to this issue, reflecting on the national and international issues that challenge Christian faith and invite loving response.

And finally, learning for ministry requires shared vision arrived at through corporate discernment. This involves the habit of shared and prayerful reflection, through which a church or group of churches examine specific aspects of their common life for their faithfulness to the gospel, and discern the direction for their ministry under the guidance of the Holy Spirit. Moreover, when the discipline of reflection becomes embedded in the life of the church it enables the process of adaptive change. A 'healthy church', writes Robert Warren, is one that 'faces the cost of change and growth'. The practice of reflection helps to provide that environment of mutual support that enables churches to see where change is needed and rise to the challenge.[40]

Oversight
Encouraging and equipping people for ministry through the local church is an aspect of the ministry of oversight. The shape of this ministry is helpfully laid out by Steven Croft in his book, *Ministry in Three Dimensions*.[41] Croft divides the tasks of oversight in a local church context into three. First there is the establishing and guarding of a shared vision as a focus of unity; second, the enabling and equipping of all God's people for ministry; third, foundational to each of the others, 'watching over' oneself and others – something I understand as doing all that is possible to ensure everything done in God's service is empowered and directed by the Spirit and dependent on God's grace, rather than becoming an overflow of merely human zeal and enthusiasm. In an earlier piece of writing, Croft added a fourth dimension to his account

of oversight: locating and connecting the local church with the wider church community. Although this may be said to belong more properly to bishops and those in other denominations with a supervisory ministry, in the local church or group of churches, the clergy play an important role as signs to the whole church of their fellowship with all God's people.[42]

Writing for clergy and those training for ordination, Croft understandably views oversight as an aspect of ordained ministry. And as we have seen, the focus on 'recognizing' the corporate ministry of the church, representing, focusing and collecting it in order to 'bring it to be', was the central focus of the report 'Education for the Church's Ministry', which set the direction for ministerial training in the years following 1987.[43] However, as I have suggested in *Reimagining Ministry*, in many contexts this ministry is best exercised by more than one person. The 'weight' of discernment involved, not to mention the challenge of dealing with change and conflict within a congregation, suggest that oversight is best handled by a small team rather than a solitary individual.[44] Within such a team it may be that one or more with educational expertise take particular responsibility for training and equipping others for ministry.

This raises the twin questions of whether oversight is necessarily a part of the ministry of all ordained clergy, and whether it might also be exercised by lay people in the context of a team. Our experience in Monmouth, working with clergy being called to move from a traditional pattern of parish-based ministry to take on the oversight of much larger ministry areas, was that this was by no means an easy transition. In many cases it involved the painful laying down of familiar roles and a process of profound personal change. And one of the difficulties some of them faced was the need to work with fellow clergy, some of whom did not share the vision for a church in which the ministry of oversight was to be exercised by ministry area leaders. This suggests that if oversight is seen as the responsibility of a team, it may not be necessary for all clergy to be part of that team simply by virtue of their ordination. On the other hand, it may be appropriate to include some lay leaders with the necessary vision and the gifts to share in oversight.

Just as in formal programmes for discipleship, the first step in equipping the church for ministry is 'needs analysis'. In relation to ministry, however, needs analysis works somewhat differently. The two basic questions are variations of those the Church of England used for some years in assessing the quality of its training institutions: 'What is the shape of the mission to which God is calling us?' and 'What ministry is required to accomplish this mission?' At this stage attention is required to the disciplines of prayerful discernment married to clear-eyed research about the needs of the church's locality and the networks of people to whom it relates. In this process, awareness of the gifts and passions present in the congregation also plays a part. As I shared in *Reimagining Ministry*, I have vivid memories of a leadership team away-day at which we received a very clear sense of God guiding us to focus our mission on a particular area of our parish. The facts that our church school served this area, and that one of our Readers with a clear sense of calling to community engagement had grown up there, proved to be crucial elements in the way the initial vision began to come to fruition. Having said this, it is often the opportunities that spontaneously arise through invitations from the community that prove to be the drivers of mission. The experience of one of our Monmouth clergy was that, as his ministry team came together and addressed themselves to mission, opportunities arose for chaplaincy in one of the local secondary schools as well as in parts of the shopping centre, and the church was invited to play a key role in planning for a large new housing development. In each case, however, the possibilities for mission have to be met by the capacity for ministry. Prayerful reflection is needed to address fundamental questions: 'Is this really the direction in which God is guiding us?' and 'What is the shape of the ministry required to fulfil this call?'

Team-building
The next key question is: 'Who is God calling to fulfil this ministry?' As Steven Croft emphasizes, a vocational understanding is far more effective and faithful than a volunteering approach.[45] To ask 'Who is available?' gives the impression that ministry is

for anyone and is a case of individual initiative. To ask 'Who is God calling?' is both more demanding and more discerning. In his book *Good to Great*, Jim Collins makes a powerful point about team-building, based on extensive research among American businesses. He is known for his description of the 'level 5' leader, someone who exhibits the twin characteristics of personal humility and professional will. This is the leader whose focus is on the good of the company as a whole, not on the benefits to themselves of high position, who sees the necessity of a cohesive and committed team and who values and nurtures the talents of all those serving alongside her. But the second of Collins' observations is summed up in the adage: 'first who then what'. Briefly, his advice is that rather than define the task and then ask who has the gifts required to accomplish it, the focus should be on building a team of the right people. In the context of the church, these will be people with the right 'heart': a desire for God's glory before their own success or satisfaction, whose focus, like that of the main leader, is on the well-being of the whole church and the progress of God's mission.[46]

As David Pendleton and Adrian Furnham point out in their book *Leadership: All You Need to Know*, no one person is capable of exhibiting all the qualities required for successful leadership. The most effective leadership structure is likely to be a complementary team, made up of people who between them offer the necessary gifts and qualities.[47] Such a team may well need to be capable of tolerating and growing through conflict.[48] Michael Frost and Alan Hirsch recommend the fivefold understanding of leadership drawn from Ephesians 4.11, incorporating apostles, prophets, evangelists, pastors and teachers, precisely because the vision and temperament of these very different kinds of leaders potentially clash with, as well as complement, each other. It is in the way each of the leaders strikes sparks from the others that God's will and purpose is discerned.[49] Certainly, a church led on the inherited pastoral model by a single leader of one particular outlook is far less likely to be in a position to respond to the guidance and direction of the Holy Spirit when leading the church in mission.[50]

Having said all this, it is rare that a church leader has the opportunity of starting with a blank sheet of paper when assembling a ministry team. Not only are there likely to be other office-holders with a stake in the process, but the church itself forms a pool of limited size. However, the God who calls his church to participate with him in mission also supplies the people with the gifts required to respond to that call. A church leader in this country may not have the scope to hire and fire, except to a limited extent, but he can place his trust in God to draw the people whom he is calling into ministry. He will also use tools such as the Carlisle Diocese SHAPE course as a way of discovering the gifts and passions present among the congregation and encouraging people to identify and offer their gifts.[51] He may use tools such as the Belbin team role analysis to indicate the team roles present among the leaders or potential leaders, and balance these in the team as far as possible.[52] He will certainly look closely at the experience, temperaments, gifts and passions offered by those with the potential for membership of the ministry team. One of our Monmouth clergy described the way he reshaped the roles of his ministry team members, paying particular attention to the experience they brought and their contribution to the team as well as to the church's mission. A team vicar with a background in education added co-ordination of schools chaplaincy and outreach to a significant new housing development to his role as vicar to one of the smaller churches in the team. An older retired lay minister with traditional church values and a gift of administration became the guardian of the churches' worship, with a role in keeping the churches up to date with developments in liturgy. A retired teacher took responsibility for work with younger families. An associate priest, previously a senior leader in a primary care trust, with experience in organizing, family work and safeguarding, became responsible for training and supporting ministers in good practice when visiting vulnerable adults as well as taking the lead in the churches' healing ministry. Perhaps most significant of all, this particular priest recognized the need for greater time spent in prayer and discernment as the team came together and the mission began to take shape; the busier things became, the more extensive the opportunities, the more time was needed for prayer.

Supervision

In many congregations, writes Steven Croft, the model for training and deployment is high initial training followed by low or non-existent ongoing support. This he calls the 'sink or swim' model![53] In contrast, Croft points out that very few lay ministry roles require vast amounts of initial training. In some cases there are important aspects of life and ministry of which the potential lay minister should be aware: a pastoral carer should understand such aspects of human life as the experience of bereavement, and such aspects of good practice as the maintenance of boundaries and safeguarding procedures; and evangelists should understand something of the theology of God's mission. But in most cases low initial training is sufficient and the emphasis falls on high ongoing support. This means that one of the key tasks of oversight is supervision.[54]

'In a nutshell,' write Jane Leach and Michael Paterson, 'pastoral supervision is a relationship between two or more disciples who meet to consider the ministry of one or more of them in an intentional and disciplined way.' They go on:

> Pastoral supervision is practised for the sake of the supervisee, providing a space in which their well-being, growth and development are taken seriously, and for the sake of those among whom the supervisee works, providing a realistic point of accountability.[55]

Frances Ward calls supervision a 'space to play': it is a place for the minister to step aside from the immediate pressure of decision-making in order to rerun aspects of the ministry in a safe environment, in which the supervisor helps the supervisee to focus on the issues involved, and to bring theology into play in order to discern God's presence.[56] Supervision has overlaps with and includes elements of counselling, spiritual direction and work consultancy, but it is not the same as these things. Its primary method is reflection, and in a Christian context, theological reflection. The 'space' that Leach and Paterson, and Ward, write about is the space provided for reflection.

The supervisor may be a more experienced colleague. In some cases she may be the minister's line manager, especially if the relationship is that of vicar and curate. On the other hand, it may be best to keep supervision and line management separate and find a supervisor who is not personally involved in the ministry context. Peer supervision is where a group of people supervise each other by reflecting together on critical incidents and situations brought by members of the group.

A minister has had a difficult encounter with a member of the church. She knows she has made some mistakes but is bruised by the encounter and needs to think it through. A session with her supervisor provides a safe space in which to do this. The supervision session has three aspects:

- Resourcing: the supervisor provides a supportive, listening ear. She offers the gift of attentive listening, enabling the minister to 'offload' the difficult episode.
- Developmental: the supervisor helps the minister to explore the various aspects of the situation – the parishioner's (possibly unrealistic) expectations; the parishioner's difficult family situation; the dynamics of the church group of which the parishioner is a part; the minister's assumptions about what the parishioner's needs were; the details of the conversations that took place. Because the supervisor is outside the situation she can much more easily hold together its different aspects and guide the minister through it.
- Qualitative or managerial: the supervisor helps the minister identify any mistakes, with a view to avoiding them in future.

These aspects of supervision will all be present, but in different proportions depending on the situation under review. The ultimate question, which unites all three aspects, is: 'Where is God in the situation?'

Supervision aims to help the supervisee develop a mature 'wisdom' for ministry. One aspect of this is the development of a broader perspective. Using the example above, it is possible to discern a number of stages:

- Self-centred, where the main question is: 'Am I getting it right?' At this stage the supervisor would aim to help the minister to see that any mistakes she may have made are not the only factor in the situation.
- Other-centred, where the emphasis is on meeting others' perceived expectations. At this stage the supervisor would want to help the minister see that the parishioner's expectations may not have been appropriate, and that there are limits to the help she could reasonably be expected to offer.
- Process-centred, where the minister is beginning to be in a position to evaluate her own ministry more clearly. The supervisor can help her to look at the dynamics of the conversation, her underlying assumptions about what might have been the real needs and what would be a reasonable outcome.
- Context-centred, where the supervisor is helping the minister to see the whole situation in its wider context – in the life of the church, the parishioner's family and so on – and above all, to identify where God might be at work. When the minister is able to do this for most of the situations she faces in ministry, she is ready to become a supervisor herself!

Finding time for supervision in the midst of a busy ministry is not easy, but it should always be a priority. Supervision acts as a regular check on the progress and direction of the ministry. In the worst-case scenario, it allows the supervisor to bring correction when something is going wrong. In the best case, it renews vision and enthusiasm. In all cases, it acts as a reminder to the minister of her accountability to the church and ultimately to God; it should also act as necessary support, as well as the opportunity to take time out to refocus amid the multiple demands of ministry.[57]

More than anyone else in the church, ordained ministers need regular supervision. Qualified counsellors are required to work under supervision. In the course of their ministry they may receive projections from their clients, which they need to identify and work through. They may find themselves dealing with issues that affect them personally, and they need to be able to put the personal impact of the issue to one side in order to focus on the client. They may face situations in which it is difficult to be sure whether they responded in the best way or asked the best questions. The purpose of supervision is to allow them to reflect on all these issues with an experienced colleague.

Ordained ministers meet all these situations *and much more besides*. Whereas counsellors work with individuals, ordained ministers work with groups as well as individuals. Usually counsellors have a contract whereby they are able to limit their time commitment; ordained ministers find it much more difficult to maintain appropriate boundaries. The expectations placed on counsellors are much more limited and easier to understand than those placed on ordained ministers. For all these reasons, and especially when they themselves have the task of supervising others, ordained ministers need to find that necessary space for supervision.

Training

Finally, we come to training! Since, as Croft writes, the most advantageous pattern is likely to be low initial training and high ongoing support, and, as Hawkins recommends, the best learning opportunities are those that arise from the exercise of ministry, much of the training required is likely to be light-touch and take the form of reflection on ministry itself. Ministry is a practice, and practices comprise three basic elements: the skills required to participate; the core values, attitudes and dispositions that uphold and connect the community of practice; the knowledge base required for each of these. The practice of Christian ministry, or of one of its many facets, likewise requires proficiency in the required skills: attentive listening, public speaking, group facilitation, conflict management and so on. It also requires the attitudes and dispositions that ensure that these skills are exercised in a way that reflects the church's calling as a sign, agent and foretaste of God's kingdom. Moreover, each of these is undergirded with a certain knowledge base, which allows the minister to understand what he is called to and why.

Etienne Wenger writes about the approach to teaching and learning that best enables people to participate in communities of practice:

If we believe that knowledge consists of pieces of information explicitly stored in the brain, then it makes sense to package this information in well-designed units, to assemble prospective recipients in a classroom where they are perfectly still and isolated from any distraction, and to deliver this information to them as succinctly and articulately as possible . . . But if we believe that knowledge stored in explicit ways is only a small part of knowing . . . then the traditional format does not look so productive. What does look promising are inventive ways of involving students in meaningful practices, of providing access to resources that enhance that participation . . . and of involving them in actions, discussion, and reflections that make a difference to the communities they value.[58]

Certain general principles emerge from this passage, and from the whole of our consideration of effective learning:

1 Use experience. Each of the would-be ministers brings vast resources of existing experience from their past history, place of work and involvement in the life of the church. New steps in ministry and the learning that goes with them must draw on this experience, make sense in terms of it and allow the minister to reinterpret and re-evaluate it.
2 Build on 'ordinary' theology. The aspiring minister also brings her own existing understanding of Christian faith. This understanding, and above all her commitment to service and prior experience of God at work in her life, play a key part in shaping her understanding of the ministry to which she is called. Most of her 'ordinary theology', however, will be implicit. It is important that she has the opportunity to make this explicit, to recognize her own beliefs in order to build on and in some cases re-evaluate them.
3 Bring ministry and learning together. Use the ministry itself as the occasion for learning.
4 Do it together. The reservoir of past experience is far greater when it is the combined experience of several people on the same journey of discipleship and ministry. Trainees preparing for or taking their first steps in ministry learn enormously and

receive encouragement from one another, learning from each other's mistakes and so on. Within the group there is also likely to be a spectrum of theological views on many topics, sharing of which encourages each member of the group to think out more clearly what they themselves believe. Finally, learning through shared tasks strengthens the disposition of respect for one another's contribution, and enables each member of the group to reflect on and value their own, building up the Body of Christ in love.

5   Use the tool of reflection. In this book I have used the pastoral cycle as a standard method of theological reflection. There are many more, some better fitted to particular situations than others. Standard methods are particularly useful in a group learning context, where it is helpful to structure the work of the group, enable everyone to work together and keep an eye on the time available. The particular strength of reflection is that it brings knowledge, skill and attitude together, focusing on all three together.[59]

Aside from standard methods of group reflection, the methods available are as rich and varied as the field of adult education, and it is worth exploring. Off-the-shelf courses and video introductions are widely available, but it is helpful to engage in thoughtful planning to ensure that the resource really meets the particular need at the time. Expertise in adult education can help in deciding on the best possible methods of learning. And as Wenger emphasizes, the most effective learning for ministry takes the form of ministry itself, as long as opportunities are made for reflection alongside.

In the past I have used something as basic as shared reading and reflection as a means of training. As we began our mission to the area of our parish on which we believed God had led us to focus, I began to think about how a church might come into being there and what it might look like. This was some years before the days of fresh expressions, but I was aware that the cultural difference between this particular neighbourhood and the worshipping style of our Sunday services was a considerable one. I decided to ask the Reader who was clearly being called to involvement with the community to read with me Vincent Donovan's book *Christianity Rediscovered*, and together we explored Donovan's experience of cross-cultural mission and its possible relevance to our own time and place.[60] The one change I would make if I could revisit that time would have been to do this exercise with the whole leadership team. In this way we would have been able to draw on the insights of the whole team and they would all have grasped the challenge facing the one particular Reader as she began to think through the implications of her own particular calling. At the present time I approach the teaching of leadership by asking my students to do a series of reflective exercises based on their reading, which then become the basis for small-group work, in which group members are able to draw on their varied experiences of leadership.

The one thing to remember is that, as with the examples of discipleship learning we looked at in the previous chapter, these are interventions. A single session, if it enables 'deep learning' bringing new insights that transform people's outlook, may be as effective as a whole course.

Conclusion

As will appear obvious, I am standing on the back of work done by many others and drawing on a wide variety of resources. But behind all the specifics of learning for discipleship and ministry lies one pressing question: How does the church make the transition from the mindset of clericalism, in which all the responsibility for and most of the work of ministry falls on the ordained clergy, and in which the assumption that ordained ministry is the church's chief or only resource is embedded in its institutional structures, to a mindset that assumes active participation of all God's people as 'missionary disciples'?

I have suggested that a more widespread acquaintance with the field of adult education and learning can make a contribution to this transition, not only because it will directly equip the church for discipleship and ministry but also, indirectly, because knowledge of the way adults learn provides a window on to a renewed and transformed style of relationships, in which all are valued on the journey of faith and all enabled to play their part in mission. It also locates the developing field of theological reflection in relation to the methods of adult education and the process of experiential learning more generally, enabling us to recognize the place of TR at the heart of Christian learning. This in turn means that Christian learning ceases to be the province of those who possess the necessary skills in verbal reasoning to benefit from traditional teaching methods, and opens it to the whole church. In the words of Sylvia Wilkey Collinson, it 'provides a solution to every caring teacher's problem, that of encouraging those not gifted academically to learn and operate successfully at their own level of giftedness'.[61] Finally, the recognition that ministry is a practice requires a rethink of our assumptions about who is qualified to take part in ministry and how they can most effectively be trained and supported.

The implications of this for the way the church selects and trains people for licensed ministry are enormous, and there is not space here to deal with this in the detail it requires. Suffice it to say that in the case of the Church of England, the Common Awards programme represents a measure of progress in this area, aiming explicitly at the development of character and recognizing reflection on practice as a key ministerial skill, if not quite placing TR at the heart of the learning.

Is this call to recognize the vital role of expertise in teaching and learning another burden on already hard-pressed clergy? Is it yet another area of expertise in which they are to be required to become proficient? I do not think so. Rather I see it as a key to greater fruitfulness. At the most basic level, TR is a vital tool for their own ministry, enabling them to step aside in order to discern the presence and call of God in the midst of the varied demands made on them. Used with members of their congregations, it has the potential to encourage ownership and commitment to the church's ministry and release energy for mission. Ordained ministers willing to make the transition from the role of 'expert' on whom the whole work of the church depends, to that of reflector or 'people's theologian', equipping the church with tools and strategies for shaping and reshaping meaning together, enabling all its members to relate Christian faith to the challenges of their own lives, will themselves face the challenge of adapting to a new role. But they will find themselves at the heart of an enterprise guided and directed by the Holy Spirit, through which God is bringing transformation both to the church and to the world around.

Notes

1 Peter Hawkins and Robin Shohet, *Supervision in the Helping Professions*, Milton Keynes: Open University Press, 2006.

2 Frances Ward, *Lifelong Learning*, London: SCM Press, 2005; Jane Leach and Michael Paterson, *Pastoral Supervision: A Handbook*, 2nd edn, London: SCM Press, 2015.

3 Hubert Dreyfus and Stuart Dreyfus, 'From Socrates to Expert Systems: The Limits of Calculative Rationality', in Hubert L. Dreyfus, *Skillful Coping: Essay on the Phenomenology of Everyday Perception and Action*, ed. Mark A. Wrathall, Oxford: Oxford University Press, 2014, pp. 25–43.

4 Dreyfus and Dreyfus, 'From Socrates to Expert Systems', p. 34.

5 Norman Ivison (director), *Expressions: The DVD*, London: Church House Publishing, 2006.

6 Chris Stoddard and Nick Cuthbert, *Church on the Edge*, Milton Keynes: Authentic Media, 2006.

7 George Lings, *Living Proof – A New Way of Being Church?*, Sheffield: The Sheffield Centre, 1999.

8 Michael Moynagh, 'Good Practice is Not What it Used to Be: Accumulating Wisdom for Fresh Expressions of Church', in Steven Croft (ed.), *The Future of the Parish System*, London: Church House Publishing, 2006, pp. 110–24.

9 www.freshexpressions.org.uk/guide.

10 Michael Moynagh, *Church for Every Context: An Introduction to Theology and Practice*, London: SCM Press, 2012, pp. 200–5.

11 Archbishops' Council, *From Anecdote to Evidence*, London: Church House Publishing, pp. 14, 27, www.churchgrowthresearch.org.uk/UserFiles/File/Reports/FromAnecdoteToEvidence1.0.pdf.

12 Joseph Dunne, '"Professional wisdom" in Practice', in Liz Bondi et al., *Towards Professional Wisdom*, Farnham: Ashgate, 2011, p. 17.

13 Aristotle, *Nichomachean Ethics*, trans. Roger Crisp, rev. edn, Cambridge: Cambridge University Press, 2014, pp. 115; 1144b.

14 Peter Senge, *The Fifth Discipline: The Art and Practice of the Learning Organisation*, 2nd edn, New York: Random House, 2006, p. 163.

15 Church of England Ministry Division, 'Formation Criteria for Ordained Ministry in the Church of England', May 2014.

16 'Assumptive frameworks' is the term used by Thomas Hawkins in *The Learning Congregation*, Louisville, KY: Westminster John Knox Press, 1997.

17 Much of what follows is based on Hawkins, *The Learning Congregation*, pp. 58–60.

18 Advisory Council for the Church's Ministry (AACM), Occasional Paper 22, 'Education for the Church's Ministry', 1987 § 29.

19 Hawkins, *Learning Congregation*, p. 11.

20 As a general rule, the higher one goes in a hierarchical organization such as a denomination, the greater is the tendency to overperformance. For the Church of England in particular, this means that the way episcopacy currently functions is one of its greatest weaknesses. See further the final two chapters in Stephen Pickard, *Theological Foundations for Collaborative Ministry*, Farnham: Ashgate, 2009.

21 Ronald Heifetz, *Leadership Without Easy Answers*, Cambridge, MA: Belknap Press, p. 126.

22 Hawkins, *Learning Congregation*, pp. 61–2.

23 Dreyfus and Dreyfus, 'From Socrates to Expert Systems', pp. 25–46.

24 Etienne Wenger, *Communities of Practice*, Cambridge: Cambridge University Press, 1998, p. 4.

25 Michael Polanyi, *Personal Knowledge*, London: Routledge & Kegan Paul, 1958; Thomas Kuhn, *The Structure of Scientific Revolutions*, 4th edn, Chicago: University of Chicago Press, 2012.

26 Edward Farley, *Theologia*, Philadelphia, PA: Fortress Press, 1993, pp. 33, 35, 39.

27 Mark McIntosh, *Divine Teaching*, Oxford: Blackwell, 2008, p. 7.

28 Peter Groves, 'Playing Football at Mansfield Park: Christian Doctrine and the Local Church', in Shaun Henson and Michael Lakey (eds), *Academic Vocation in the Church and Academy Today*, Farnham: Ashgate, 2016, pp. 54–7; quotation from p. 57.

29 Kathryn Tanner, *Theories of Culture*, Minneapolis, MN: Fortress Press, 1997, p. 69.

30 Tanner, *Culture*, p. 71; see Helen Cameron et al., *Talking About God in Practice*, London: SCM Press, pp. 54–6.

31 Jeff Astley, 'In Defence of "Ordinary Theology"', *British Journal of Theological Education* 13.1, 2002, pp. 21–35; quotation from p. 25. See also Astley, *Ordinary Theology*, Aldershot: Ashgate, 2002.

32 Wenger, *Communities of Practice*, p. 4.

33 Mike Higton, 'Theological Education Between the University and the Church: Durham University and the Common Awards in Theology, Ministry and Mission', *Journal of Adult Theological Education* 10.1, 2013, p. 31.

34 See the responses to Kuhn's theory in Imre Lakatos and Alan Musgrave, *Criticism and the Growth of Knowledge*, Cambridge: Cambridge University Press, 1970.

35 Charles Taylor, *A Secular Age*, Cambridge, MA: Belknap Press, 2007, esp. pp. 539–93.

36 For a more detailed exploration of the place of the incarnate Jesus and the Holy Spirit in relation to issues of knowledge and truth, see my earlier book, *Divine Revelation and Human Learning*, Aldershot: Ashgate, 2004.

37 Christian A. B. Scharen and Eileen R. Campbell-Reed, *Learning Pastoral Imagination: A Five-Year Report on How New Ministers Learn in Practice*, Auburn Studies Bulletin 21, http://auburnseminary.org/wp-content/uploads/2016/02/Learning-Pastoral-Imagination.pdf, pp. 18–23.

38 ACCM, 'Education for the Church's Ministry', § 29.

39 For a more extensive treatment of *koinonia*, see my *Reimagining Ministry*, London: SCM Press, 2011, pp. 118–25.

40 Robert Warren, *The Healthy Churches Handbook*, London: Church House Publishing, 2004, pp. 31–5.

41 Steven Croft, *Ministry in Three Dimensions*, 2nd edn, London: Darton, Longman & Todd, 2008, pp. 139–92.

42 Steven Croft, 'Leadership and the Emerging Church', in *Focus on Leadership*, a collection of papers from the launch of the Foundation for Church Leadership, January 2005, pp. 7–39.

43 ACCM, 'Education for the Church's Ministry', § 29.

44 Heywood, *Reimagining Ministry*, pp. 191–2.

45 Croft, *Ministry in Three Dimensions*, p. 176.

46 Jim Collins, Good *to Great*, London: Random House, 2001, pp. 17–64.

47 David Pendleton and Adrian Furnham, *Leadership: All You Need to Know*, Basingstoke: Palgrave Macmillan, 2012, pp. 74–117.

48 For the necessity of conflict as an element in the life of any team, see Patrick Lencioni, *The Five Dysfunctions of a Team*, San Francisco: Jossey-Bass, 2002.

49 Michael Frost and Alan Hirsch, *The Shaping of Things to Come*, Peabody, MA: Hendrickson, 2003, pp. 165–81.

50 See Croft, *Ministry in Three Dimensions*, pp. 4–5.

51 'Your Shape for God's Service', originally developed by Amiel Osmaston for the Diocese of Carlisle and now available online from several places, including Carlisle Diocese, CPAS and the Arthur Rank Centre.

52 Meredith Belbin, *Team Roles at Work*, 2nd edn, London: Routledge, 2010; and see www.belbin.com/about/belbin-team-roles.

53 Croft, *Ministry in Three Dimensions*, p. 178.

54 In fact 'supervision' and 'oversight' are the same word, the one based on Anglo-Saxon roots, the other Latin. The 'Greek' version is *episcope*, which is the root of our word 'bishop'.

55 Leach and Paterson, *Pastoral Supervision*, p. 1.

56 Ward, *Lifelong Learning*, pp. 88–95.

57 For greater detail, see Leach and Paterson, *Pastoral Supervision*; and Hawkins and Shohet, *Supervision in the Helping Professions*, pp. 56–103.

58 Wenger, *Communities of Practice*, pp. 9–10.

59 For a variety of methods, see Charles Chadwick and Phillip Tovey, *Growing in Ministry Using Critical Incident Analysis*, Cambridge: Grove, 2003, now available only as a download; Patricia O'Connell Killen and John de Beer, *The Art of Theological Reflection*, New York: Crossroad, 1994; Judith Thompson, *The SCM Studyguide to Theological Reflection*, London: SCM Press, 2008; Helen Cameron et al., *Theological Reflection for Human Flourishing*, London: SCM Press, 2012; Cameron et al., *Talking About God in Practice* and Leach and Paterson, *Pastoral Supervision*. For reflection in general, see Roger Walton, *The Reflective Disciple*, London: Epworth Press, 2009.

60 Vincent Donovan, *Christianity Rediscovered: An Epistle from the Masai*, London: SCM Press, 1978.

61 Sylvia Wilkey Collinson, *Making Disciples: The Significance of Jesus' Educational Methods for Today's Church*, Eugene, OR: Wipf & Stock, 2006 (originally Milton Keynes: Paternoster Press, 2004), pp. 103–40.

Index of Names and Subjects

academic theology 71, 99–100, 160, 167–8, 185, 187, 196–205
Acts, book of 16, 27, 29–30, 98–9, 103, 104, 105, 125, 126
adaptive change 1, 2–4, 6, 151–7
adult learning 46–8, 48–59
After Sunday 156–7
aims and objectives 134–40, 140
Aisthorpe, Steve 11
Alpha course 130
analogy 91–3
Aristotle 35, 62, 64, 111, 118n, 188–9
Astley, Jeff 70, 198–9

Bartlett, Sir Frederic 88
Bass, Dorothy 162–5
Baumohl, Anton viii
Belbin team roles 211
Bible *see* Scripture
Bonhoeffer, Dietrich 37, 42, 91
Brookfield, Stephen 53–4
Brueggemann, Walter 122
Brunner, Emil 15

Carlisle Diocese 9, 211
chaplaincy xi, 1, 4, 179, 209, 211
character 7, 20, 59–71, 77–8, 110–11, 115–16, 136, 141–2, 165–8, 175–6
'Character Education in UK Schools' 63–6, 69
'Character Nation' 63–6
Christian practices 161–5

Christianity Rediscovered 217–18
Church of England
  and discipleship 7
clericalism xi, 5, 9–11, 13, 21, 159–60, 218
collaborative ministry 104–8, 125, 157–60, 190–4
Collins, Jim 210
Collins, John 12
Collinson, Sylvia Wilkie viii, 26–8, 30, 69, 219
Colossians, epistle to xii, 13, 29, 32–4, 41, 45, 91, 98, 110, 111, 120, 121, 201
Common Awards 67–9, 204, 219
community of practice 22, 160–76, 184–6, 198, 203, 215–16
conflict 84, 112
congregation, role in learning 59, 102–8, 125–6, 144–60
Cooling, Trevor 173–4
Corinthians, epistles to 15, 16, 17, 29, 31, 36, 79, 99, 108, 110, 119, 120
Cray, Graham 105
critical incidents 83–6, 92
Croft, Stephen 126, 207–9, 212, 215

Dearing Report 45
defensive routines 157
Demos 63–6, 69
Deuteronomy, book of 97
Dewar, Francis 15–16, 18

223

diakonia 12
discipleship
 definition 13
 and ministry 5, 11–19
Divine Revelation and Human Learning 87–93
Dreyfus, Hubert and Stuart 180–2, 194
Dunne, Joseph 112, 188
Durham University 67
Dykstra, Craig 162–5

'Education for the Church's Ministry' (ACCM 22) 66–7, 192, 208
'Education for Discipleship' 7–9
'Education for Ministry' method of theological reflection 87
Emmaus course 126, 135–6, 155, 162, 176n
Enlightenment 60, 62–3, 68, 165, 194–200
Ephesians, epistle to 14, 15, 29, 31, 38, 41, 104, 106, 110, 119, 120, 210
evaluation 142–4
exemplars 42, 90, 99, 110, 164

Farley, Edward 66, 196–7
feelings 20, 64, 67, 70, 77–9, 84–8, 91–2, 100, 111, 114, 123, 166, 182–4, 188, 195, 196
foundational domain of spirituality 164
fresh expressions of church 1, 184–6
Fresh Expressions website 184–6
'Fruits of the Spirit, The' 65–6, 68
funerals as a 'practice' 182–4

Gallagher, Rob viii, 81–116, 168
Genesis, book of 96, 97
Gilchrist, Alison 149
Goleman, Daniel 118n

Green, Laurie 116n, 123, 128, 159–60
groups, learning in 54–7
'Growing Disciples' 9

habitus 66–70, 118n, 120
Hawkins, Thomas viii, 2, 128, 151–2, 158, 193, 215
Healthy Church Handbook, The 150, 154, 207
Heifetz, Ron 193
heroic leadership 104–5, 191–4
hierarchy 4, 107, 158–9, 191–4, 221n
'Higher Ambitions' 46
Hind Report 7, 67
Hodges, Janet 150
Holy Spirit 4, 98, 99, 101, 103, 104, 134, 200, 207, 210, 220
 empowering mission 12, 18–19, 44, 105–6, 153, 159, 176, 208
 role in theological reflection 28, 92, 108–11, 124
 empowering transformation 14, 20, 31, 33, 37, 38, 43, 59, 61, 62, 91, 94, 115, 119, 120, 121, 122, 123, 124, 143, 161, 171, 197, 206
hospitality 79, 122, 149–50, 151, 163, 164–5, 171, 172, 173

identity 49–50, 110–11, 124, 170–1
intuition 86–93

Jesus
 exemplar of human identity 33, 37, 61, 90–1, 110, 116, 119, 124, 164–5, 175
 teaching methods 26–8, 125
 as ultimate truth 34, 41, 109, 200
John, gospel of 16, 25, 34, 44, 103, 108, 109, 124, 206
Jubilee Centre 63–6, 69

INDEX OF NAMES AND SUBJECTS

kingdom of God 4, 13, 16, 18, 20, 25–7, 40–5, 62, 90, 101, 122, 132, 159
koinonia 43, 99, 122, 158, 206
Kolb, David 76, 89, 116n, 123
Kuhn, Thomas 89, 91, 195, 200

Lawrence, James 154–5
leadership 6, 22, 25, 104–7, 158–60, 180, 187, 191–4
learning, action-reflection approach 28, 29, 33
learning cycle 21, 33, 123–4, 140–1, 205
'Learning for Life' 60–1, 63
learning organization 2, 6, 71, 104–8, 151–7, 193
learning styles 141
lectio divina 77, 100
Lewis, C. S. 121–2
Lings, George 185

MacIntyre, Alasdair 21–2, 59–64, 94, 165–7, 180
Mark, gospel of 25–8, 36, 40, 71n, 86, 103, 104, 105, 155, 197
Matthew, gospel of 25–9, 31, 36, 40, 41, 103, 119, 120, 122, 174
Messy Church 1, 142
metanoia 3, 37, 62, 71, 122
Methodist Church 7
ministry
  and discipleship 5, 12–19
  licensed ministry 5, 7
  of the whole church 5, 8, 10, 11–19, 205–20
  in the whole of life 18–19
ministerial training
  academic model 5
mission 1, 3, 5, 8, 11–13, 14, 15, 44
Mission-shaped Church 1
Monmouth Diocese 204–5, 209, 211

Morisy, Ann 1, 17, 124, 164
Moynagh, Michael 185–6
Murdoch, Iris 77–8
Myers, Joseph 56–7

Newbigin, Lesslie 14, 43–4, 175
New Wine 162

On Fire 162
'ordinary theology' 70, 129, 198–9, 202, 216
oversight 207–9

paideia 68–9
parables 90, 96, 98, 120, 125
participation and reification 146–8, 149
pastoral cycle 75, 76–81, 116n, 123–4, 128, 156, 173, 217
Pastoral Supervision: A Handbook 179, 212–13
Paul xii, 13–14, 20, 29–38, 42, 45, 61, 79, 90–1, 99, 104–5, 108, 110, 119, 120, 124, 186, 201
people's theologian 159–60, 174, 219
Peter 98–9
Philippians, epistle to 14, 17, 34–7, 42, 48, 72n, 99, 104, 108, 111, 120
phronesis see practical wisdom
Pickard, Steven 72n, 107, 160
Pilgrim course 126–7, 160, 162, 176n, 206
pluralism 2, 34
Polanyi, Michael 88, 92, 114–15, 167, 195
practical wisdom 34–7, 62–3, 72n, 99, 180, 186–90, 196
practices 21–2, 147–8, 160–76, 179–90
Proclamation Trust 162

Quinlan, Kathleen 63–70

reflexivity 70, 78, 92–3, 188
reimagining ministry 2–4
Reimagining Ministry vii, xi, 4, 208, 209
'Released for Mission' 3, 5
Ripon College Cuddesdon 204
Robbins Report 45
Rogers, Jenny 51–2
Romans, Epistle to 15, 17, 29, 31, 36, 41, 43, 110, 119, 120–1, 124

Sabbath 40, 122, 132, 163, 165, 171
Schön, Donald 106–7, 114
Scripture 21, 79, 114–15, 127
 role in theological reflection 93–102, 103, 109, 123, 175
Senge, Peter 157, 190
'Serving Together' 10, 11
'Setting God's People Free' xi–xii
SHAPE course 130, 211
Shaping the Future 7, 13, 67
Smith, David 173–4
St Albans Diocese 10
St Margaret's Liverpool 81–3
Stop the Traffick 128
Street Pastors 1, 80, 131
supervision 212–15
Supervision in the Helping Professions 179

tacit knowledge 88–93, 112, 115, 119–20, 122, 168–9, 172
Taylor, Charles 200

Taylor, John V. 105
teambuilding 209–11
theological reflection 6, 20–1, 69–71, 75–116, 128–9, 139, 148–151, 151–7, 161, 172–3, 184, 186–8, 192–3, 207, 217–19
Tomlin, Graham 14, 38
Tough, Allen 47, 49
transformation 16, 21, 30–4, 39, 44–5, 52–3, 61, 70, 73n, 119–23, 170–1

'Umoja' programme 156
United Reformed Church 7

Varley, Liz 155
virtue *see* character
vocation 15, 18–19, 51, 203, 209
vocational domain of spirituality 164
Volf, Miroslav 18–19

Walton, Roger 56, 107–8
Ward, Frances 95, 179, 212–13
Warren, Robert 150, 207
Wenger, Etienne 146, 168, 169, 171, 195, 215–16, 217
What If Learning 65–6, 173–4
Williams, Rowan 12
Wright, Tom 19, 73n, 101